Intermediate GNVQ Engineering

Colin Chapman
Gillian Whitehouse

Longman

Pearson Education Limited
Edinburgh Gate
Harlow
Essex CM20 2JE, England
and Associated Companies throughout the world

ISBN 0 582 38138 X

British Library Cataloguing-in-Publication Data
A catalogue record for this book is available from the British Library.

Set by   in
Printed in Malaysia,LSP

Contents

Preface

This book has been written to support the government's Curriculum 2000 initiative, which has the broad aim of increasing the breadth of the post-16 curriculum that can be made available to students. One of the key elements of the initiative is to provide high-quality vocational courses, including Intermediate GNVQs, in a number of subject areas including Engineering.

To take this course you do not need to have previous experience of engineering, but you will need an interest in engineering and in exploring new ideas. As well as learning some of the most important concepts and techniques in engineering, you will also develop a range of practical skills, and have the opportunity to improve your key skills in communication, application of number and use of IT.

There are three mandatory units for the course. These are:

1. Design & Graphical Communication
2. Application of New Technology in Engineering
3. Making Engineered Products

To complete the qualification you will need to complete three optional units offered by an awarding body (Edexcel Foundation including BTEC; AQA including City and Guilds; OCR including RSA Examination Board). These may be specialist units, which focus on particular career pathways for example:

- electronics
- motor vehicle technology
- engineering drawing

or more general ones such as Science and Mathematics.

This book contains chapters covering each of the three mandatory units. It therefore provides an essential resource for anyone taking an Intermediate GNVQ in Engineering, and will also be useful to students on a Foundation GNVQ who study the same mandatory subjects in less depth.

An Intermediate GNVQ in Engineering will give a broad understanding of the area, and encourage the application of that knowledge and understanding to practical situations. This book is designed to support those aims, as well as a detailed coverage of the topics required by the unit specifications.

Assessment will include up to two-thirds of the total units for a qualification, these being internally assessed through tests, assignments, projects or case studies. At least one third will be externally assessed by similar means. Throughout the book students will find a number of self-assessment exercises that will assist them in their preparation for undertaking the unit assessments. The book will also form a superb reference source for open assessments.

Design and Graphical Communication

This unit introduces design and graphical communication within engineering. The chapter covers a variety of communication techniques appropriate to a wide range of design applications. It is important to understand the process of design and be familiar with many graphical methods in order to develop your design expertise and the ability to select and use a method of communication that is appropriate to its application. For example, sketches that are appropriate for the communication of ideas may be inappropriate for workshop drawings and formal drawings will be inappropriate for presentation and marketing applications.

Design and graphical communication involves thinking about the needs of your client, developing a design specification from the client's design brief, and working with a wide range of media including that available through information technology (IT). IT software is particularly appropriate for charts, graphs and the presentation of information taken from spreadsheets. Many software packages are available for both modelling and drawing using BS and ISO standard symbols and conventions. It is important to have access to IT hardware and software that are suitable for the user and the task to be carried out. Some of the best and most highly regarded computer-aided design and draughting (CADD) packages offer too much sophistication for may students and simplified and more appropriate versions are often available.

The areas covered in this unit are:

- Designing for customers and clients.
- Sketching, drawing and CAD for conceptualising and presenting design solutions.
- Diagrams and charts for communicating information.
- Schematic and circuit diagrams.
- Engineering drawing

After studying this unit you should be able to:

- Analyse a customer's design brief and understand the key features for an engineered product.
- Understand that there may be more than one solution that meets the customer's needs.
- Produce a design specification which includes details and decisions about the intended product.
- Use your design specification to produce a design solution that will meet the customer's design brief.
- Select a design solution from initial design solutions.
- Produce and interpret engineering drawings.
- Interpret electrical and mechanical engineering drawings to explain the function of the components and features used.
- Choose drawing techniques that take into account the purpose of the drawing and the intended audience.

1.1 Designing for customers and clients

Design in the real world is rarely a 'blue sky' activity where a designer or an inventor sits and waits for great ideas just to happen. Design is said to be 5% inspiration and 95% perspiration; it is a creative activity that has to be practised and worked at.

Understanding the process of designing

Designing is, in reality, a very complex activity. It involves thinking and doing and time to relect followed by more thinking and more doing in a continual process. In order to try to understand this process, and to structure it, designing is looked at as a process model. This is a way of visualising design in an illustrative form. Any model of this nature will, however, have some shortcomings. It is never possible to have a visualisation of such a complex process that truly reflects all circumstances.

In its simplest form the process of designing can be seen as a linear activity with a start and an end (see Fig. 1.1) The reality, however, takes on a more cyclic form or what has also been called the 'design loop'. The real process, as a model, looks more like that shown in Fig. 1.2. The model is trying to show how the various aspects of designing link and feedback to each other. For example:

- Investigation will involve looking at how the product can be made
- The initial ideas will be evaluated and this will result in development and refining
- prototypes will lead to new ideas and further evaluation
- The final evaluation will certainly cause the designer to look again at the starting point.

To make the issues more complex, some researchers have suggested that neither model truly represents the process and

Figure 1.1 Linear design process model

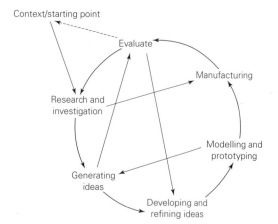

Figure 1.2 A cyclic design process model

it is in fact an 'iterative process'. This means that it is a process that progresses as a repeated interaction between the hand and the eye; thinking then doing again and again as the design moves forward.

Consider the design of a chair. If asked to design a familiar item like a chair it is not possible to start by investigating the function of a chair, as most design models would suggest. This is because the image of a known chair will immediately come to mind. It is immediately a redesign and refining process. Design is often defined as 'the reorganisation of known facts'.

Starting to design

Needs

All design must start somewhere. It often starts from an identified need that a person or group of people might have. Real basic human needs are food, water, warmth and shelter but many people have other additional and important special needs. People with disabilities, old people and small children all have special needs. Some people have needs related to the job they do, where they live, what they eat, or how they like to spend their leisure time; all of these can provide a starting point for design activity.

Contexts

Design must have a context or a location. The context could be a public place like a park or bus station or it could be closer to home such as a bedroom or a kitchen. The context will determine some aspects of the design. Somewhere to sit while waiting for a bus will be different from somewhere to sit within the home.

Existing products

Most product design is actually about improving or remodelling existing products. The aim may be to improve the product in terms of performance, to make it cheaper, or simply to regain credibility in terms of fashion or style. Whatever the reason the reality will be to regain a share of the market and sell more. It is always important, therefore, that designers fully understand the product, and for that reason it is often necessary to carry out a product analysis.

A product analysis will determine:

- *The product's purpose* – A product can only be evaluated against its original design intention or design specification.
- *How the product achieves its purpose* – How does the product function or operate for it to do what is intended?
- *The materials used* – Why has a particular material been chosen for a component and what are the properties that make it suitable?
- *The process involved in the manufacture of the product* – By discovering how a product has been made and assembled it is possible to understand much of why it is like it is.

Design in industry

Industrial designers normally work in a team so that an assignment can be broken down into manageable tasks. Team work has many benefits; ideas can be shared, discussed and refined, and in this way all the members of the team develop a greater understanding of the complete product and the implications that their decisions are likely to have for others. Design activity often starts with brainstorming sessions. This is where designers, and sometimes their clients, get together and toss ideas around among themselves. Brainstorming should take in the wildest and widest range of ideas no matter how bizarre they may at first appear to be. It is often through brainstorming that innovative design ideas develop and new and successful products reach the market.

Design briefs

Designers usually work from a design brief in response to the needs of a client or customer. A design brief is a clear statement of intent such as: 'Produce a design for a cooling system for a specific piece of electronic equipment.' From the design brief the designer is able to develop a design specification that will contain the key features of the product and set out precisely what the design must be able to achieve. There will always be a wide range of things to consider in relation to any product or component that is being designed although many of these considerations will be common to all products.

Function and aesthetics

It is interesting to consider these aspects of design together as they are so often said to conflict with each other.

- *Function* is about what the product should be able to do.
- *Aesthetics* is about what the product looks like and how it appeals to the consumer.

There are may instances where aesthetics is of no real consideration, but function is always important. There is little need to consider the aesthetics of the internal components of a pump or an engine that can never be seen, but often they must function without attention for long periods of time. Nevertheless, in the nineteenth century, many functional industrial components, including pumps and engines, were designed to have a great deal of unnecessary aesthetic ornamentation.

When designing a chair, for example, it is important to consider fully the function and the intended purpose. It is to be used for sitting at a table for relaxation, for working at a desk, or for some other function? These functional points will affect the design, so they must be clear in the mind of the designer.

Figure 1.3 shows an example of how the design of a simple component might be explored in relation to its function. The component is a finger-operated release catch. The functional surfaces are shown at A, B, C and D. Having first established the function, the design can now be explored and possible solutions examined.

All the designs shown are functionally acceptable so how can the designer now decide which to take forward and develop further? The considerations must go beyond the function and the following points need now to be considered:

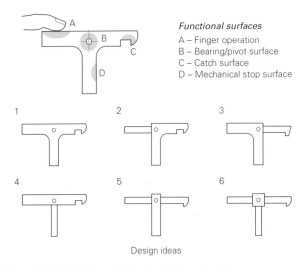

Functional surfaces
A – Finger operation
B – Bearing/pivot surface
C – Catch surface
D – Mechanical stop surface

Figure 1.3 Illustrations of simple catch mechanism

- *Size* – How big it will be; in this case this is determined by the user. This is to be a finger-operated catch so the size must suit the user's finger. This is an **ergonomic** decision. Ergonomics is 'the study of man within his working environment' and this is informed by data about people known as **anthropometric** data.
- *Cost, manufacturing method, scale of production* – The designer must be constantly aware of all of these points. The cost will be mostly determined by the method of manufacture which will in turn be determined by the quantity required over a given time period, i.e. the scale of production. In the example shown in Fig. 1.3 it would be easy and cheap to produce design 4 if only one or just a few catches were required. Stock material and bench manufacturing processes could be used. If it was necessary to mass produce this component then design 1 would be more suitable and large-scale manufacturing processes such as injection moulding or die casting could be considered. The economics of manufacture must always balance the large investment in tooling and automation with the long-term return on the investment made. The production cost of any component that can be made by a single process will be very low, but the investment costs for that process will always be very high.

Design and economy

Figure 1.4 shows a special screw to be manufactured in brass. The initial design is suited to two different methods of production but a modified design has had to be adopted for the economy of mass production.

- Method A is suitable for up to 5000 components per year using standard milling and turning processes.
- Method B includes an investment in hot pressing in order to form, rather than machine, the head of the screw. The process is quicker and less material is used so the production costs are reduced. This is suitable for batch production up to 50 000 components per year.
- For mass production, 200 000 components per year (method C), it has been necessary to modify the design of the component and produce a fabricated or assembled version in order to take advantage of manufacturing processes that will further reduce costs.

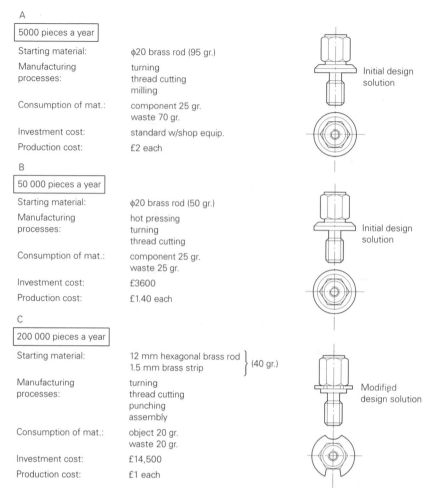

A

5000 pieces a year

Starting material:	φ20 brass rod (95 gr.)
Manufacturing processes:	turning thread cutting milling
Consumption of mat.:	component 25 gr. waste 70 gr.
Investment cost:	standard w/shop equip.
Production cost:	£2 each

Initial design solution

B

50 000 pieces a year

Starting material:	φ20 brass rod (50 gr.)
Manufacturing processes:	hot pressing turning thread cutting
Consumption of mat.:	component 25 gr. waste 25 gr.
Investment cost:	£3600
Production cost:	£1.40 each

Initial design solution

C

200 000 pieces a year

Starting material:	12 mm hexagonal brass rod 1.5 mm brass strip } (40 gr.)
Manufacturing processes:	turning thread cutting punching assembly
Consumption of mat.:	object 20 gr. waste 20 gr.
Investment cost:	£14,500
Production cost:	£1 each

Modified design solution

Figure 1.4 Illustrations of special screw development (from Eskild Tjalve (1979) *A Short Course in Industrial Design*, Newnes-Butterworth)

It is quite common practice for a simple and functionally suitable design to have to be changed to something more complex to take advantage of reduced manufacturing costs. An investigation of the small fittings used in cars for fixing upholstery and trims will reveal many complex components that are only economic due to the large scales of production within the car industry.

- Can assembly be achieved without component stress or time-consuming adjustments?
- Do the tolerances of mating and functioning components ensure the required fit in all instances and at an acceptable degree of wear on 'running' components? (See also page 63, 'Tolerances'.)

Designing for quality, safety and maintenance

Many manufacturing companies have ISO 9000 status; this means that they perform to an international standard of quality. Quality is not only about quality of manufacture – the quality of a product can only be assured when it is an integral part of the product's design. It is the aim of a quality assured company to produce products that are 'right first time every time'.

As a designer you need to consider:

- How quality can be assured through the design.
- Service and maintenance.
- All aspects of safety and conformity with any relevant regulations, standards and procedures.

For a product to be of the highest possible quality, safe in use and maintainable it is important to address the following issues:

- Are standard components that are specified for use up to your company's quality standards?

Figure 1.5 Superbike racing

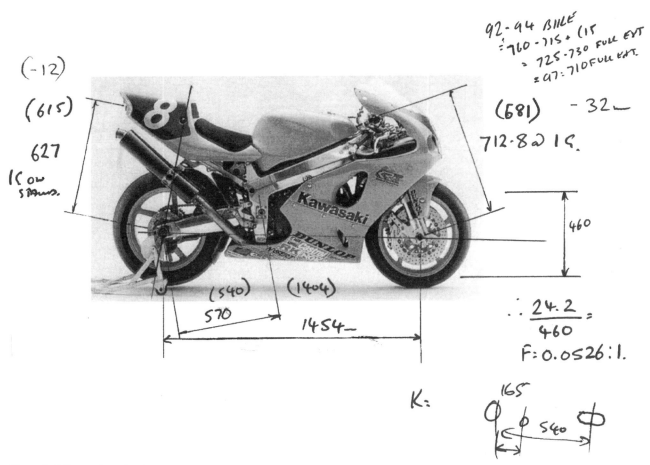

Figure 1.6 Research and notes

- Has the design included provision for lubrication and/or cooling?
- Can the product be accessed for maintenance and servicing?
- Are servicing instructions clear and, if appropriate, multilingual?
- Are spare parts and standard components readily available?
- Does the product in all aspects conform to the appropriate BS or ISO standards for performance and safety?

Engineering design case study: North Moor Engineering

This case study underpins the comments made earlier regarding the real nature of design and design development. In this example it is clear that the process of designing is a process of design – prototype – test – modify – and design again. It is a cyclical process and a process of continual interaction of hand and eye; of thinking and doing.

North Moor Engineering are motor sport engineers. They specialise in racing motor cycles at the highest competitive level. This design case study centres around a small aspect of the continual process of improvement that is needed to stay competitive in world-class superbike competition.

Superbikes (Fig. 1.5) represent the state of the art within motorcycle engineering. On the face of it they are fine examples of complex engineering; however, they become even more complex when trying to understand the geometry, and the continual stresses and weight transfer that takes place in controlling 150 brake horsepower capable of accelerating to 60 mph in 3.8 seconds.

The task facing North Moor Engineering was how to improve the handling characteristics of the bike by increasing the wheel base length and adjustment. The ability to provide fine adjustment to the length of a bike means that its performance can be optimised to suit different tracks and conditions. It is known that stability can be improved by extending the wheel base but there is a danger that rear tyre grip may be lost because of the reduced weight transfer to the wheel as the centre of gravity moves forwards.

The focus of redesign was the swinging arm. This is the aluminium fabrication that secures the rear wheel to the bike. The idea of extending this and providing more adjustment is simple enough but the unknown consequences centred around the rigidity of the arm itself and the effect upon stability.

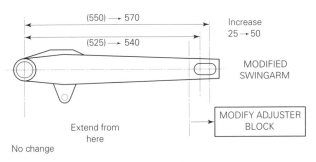

Figure 1.7 Design sketch of the swinging arm

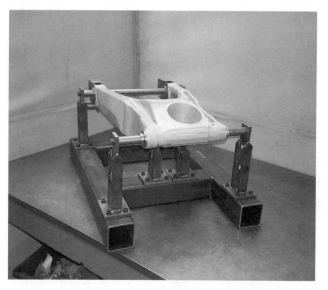

APPROX 4mm

REMOVE ANODISING BEFORE ASSEMBLY

MATERIAL :- ALUM ALLOY NS4
HARD ANODISE BEFORE ASSEMBLY

B- HOLE M8 P1.25mm THROUGH.

FAB + MACHINE

30mm ADJUSTMENT

is this enough ?

RIGID PULL ADJUSTER BLOCK

MATERIAL :-
ALUM ALLOY
7075TF
HARD ANODISE.

M8 PULLSCREW

MATERIAL :-
EN 24T
MILD
STEEL
HEAT TREAT
+ NICKEL PLATE

4mm A/F
SOCKET
RECESS

Figure 1.8 Design sketch of adjuster

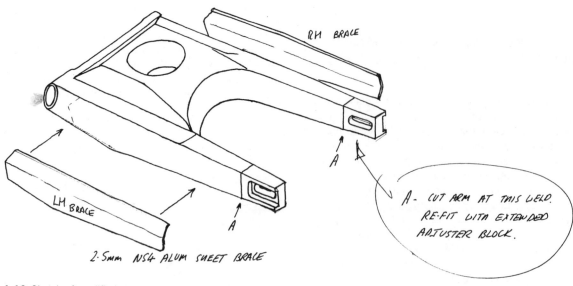

Figure 1.9 Swinging arm

The first stage was to carry out some research and look at the effect that this would have on the overall scale and geometry (Fig. 1.6).

A design sketch of an extended arm followed. This provided sufficient information to be able to fabricate the first prototype and provide some information on the effect that this might have. Figure 1.7 shows how the increase in length also provides an increase in adjustment from 25 m to 30 mm.

Initial trails were very promising, the changes in geometry were actually cancelling the effect of transferring the weight from the rear wheel. Attention was now transferred to the design of the adjuster. The design ideas at this stage are shown in Fig. 1.8. The sketches contain notes relating to how manufacture could take place and how much adjustment could be achieved. There is particular reference to anodising and heat treatment. These are important aspects of components that are subjected to stress.

The design worked well but it was evident that further improvements could be made to the rigidity of the swinging arm. Figure 1.9 shows the prototype swinging arm mounted

RH BRACE

LM BRACE

A

A

A- CUT ARM AT THIS WELD.
RE-FIT WITH EXTENDED
ADJUSTER BLOCK.

2.5mm NS4 ALUM SHEET BRACE

Figure 1.10 Sketch of modified arm

Figure 1.11 Modified arm

Figure 1.12(a) Superbike ready for racing

onto the fixture that is used for machining and for checking the alignment.

In order to improve further the rigidity of the arm it was decided to add more small panels to the fabrication. These were developed through sketches and through card modelling. The modified arm can be seen in Figs 1.10 and 1.11.

Figures 1.12(a) and 1.12(b) show a bike with its tyre warmers on in preparation for a race. Figure 1.12(b) shows clearly the new swinging arm assembly in place.

Figure 1.12(b) This photograph shows details of the swinging arm assembly

1.2 Sketching, drawing and CAD for conceptualising and presenting design solutions

Sketches can be used to develop and clarify your own ideas and as a means of communicating those ideas to others. Either way it is important to be able to sketch clearly and quickly. Freehand sketches should enable you to use a piece of paper or a note pad as an extension of your brain and your thinking processes. It does not matter if things get refined later or even rejected completely, it is more important to get the ideas down on paper than it is to spend time making them look like works of art.

Some of Alec Issigonis' now famous 1950s' sketches of the Morris Mini Minor were said to have been made on a restaurant table cloth (Fig. 1.13). These ideas are regarded as a milestone in small car design. Issigonis' designs were so successful that they continue to influence car design today.

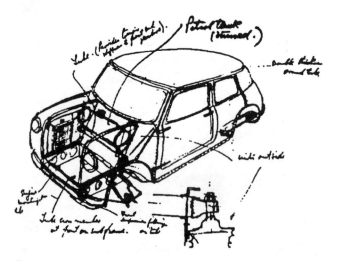

Figure 1.13 Original sketch of the Mini by Alec Issigonis

Freehand sketching

The ability to sketch can be greatly improved by practice and by learning a few techniques, but first let us consider the equipment to use. Professional graphic designers use a range of pens and pencils for making drawings, but for preliminary sketches, within the context of engineering design, softish pencils such as 'B' or '2B' are good and many designers use an ordinary ball-point pen. Few use felt or fibre-tip pens unless they wish to colour or render their drawings at a later stage. It is important to use the drawing instrument that flows easily and enables you personally to work easily.

To learn how to sketch fluently, start by drawing simple, flat geometric shapes. Simple shapes are built up from either straight or curved lines. The key to drawing straight lines is to look where you are going and not at the point of the pencil or pen that you are using. Try drawing long straight lines vertically and horizontally to join dots at either end of an A4 sheet of paper, and look at the dot not at the pencil. Follow this by drawing right angles and work up to drawing squares and rectangles (Fig. 1.14).

Curves and circles can be constructed within squares based around the fact that a circle will touch a square in four places at a mid point along each side. Try drawing circles in squares and ellipses inside rectangles. Use a flexible wrist action to draw curves (Fig. 1.15). Don't push the pencil but turn the paper round so that the pencil flows easily, and try to avoid drawing circles with points. Bring it all together by sketching some familiar three-dimensional objects (Fig. 1.16). Always begin with the overall outside shape and ensure that these proportions are correct, then identify the simple shapes that make up the complex one and work on it a little at a time.

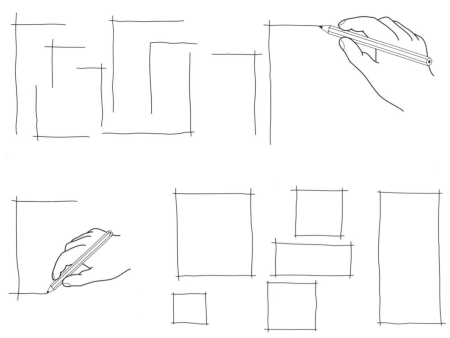

Figure 1.14 Sketches of squares and rectangles

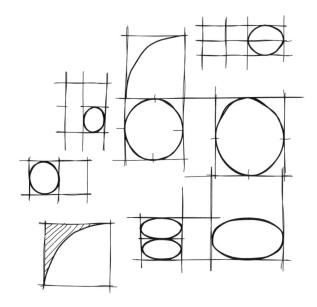

Figure 1.15 Sketches of curves and circles

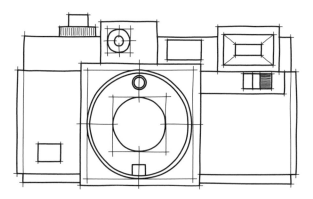

Figure 1.16 Sketch of a camera

Three-dimensional, or pictorial, sketches use a technique called 'crating'. This involves drawing an overall rectangular form (a 'crate') that would just contain the object that you intend to draw, rather like a close-fitting fish tank. You can then draw the object inside the crate; this technique helps to keep the proportions correct and the sides parallel.

Pictorial drawings are most commonly 'oblique' or 'isometric'. Perspective drawing is another common form of pictorial drawing but it is unlikely to play a large part within the context of engineering. Oblique drawings have a 'correct' front face with right-angled corners and side edges that slope back at 458. In isometric drawing, which is the more popular of the two, the drawing is tipped forwards and the front and side edges slope at 308. For oblique drawings the depth of the drawing has to be shortened in order for the object to look right (Fig. 1.17).

Circles and curves are dealt with as before but this time an outer square is drawn first (oblique or isometric). An oblique or isometric circle will touch the sides of the 'square' halfway along their lengths.

Developing and communicating design solutions

Freehand sketching is the best method of exploring and communicating ideas. It is far easier to work on design detail in sketch form on paper than it is to work things out in your head or try to describe them. Initially you might generate and record ideas just for yourself but as they develop there will be a need to communicate them to others.

Use your initial sketches for reflection and development. Make yourself develop alternatives and variations. Design is about looking, reflecting and considering. It is also about working with others and bouncing ideas around – and this means communicating. Few designers operate on a 'eureka' basis. Issigonis didn't sketch on that table cloth for his benefit alone, he needed to communicate and share his ideas with colleagues.

Figure 1.18 shows some sketches which look at possible ways of locating the hinge pin of a cover. Clearly there needs to be more consideration given to materials and manufacturing processes before further design decisions can be taken. As designs develop they have to be informed by the possible manufacturing stages, but initially it is important that all possibilities are considered.

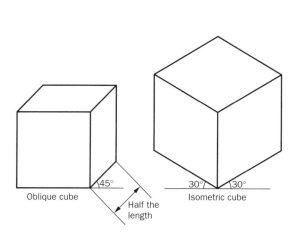

Figure 1.17 Oblique and isometric sketches

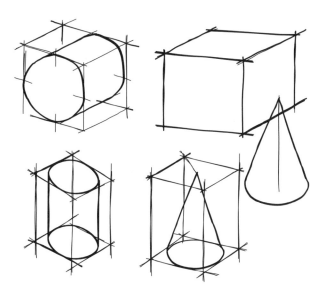

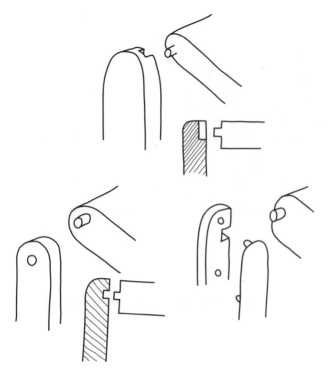

Figure 1.18 Sketches of hinge arrangement

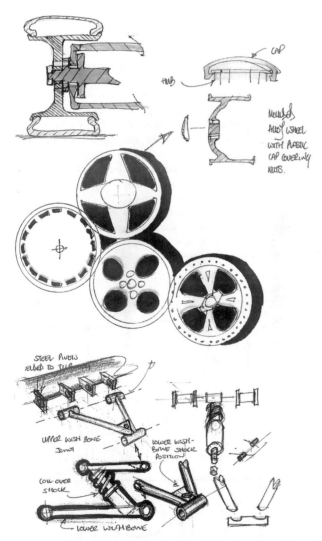

Figure 1.19 Sketches of a concept car (*reproduced courtesy of* Tom Morgan (De Aston School, Market Rasen))

Figure 1.19 shows examples of a designer's work, exploring potential variations for sports car wheel hubs and also looking at the possible construction of a suspension unit. You can see that materials and processes are receiving consideration as well as form and appearance. Here two aspects of the same product have different priorities. While wheels are clearly a functional part of a car, their appearance also makes a statement about the type of car: sports car, family car, city car, etc. The suspension units are primarily functional and here the form follows the function.

Presentation design solutions

All engineered products are becoming increasingly complex and expensive, whether a kitchen appliance, a machine tool or a military aircraft. In order to demonstrate to a client that the design brief has been satisfied it is often necessary to produce a prototype model or presentation drawing. This process must take place long before the actual product exists so that the designer can ensure that the customer will be satisfied befor any major financial commitments are made. Presentations of designs are also used by marketing departments to enable them to create a demand even before production is underway. This will mean that product sales will peak faster and provide the designer's with a quicker return on investment.

Visual images are powerful inducements for clients and for a client's potential customers. The selection of the presentation format is an important consideration if you wish your design be persuasive as well as informative. Presentation drawings can take many forms and can have the advantage over the finished product in that they can be used to highlight and exaggerate particular selling features. There are many examples commonly used in advertising and display that are also appropriate when presenting design solutions. Cars are often shown to be sleek and fast by presenting them low to the ground and by using 'quick' lines and blurred backgrounds. Objects presented with shadows look more solid and tend to lift themselves from the page; another technique is to use 'washed out' versions of earlier design ideas or products as a background to your chosen design solution. The effect of this is to tend to 'lift' the design and persuade a client that your chosen solution is the better alternative.

Figure 1.20 shows a sequence of illustrations of the stages in making a presentation drawing of a blow-moulded bottle for hand cream using marker pens.

1. The outline has been drawn on top of a feint pencil line using a fine fibre-tipped pen. A light-coloured marker pen is used to add the first areas of colour to the cap and the body of the bottle. The front of the body is flat, so this is left unmarked.
2. With a strip of tape placed down one side, the front can now be streaked across with quick movements. Streaking suggests a flat surface.
3. Further work with the same markers deepens the colours of the bottle and the cap on the left-hand side. This suggests depth of form and a right-hand light source.
4. Finally some black lines are added, also on the left, and white crayon is used to highlight the top edge of the bottle and separate it from the top. The finishing touch is

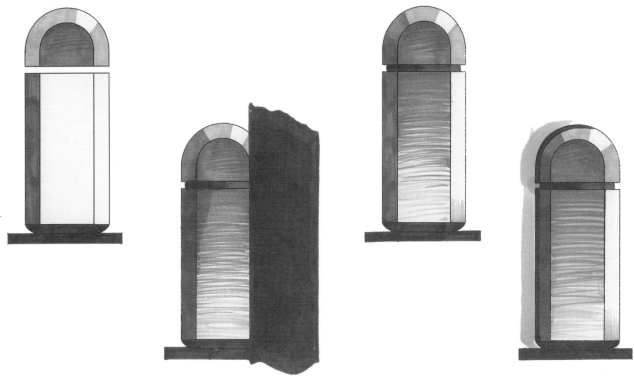

Figure 1.20 Marker rendering

a suggestion of shadow which is used to lift the product from its background.

Another presentation technique is airbrush rendering. This can be very time consuming as the majority of the work is involved in creating templates and masks. It is essential that the work is planned in the finest detail and that it is well practised (Fig. 1.21).

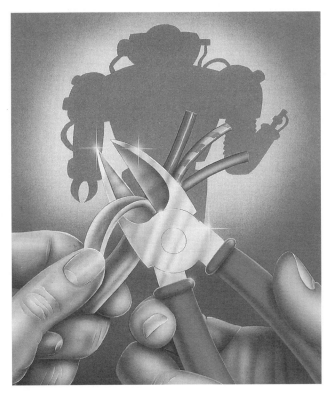

Figure 1.21 Airbrush rendering (*reproduced courtesy of Dave Eastbury*)

Computer-aided design (CAD)

Computer software can be used to aid the designer at many stages of the process of design and during the eventual transfer to manufacturing and process control. Design software is by its nature more sophisticated than computer draughting packages that may only support engineering drawing. The process of designing is a process of rearranging, visualising and making decisions and it should not be confused with inventing. If a design exists then it can be reworked and developed or imported and included. If it exists on a computer then the process can be done faster and more economically.

Consider the followings ways that CAD can assist the design engineer:

- Enables modification and reworking of existing designs.
- Provides access to libraries of standard features and components.
- By plotting the paths of moving features for clearance and collision detection.
- Aids design decision making by supporting the ability to visualise completed components and products.
- Enables engineering analysis of components subject to stresses and fatigue.
- Allows information to be shared electronically via communication networks such as e-mail, video conferencing and the Internet.

Access to libraries of standard components helps to speed up the process (Figs 1.22 and 1.23). The library file can also be used to show available stock and preferred components.

Parametric design software enables the design engineer to plot the path of moving parts to see how they could potentially interfere with other aspects of the design. Software of this nature is also used to design manufacturing cells to avoid clashes between robot operations.

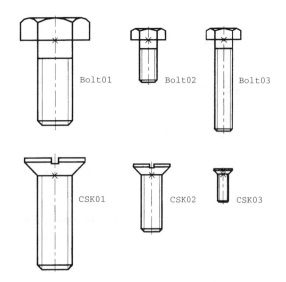

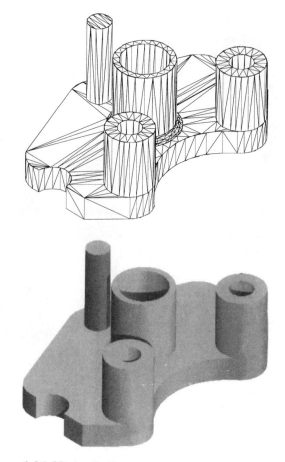

Figure 1.22 Extract from a library of standard bolts and screws

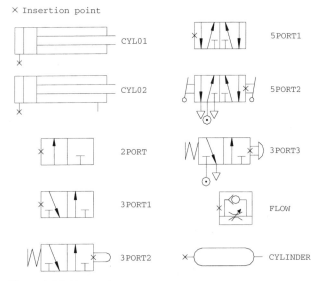

Figure 1.23 Extract from a library of standard pneumatic circuit symbols

Figure 1.24 3D visualisations

The interpretation of computer-generated images into three-dimensional forms enables the designer better to visualise and communicate the outcome. Figure 1.24 shows wire frame and solid model interpretations of a cast component. While the solid model is the easier to visualise, because it is closest to reality, it is expensive in terms of hardware requirements and processing time, making it slow to manipulate on the screen. Designers often stop at the wire frame stage. Wire frame modelling as a 'language' for communication is very popular and has the advantage of being able to see features behind and on the rear surface of components. By using colour to identify different components and surfaces, wire frame assemblies become easy for the trained designer to interpret.

Self-assessment tasks

1. Using the freehand sketching techniques described at the beginning of this section make some sketches of familiar rectangular items such as televisions, stereo systems, computer systems, etc. Look carefully at the proportions and sides that are parallel.
2. Take the best of your sketches from Task 1 and turn it into a three-dimensional oblique drawing. Do not use any drawing instruments.
3. Using isometric techniques, sketch a compact camera.
4. Using sketches and notes carry out a study of a simple mechanical device such as a stapler, can opener, pencil sharpener or hole punch.
5. For what purpose might a designer produce a presentation drawing?
6. Using any technique that you feel is appropriate, make a presentation drawing of a product that you are working on as part of your course.
7. Make a list of the advantages and disadvantages of using computer systems as an aid to designing and communicating design ideas.
8. What are the advantages of using computer-generated wire frame modelling over other graphic and prototyping techniques?

1.3 Diagrams and charts for communicating information

Manufacturing industries, as they become international and develop international markets, become increasingly complex and have an ever greater need to communicate information. Non-verbal communication takes place within organisations, between organisations, and between organisations and their customers and suppliers irrespective of national boundaries or language. The mode of communication adopted will depend upon two key considerations.

- **Who** is it for? – 'The target audience'
- **What** does it need to say? – 'The message'

By addressing these questions it is possible to determine the most appropriate mode of communication: it could be a written report and in another case a picture. Quite often the most appropriate form lies between the two extremes and involves both graphic images and text.

Data charts

Manufacturing and planning data charts are used to display information that frequently needs to be referred to. Such charts are presented within handbooks or are produced with a wipe-clean surface to be displayed on walls near to the appropriate process. Cutting speeds for machine tools, drilling sizes for screw threads and temperature settings for heat treatment are typical of the types of information that may be presented in this manner. The chart shown here (Fig. 1.25) shows the speed settings for drilling operations in columns (vertically) according to the cutting speed of the material, and in rows (horizontally) according to the diameter of the drill.

Metric series	CUTTING SPEEDS Approximate							Metric series
ft/min	30	40	50	60	70	80	90	100
m/min	9	12	15	18	21	24	27	30
diam/mm	Revolutions per minute							
·5	5817	7756	9695	11634	13573	15512	17451	19390
1·0	2909	3878	4847	5817	6786	7756	8725	9695
1·5	1942	2589	3237	3884	4532	5179	5826	6474
2·0	1456	1942	2427	2912	3397	3883	4369	4854
3·0	970	1294	1617	1940	2264	2587	2911	234
4·0	728	970	1213	1455	1698	1940	2183	425
5·0	582	777	970	1164	1359	1553	1747	941
6·0	485	647	808	970	1132	1294	1455	617
7·0	416	555	693	832	970	1109	1248	386
8·0	364	485	606	728	849	970	1091	213
9·0	324	431	539	647	755	962	970	078
10·0	291	388	485	582	679	776	873	970
11·0	265	353	441	529	617	706	794	882
12·0	243	324	404	485	566	647	728	808
13·0	234	299	373	448	522	597	672	746
14·0	208	277	346	416	485	554	623	693
15·0	194	259	323	388	453	517	582	647
16·0	182	243	303	364	424	485	546	606
17·0	171	228	285	342	399	456	513	571
18·0	162	216	269	323	377	431	485	539
19·0	153	204	255	306	357	408	459	511
20·0	146	194	242	291	340	388	436	485
21·0	139	185	231	277	323	370	416	462
22·0	133	177	220	265	309	353	397	441
23·0	127	169	211	253	295	337	380	422
24·0	121	162	202	242	283	323	364	404
25·0	117	155	194	233	272	310	349	388

Figure 1.25 Typical data sheet

Graphs

A graph is one of the most common method of displaying information (Fig. 1.26). In its simplest form a graph will just show the relationship between two factors such as time and distance. Conventionally, when time is displayed upon a graph, it occupies the horizontal or 'x' axis. The vertical axis is called the 'y' axis. For example, vehicle A travelling at a constant speed appears as a straight line on a distance/time graph whereas vehicle B which is accelerating or changing its speed will generate a graph that is curved.

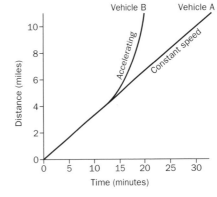

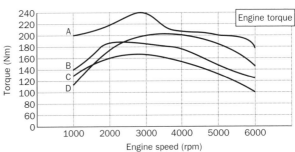

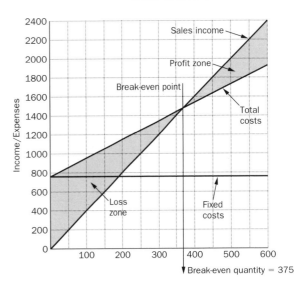

Figure 1.26 Examples of graphs

The other two graphs shown in Fig. 1.26 have different information to communicate. The graph showing engine performance has the torque versus engine speed of four engines (A, B, C, and D) plotted on it. The purpose of the graph is to compare the torque capability of the four engines.

The break-even analysis graph is used to determine one essential piece of information, the point where loss changes into profit: a most crucial point for any business.

Graphs are used extensively within newspapers and the media to show trends rather than for extracting detail. The upwards slope of a graph indicates increase whereas a downwards slope shows decline. They are not intended to be 'quantitative'; this means that you can't read off the graph any numerical values as you could in the three graphs shown in Fig. 1.26.

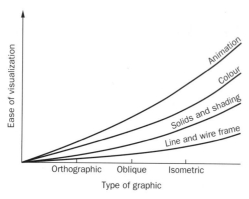

Figure 1.27 Types of graphical communication and their relative ease of visualisation

The graph shown in Fig. 1.27 has no quantifiable information on the axes but it does enable some important comparisons to be made that are particularly relevant to this unit.

Bar charts

Bar charts are used to display information in a more accessible form than a graph. In its simplest form a bar chart is more properly known as a 'histogram', which is really a graph that is drawn in steps rather than as a curve. The histogram shown

in Fig. 1.28(a) is the sort that appears in holiday brochures showing the temperature of a resort at different times of the year. Again time, in this example in months, is shown conventionally along the x axis.

Bar charts can be displayed in three-dimensional form and either vertically or horizontally. The bar chart in Fig. 1.28(b) shows how the UK workforce is divided up. The 'message' being conveyed is that manufacturing industry has to earn enough to cover the costs of other people within the economy, particularly those in service industries.

Pictograms are another form of bar chart, using images to represent the message of the chart. In Fig. 1.29 the shape of a person is used to represent people employed within various aspects of manufacturing.

In Fig. 1.30 all of the 'bars' are the same size, representing 100% of taxation, and the chart is used to compare how the taxation in a number of countries is made up from a range of taxation sources. You can see that as a percentage of total taxation, income tax in the UK is similar to that in Japan, Italy and Germany and less than that of Canada and the United States. The chart does not, however, say how much taxation is collected or how much income tax is paid in those countries as a percentage of income. It is important to remember that the message being portrayed is the chosen message of the originator of the information and not necessarily the whole story.

Pie charts

Pie charts are limited in that they can only show how things are divided up. Often when the aim is to draw attention to a particular aspect, that slice of the pie is drawn separately. The UK taxation example in Fig. 1.30 can be represented as a pie chart, as shown in Fig. 1.31; the 30% that is income tax has been highlighted.

Computer-generated graphs and charts

Spreadsheets and databases usually have the facility to produce graphs from the data stored within them.

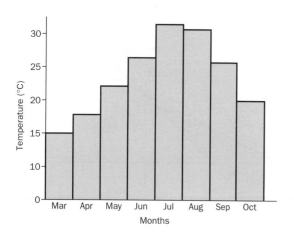

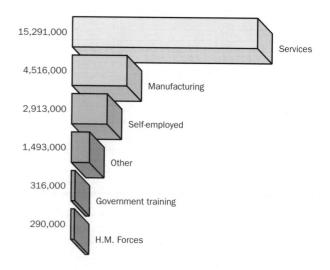

Figure 1.28 Examples of (a) histogram and (b) horizontal bar chart

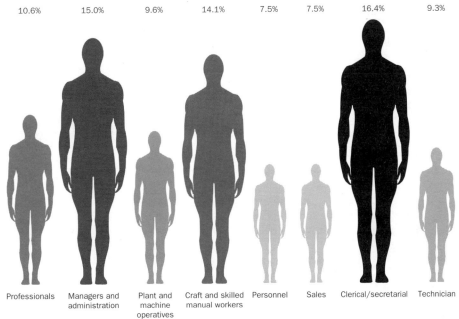

10.6%	15.0%	9.6%	14.1%	7.5%	7.5%	16.4%	9.3%
Professionals	Managers and administration	Plant and machine operatives	Craft and skilled manual workers	Personnel	Sales	Clerical/secretarial	Technician

Figure 1.29 Examples of a pictogram

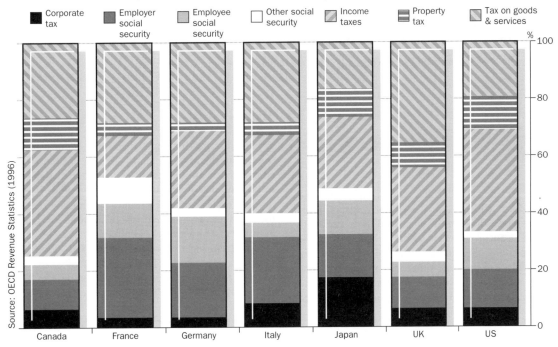

Figure 1.30 Taxation bar chart

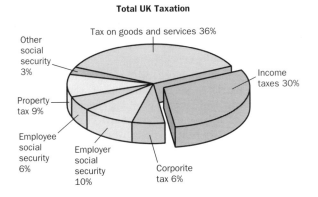

Figure 1.31 UK taxation pie chart

Figure 1.32 shows graphs and charts generated by Microsoft Excel (a commercially available spreadsheet package). Once data has been entered into the computer it can be organised, manipulated and displayed in a number of ways including:

- Spreadsheets
- Databases
- Tables
- Charts
- Graphs
- Bar charts
- Pie charts.

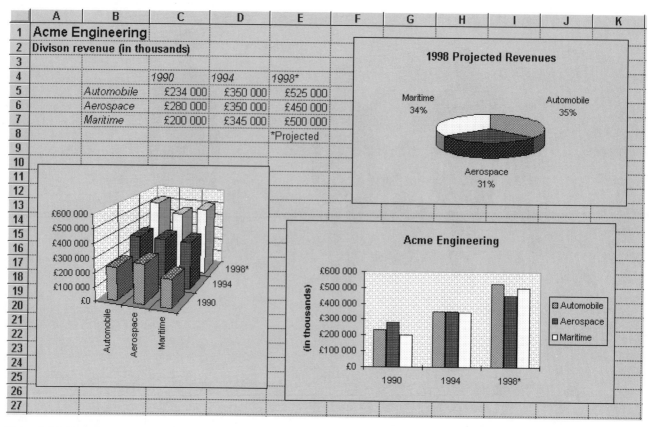

	A	B	C	D	E	F	G	H	I	J	K
1	Acme Engineering										
2	Divison revenue (in thousands)										
3											
4			1990	1994	1998*						
5		Automobile	£234 000	£350 000	£525 000						
6		Aerospace	£280 000	£350 000	£450 000						
7		Maritime	£200 000	£345 000	£500 000						
8					*Projected						
9											
10											
11											

Figure 1.32 Example of using Microsoft Excel to display same data in different graphical formats

Block diagrams

Block diagrams are used very widely within engineering to show in graph form concepts, processes and organisational structures. The block diagram in Fig. 1.33 is a graphical representation of 'concurrent engineering'. It shows how the elements overlap along the time axis (left to right) and are therefore taking place at the same time, i.e. concurrently. The block diagram is a powerful means of communication, to describe the process verbally would be long and could lead to confusion.

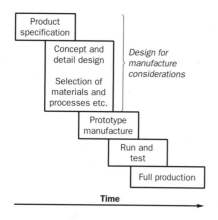

Figure 1.33 Concurrent engineering

There are no strict rules that apply to most block diagrams other than the need for clarity and the convention that if time is involved it progresses either from left to right or from top to bottom. The block diagram shown in Fig. 1.34 describes a product cycle and therefore has no time line. The diagram is used to indicate how and where information technology has been integrated within the production cycle.

Manufacturing processes may be controlled by a 'precedence network'. This is a form of block diagram that adheres to certain conventions as set out in BS 4335 and summarised within PP7307. Precedence networks are used to control processes that have crucial start, finish and delay requirements. For example in Fig. 1.35 'process B' cannot start until 'y' days after 'process A' has started. This is called a 'lag start'.

Flow charts

Flow charts are a form of block diagram used to organise sequences of events. They are commonly used when writing computer programs and when planning operations that involve decisions of a 'yes/no' nature. Flow charts are also frequently used for diagnostic purposes where a fault-finding procedure must be adhered to. Within PP7307 there is an example of a flow-charted procedure for checking a faulty 13 amp electrical plug (Fig. 1.36).

Flow charts should proceed downwards or from left to right. The 'yes' outcome from any decision should follow the

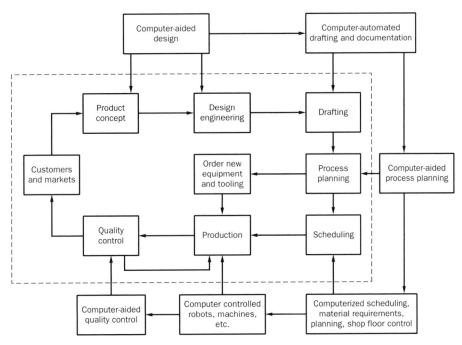

Figure 1.34 Computer integration within the product cycle (*after* Groover and Zimners Jr (1984) *CAD/CAM: Computer-Aided Design and Manufacturing*, Prentice-Hall)

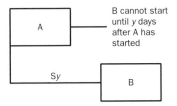

Figure 1.35 Examples of a precedence network

principal direction of flow. Arrows may be used to indicate flow direction and increase clarity but these should be kept to a minimum. Flow chart templates that contain all of these standard symbols can be purchased from stationers. The example chart shown here includes most of the commonly used symbols (see Table 1.1).

Table 1.1 Flow chart symbols

Symbol	Name	Meaning
⬭	Terminator	Stop or start, or exit from the process
▭	Process	Any predefined process or operation
◇	Decision	Resulting in 'yes' or 'no' and leading to one of two paths
▱	Data (*not used in Fig. 1.36*)	An input or output of data to or from the process
⬡	Manual input	Manual or other interruption to the process

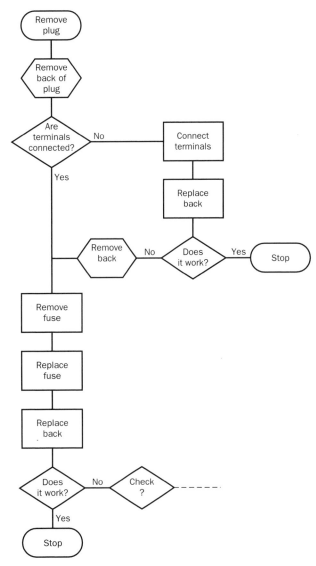

Figure 1.36 Flow chart to analyse a mains plug which is not working

Self-assessment tasks

1. Outline the reasons for using diagrams and charts when communicating information. Give examples from your own experience of occasions when you have referred to a diagram or a chart for information.
2. What criteria should be used to determine the most appropriate type of diagram or chart to use for a particular application.
3. Refer to the information presented in the graph of engine performance in Fig. 1.26. What can you say about the performance of engines A and D?
4. What does the graph in Fig. 1.27 tell you about communication of information?
5. Refer to the information given in the bar chart in Fig. 1.28(b) and the pictogram in Fig. 1.29. Draw a histogram showing the actual numbers of people employed within the various aspects of manufacturing industry in 1993.
6. Produce a pie chart to show how your typical day is divided up into a range of activities.

7. (a) Enter the following information on bicycle sales into any spreadsheet that you are familiar with, and from it produce a range of graphical interpretations.

	1995	1996
1st quarter	1,760	2,140
2nd quarter	3,450	4,025
3rd quarter	1,134	1,560
4th quarter	8,784	10,234

   (b) Comment upon the seasonal nature of these figures in relation to the particular product.
8. Produce a block diagram of any production process that you are familiar with.
   (a) Why should it be crucial within some processes that operations overlap or do not start before a certain point is reached?
   (b) Produce a block diagram in a form that illustrates this using an example of a process that you are familiar with.
9. Produce a flow chart guide to replacing a tap washer or repairing a bicycle puncture.

1.4 Schematic and circuit diagrams

Schematic drawings and circuit diagrams are used to show the arrangement of components within electrical, electronic, hydraulic and pneumatic systems. The various systems use standard symbols that are set down in a large and comprehensive range of British Standards. These are, however, summarised in PP7307 *Graphical Symbols for use in Schools and Colleges* and this document should be referred to.

Pneumatic and hydraulic systems

It is convenient to group these two types of system together because the symbols used within them are similar. They are described as 'functional' symbols, which means that the symbol describes graphically the function of the component. Valves, whether they control fluid or air, operate in a similar manner, and are therefore represented by the same or a similar symbol.

The simplest valve is a manually operated, two-port, two-way, directional control valve. This means two connections (in and out) and two positions (on and off). It is represented graphically in Fig. 1.37.

The valve is shown connected in a flow line in its 'at rest' position (Fig. 1.37(a)); valves should always be shown at rest. The line is blocked off by two closed ports. The functionality of the symbol is explained by the notion that when the valve is operated the right-hand square is replaced by the left-hand square and so the flow line is joined (Fig. 1.37(b)).

Study the two systems shown in Figs 1.38 and 1.39. The functional nature of the symbols will become clear as you come to understand the function of the systems.

Some other points and a few useful graphical symbols are shown in Fig. 1.40.

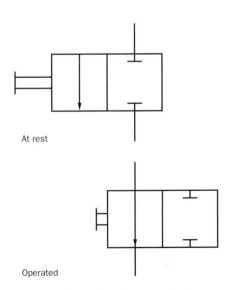

At rest

Operated

Figure 1.37 Symbol for a simple two-part, two-way, direction control valve

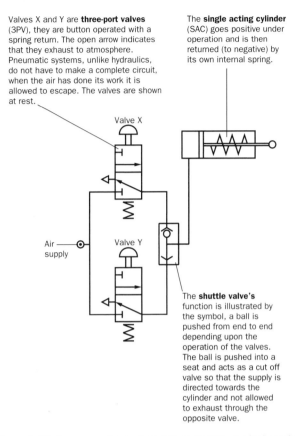

Valves X and Y are **three-port valves** (3PV), they are button operated with a spring return. The open arrow indicates that they exhaust to atmosphere. Pneumatic systems, unlike hydraulics, do not have to make a complete circuit, when the air has done its work it is allowed to escape. The valves are shown at rest.

Valve X

Air supply

Valve Y

The **single acting cylinder** (SAC) goes positive under operation and is then returned (to negative) by its own internal spring.

The **shuttle valve's** function is illustrated by the symbol, a ball is pushed from end to end depending upon the operation of the valves. The ball is pushed into a seat and acts as a cut off valve so that the supply is directed towards the cylinder and not allowed to exhaust through the opposite valve.

Figure 1.38 A pneumatic system for operating a single-acting cylinder from either one of two button-operated valves

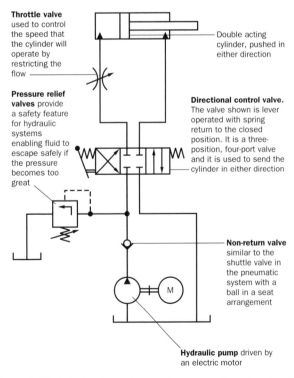

Throttle valve used to control the speed that the cylinder will operate by restricting the flow

Double acting cylinder, pushed in either direction

Pressure relief valves provide a safety feature for hydraulic systems enabling fluid to escape safely if the pressure becomes too great

Directional control valve. The valve shown is lever operated with spring return to the closed position. It is a three-position, four-port valve and it is used to send the cylinder in either direction

Non-return valve similar to the shuttle valve in the pneumatic system with a ball in a seat arrangement

Hydraulic pump driven by an electric motor

Figure 1.39 A hydraulic system for lever operation of a double-acting cylinder

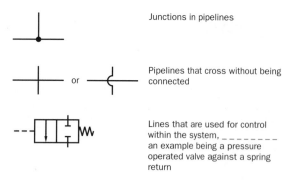

Junctions in pipelines

Pipelines that cross without being connected

Lines that are used for control within the system, an example being a pressure operated valve against a spring return

Figure 1.40 Some pneumatic and hydraulic symbols

The electronic circuits shown in Fig. 1.42 and 1.43 are based around discrete components, like those shown in Fig. 1.41. One is drawn by hand using symbol templates and the other has been drawn using a CAD software package called 'Crocodile Clips'. This software has the advantage that circuits can be both designed and tested on screen before being printed. The electronic symbols that are used are selected from the menu bar and they can be supplemented by animated icons such as the switch example shown here. As you can see, the software does not use 'dot' connections but uses a 'bridge' where lines cross similar to that used for pneumatic and hydraulic systems. The British Standard recognises this as an acceptable alternative.

Electrical and electronic systems

The principal means of communication within electrical and electronic systems is through circuit diagrams. Electronic circuits are often quite complex so it is important that the established international symbols and conventions are used:

- Circuits are 'read' from left to right and top to bottom. Where appropriate they should follow the structure:

  Input – Process – Output

- Positive supply should run along the top of the circuit and the 0 V or negative along the bottom.
- Connecting lines should be either horizontal or vertical and should cross each other as little as possible.
- Connections between lines should be made with a clear 'dot'.

Figure 1.41 shows some of the most commonly used component symbols for electronic circuits.

Integrated circuits

More commonly integrated circuits (ICs) have replaced many discrete components. An IC within a circuit can be represented with either the connections in the actual pin location or placed for the convenience of the layout and to avoid lines crossing. Figure 1.44 shows the same 555 timer circuit represented in two ways. In circuit (a) the IC is shown as it actually looks with pins numbered 1 to 8. This means that there has to be several lines crossing and the output device, the loudspeaker, is to the left of the IC. Circuit (b) is clearer and the output is in the preferred position on the right-hand side. Notice also that there is no need to show pin 5 because it is not being used.

Circuit (c) shows an amplifier IC in a circuit; it is shown in a triangular form even though it is actually a normal 8-pin IC. Again, for clarity, only the pins that are used are shown. Notice also the −9V supply.

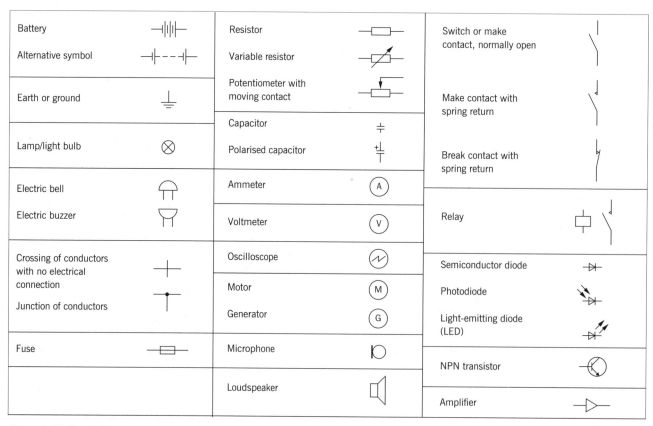

Figure 1.41 Symbols used in electronic circuits

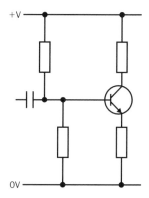

Figure 1.42 Electronic circuit based on discrete components

Communication for manufacture

A circuit diagram is part of the process of designing electronic systems and as such may not be a suitable means of communication to assist the manufacture of printed circuit boards (PCBs) or the location of components. PCB 67284 is a circuit board within a Computer Integrated Training System manufactured by TecQuipment Ltd. The circuit diagram is shown in Fig. 1.45. It is centred around integrated circuit IC1 and two amplifiers that are both located within the integrated circuit IC2. Leading away from the circuit diagram are a number of connections to voltage supplies and to external components.

Figure 1.46 shows the actual layout of the components on the component side of the PCB and the reverse side with the copper tracks making the appropriate connections. Compare the layout with the circuit diagram. The resistors have been grouped together and IC1 takes up only a small amount of space. The dominant features are the connectors CON1 and CON2. The component layout is printed on the component side of the board using silk-screening techniques. The software used to produce these three graphics is part of an integrated computer-aided design package that enables the designer to bring in standard size components and use auto-routeing technology. Auto-routeing lets the computer make the initial decisions regarding the layout and the routes of the copper track. It is possible then to print out masks for both the copper track and the silk-screening of the component side of the board.

Lastly, the computer system generates a parts list for the PCB and a simple schematic with notes for connection and fitting (Fig. 1.47).

Because these drawings are interrelated and stored electronically modifications and reissues can be monitored by the integrated computer system. This reduces the risk of errors caused by people working to and ordering from out-of-date drawings.

Schematic wiring diagram

Figure 1.48 is a schematic wiring diagram used for the installation of electronic components within a test rig. It is different from the circuit diagram because it is intended for a different audience and purpose. The various meters and

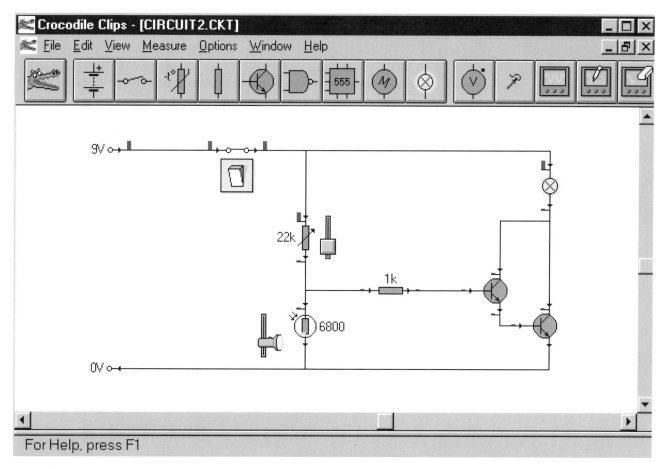

Figure 1.43 Electronic circuit drawn using a proprietary package (*reproduced courtesy of* Crocodile Clips Limited)

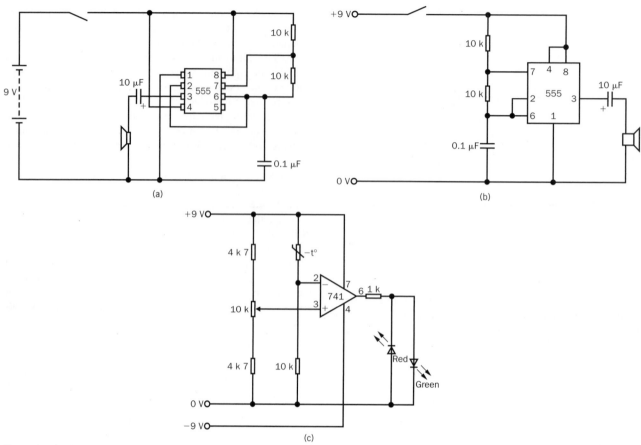

Figure 1.44 IC representation in three circuits

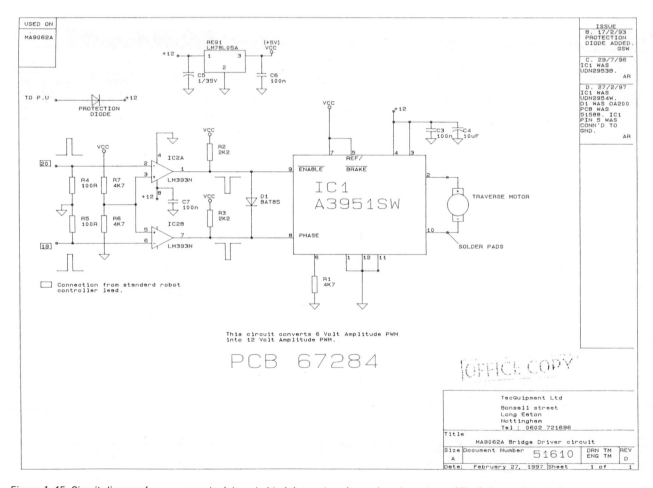

Figure 1.45 Circuit diagram from a computer integrated training system (*reproduced courtesy of* TecQuipment Limited)

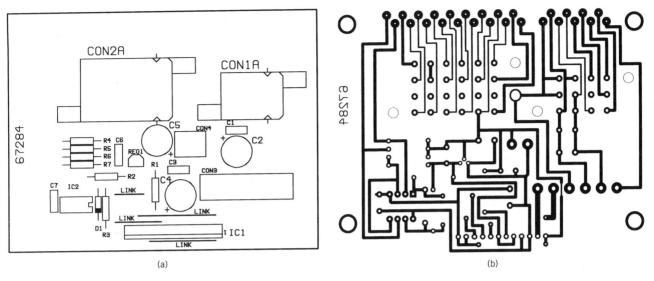

Figure 1.46 Layout of components (a) for circuit given in Fig. 1.44 and (b) copper tracks on reverse of printed circuit board (*reproduced courtesy of* TecQuipment Limited)

components are shown and these may be PCBs or housed components with terminal connectors. The schematic's purpose is to indicate the connections that have to be made and so all of the wire links are numbered at each end to avoid errors in tracking them through the diagram. For example, a connection has to be made between terminal 5 on the PF meter and terminal 3 on the amp SW. This link is shown being made by the line numbered 825. Alternatively, schematic diagrams of this type may show the connections being made using colour-coded wiring.

Measurement systems

The principal development in computer systems and integrated circuit technology is based within American companies and is predominantly located on the West coast of America. The conventional sizes that have evolved, therefore, are based upon imperial measurements. For example the standard spacing for pins on integrated circuits is actually 0.1 inches although you may see this specified as 0.245 mm. It is unlikely that the electronics industry will convert to metric standards.

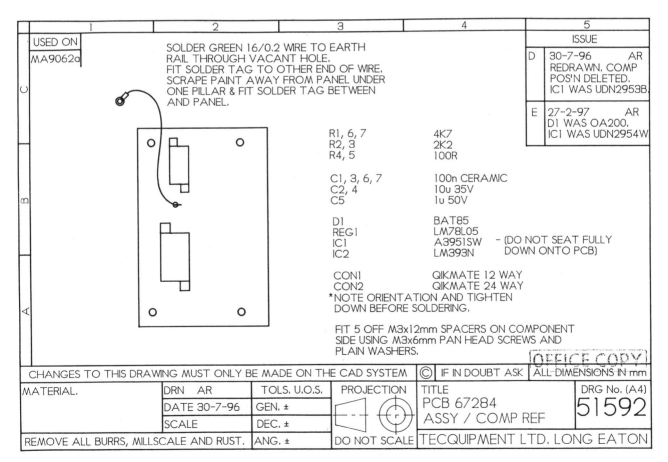

Figure 1.47 Parts list for circuit given in Fig. 1.44 (*reproduced courtesy of* TecQuipment Limited)

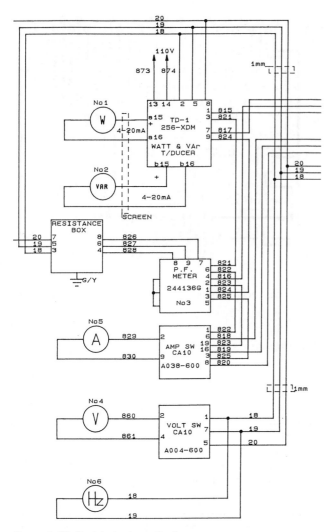

Figure 1.48 Electrical schematic diagram

Self-assessment tasks

1. Use a short sequence of illustrations to show how a button-operated, three-port pneumatic valve operates.
2. Draw a pneumatic circuit that can be used to open and close a door from two positions, i.e. from either the inside or outside.
3. Using standard components draw a circuit that will enable any one of three switches to operate a battery-powered light bulb.
4. Outline the advantages and disadvantages of the two types of representations of an integrated circuit shown in Fig. 1.44.
5. Produce a chart to show the input, process and output components commonly used in electronics.
6. Produce a schematic wiring diagram of a dynamo-generated lighting circuit for a bicycle.

1.5 Engineering drawing

The ability to ensure that manufactured products are produced to a consistently high quality is one of the main priorities within the manufacturing industry. Clear, unambiguous communication underpins the ability to provide customers with quality assurance. The need for formality within much of engineering drawing as a means of communication cannot be avoided or its importance understated. Engineering drawing as a means of graphical communication is a language and is therefore bound by rules and conventions like any spoken language: to be understood it is important for both parties to communicate using the *same* language.

Currently the formal language of engineering is set down within the three volumes of the British Standard BS 308. This publication along with many other BSI (British Standards Institution) publications is being revised as part of the development of European and International Standards. BS 308 is therefore current but will eventually be superseded. The abridged versions, PP7307 and PP7308, are intended for use within schools and colleges.

GNVQ Engineering is concerned with producing and interpreting engineering drawings. Within most engineering companies drawings are created using computer-aided draughting systems, which are vector-based software packages. This means that the software has a mathematical basis for locating points at the ends of lines and within curves. This system of drawing, unlike pixel-based or bitmapped screen graphics, can be correctly scaled and manipulated mathematically by the computer.

Computer-aided design (CAD) offers many advantages to a draughtsperson:

- Drawings can be carried out up to three times faster by using library files of standard components and copy and paste functions.
- Instant access to drawings for re-issue, modification and updating.
- Increased quality and accuracy with consistent text, lines, hatching and shading irrespective of draughtsperson.
- Access to increased range of functions not available conventionally such as re-scaling, auto-dimensioning, rotation of parts, extraction of details for removal or analysis and the combining of drawings.
- Storage is reduced in size, increased in quality and has greater security.
- Allows integration with other computer-based functions such as computer-aided manufacture (CAM), stock control, sales and marketing.

The standards and conventions of engineering drawing apply equally to CAD as they do to conventional technical drawing using a board and pencil.

Lines, text and dimensioning

The drawing shown in Fig. 1.49 is taken from PP7308 and is used to show the application of the various types of lines used

Table 1.2 British Standard line types and their use

Line type		Application	
A	Continuous thick	Visible outlines and edges	
B	Continuous thin	B1	Dimensions
		B2	Projection and leader lines
		B3	Hatching
		B4	Outline of revolved sections
		B5	Short centre lines
		B6	Imaginary intersections
C	Continuous thin	Limit of partial or interrupted view irregular	
D	Continuous thin	Sections and parts of drawings if the limit straight with zig-zags of the section is not on an axis	
E	Dashed thin	Hidden details, outlines and edges	
F	Chain thin	Centre lines, pitch lines and pitch circles	
G	Chain thin, thick at ends	Cutting planes for sectional views and changes of direction	
H	Chain thin	Outlines of adjacent parts and extreme double dashed positions of moving parts	

within engineering drawings. The line types and how they should be used are given in Table 1.2.

Lines

- Pencil or black ink should be used for all formal engineering drawing.
- Only two thicknesses of line should be used, thick lines should be twice as thick as thin lines.
- Centre lines should extend just past the outline of the drawing or relevant feature and can be extended to form leader lines for dimensions. They should cross one another and terminate with a long dash.
- Dashed lines and centre lines should meet and cross any other lines on a dash rather than a space.

Text

On many occasions text needs to be added to engineering drawings and the important consideration is clarity.

- Use only capital letters without any embellishments.
- Letters should not be less than 3 mm in height; numbers should be larger.
- Notes should be grouped together and be placed close to the relevant feature.
- Underlining should not be used.

Dimensioning

Dimensions are a vital aspect of component drawings which are intended to be used for manufacture. Mistakes, as simple as an error with a decimal point, can have disastrously expensive consequences.

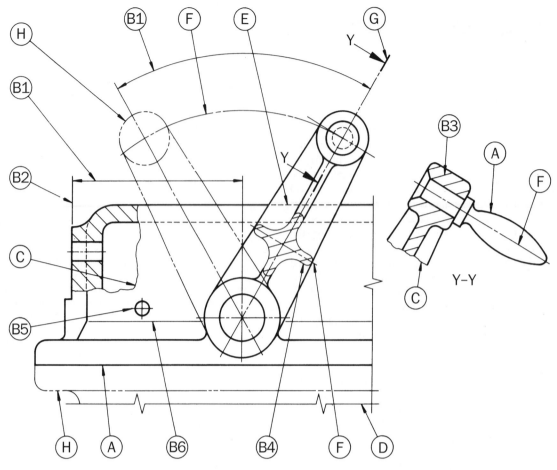

Figure 1.49 Use of different types of line in a drawing

- It should never be necessary for a dimension to be calculated, assumed or scaled from other dimensions on the drawing.
- There should be no more dimensions on a drawing than are necessary.
- Dimensions for a particular feature should, where possible, all be placed on the view that shows the feature most clearly.
- Linear dimensions should be in millimetres with the unit symbol 'mm'. This can be placed as a note, i.e. 'all dimensions in mm unless otherwise stated'.
- Examples of correct methods of expressing numbers:
  - whole numbers: **45** *not* **45.0**
  - less than 1: **0.5** *not* **.5** *or* **1/2**
  - greater than 999: **12500** *not* **12,500** *or* **12 500**
- Projection and dimension lines should be placed outside of the outline wherever possible.
- Projection and dimension lines should not cross over each other unless this is unavoidable.
- Projection lines should start just clear of the outline and extend just beyond the dimension line.
- Dimensions should be placed above the line as viewed from the bottom or the right-hand side of the drawing.
- Arrowheads should be triangular with the length approximately three times the width.

An example of a dimensioned drawing is shown in Fig. 1.50.

Orthographic projection

Orthographic projection provides the engineer with a means of accurately communicating three-dimensional forms on a two-dimensional piece of paper. Pictorial drawing – isometric and oblique (referred to earlier in this unit) – is not accurate enough. Right-angled corners are not shown true and sizes are adjusted to make the drawing 'look' right. For manufacturing purposes this can be confusing and is therefore not acceptable.

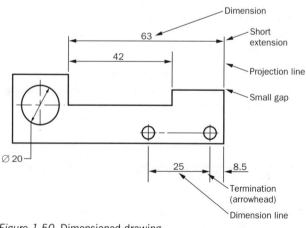

Figure 1.50 Dimensioned drawing

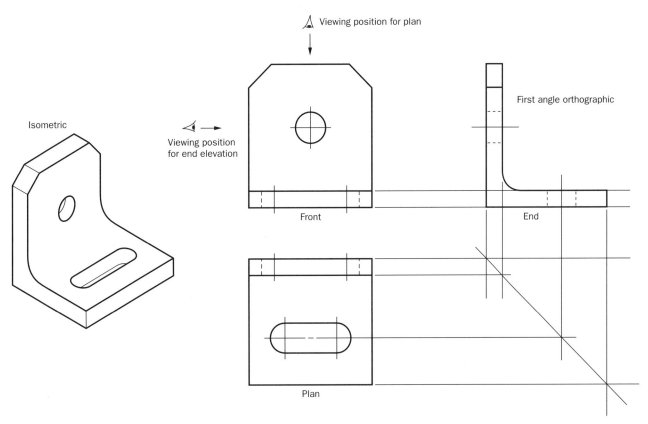

Figure 1.51 Example of first angle projection

Consider the bracket shown as an isometric drawing in Fig. 1.51 and the orthographic representation of the same object. The front view, end view and plan are drawn accurately and placed in such a position that the relationship between them is clear. This method of orthographic

Projection	Symbol	
First angle		
Third angle		

Figure 1.53 First and third angle symbols

projection is called 'first angle projection'. The views are referred to as elevations.

When viewing the front elevation from the left in order to see that end (or side) the view is projected through the bracket and shown on the right-hand side. Viewing from above the bracket in order to see the plan (or top) the view is again projected through the bracket and therefore the plan is shown below.

The notion of projecting is very important and by following the thin projection lines around you can see how the elevations relate to each other and confirm the position of aspects of the drawing.

Figure 1.52 shows the same bracket but this time drawn in 'third angle' orthographic projection. This method of projection is the more popular of the two alternatives. In third angle projection the elevation is placed adjacent to the viewing point rather than projecting it through to the opposite side.

In practice the type of projection used must be indicated on the drawing in writing or by using one of the British Standard symbols shown in Fig. 1.53.

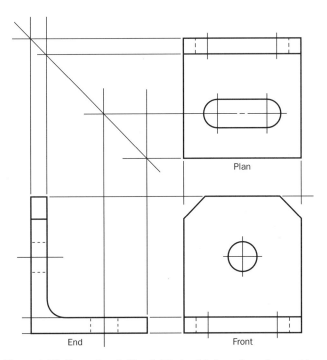

Figure 1.52 Example of Fig. 1.51 in third angle orthographic projection

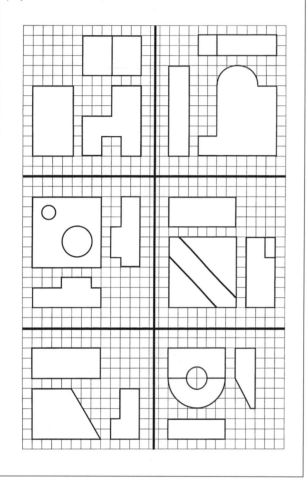

Sections and auxiliary views

It is often helpful for drawings to show views other than those mentioned above. Sectional views enable the reader to see deeper within what is drawn to locate the internal shapes of features or internal detail that is otherwise hidden from view. Three examples of sectioning are shown in Fig. 1.49 (p. 26): an interrupted view to show the inside of the main casting, a rotated sectional view to show the structure of the lever, and a section designated 'Y–Y' which shows how the handle locates within the lever. You will notice that when a part is sectioned the cutting plane is hatched with lines at 458.

Figures 1.54 and 1.55 show further examples of sectional elevations. The 3D model and sectional elevation of the foot step bearing have been generated using AutoCAD.

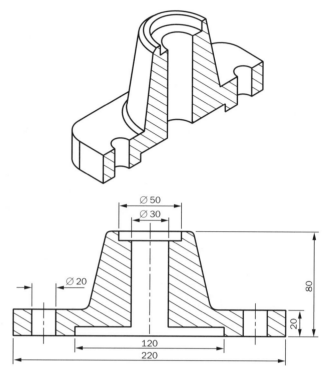

Figure 1.54 Sectional elevations

Points about sectional elevations

- The cutting plane should be clearly indicated and the sectional elevation projected in accordance with the method of orthographic projection being used.
- The cutting plane should be hatched at 458 in the sectional elevation, separated areas of the same component should be hatched with the same direction and spacing.
- Where different sectioned parts meet in a drawing the direction and spacing of the hatching should be varied (although not the 458 angle).
- Large areas need only be hatched around the edges and where they connect to adjacent parts.
- Sectional elevations can be made in more than one plane where this clarifies an aspect of the drawing (Fig. 1.55).
- By convention the following details, when they appear on a cutting plane, are not shown hatched when the cutting plane passes through them longitudinally:
  - fasteners, such as nuts, bolts, screws, washers, pins, etc.
  - shafts
  - ribs and webs
  - spokes of wheels

Auxiliary views (Fig. 1.56), like sections, are an opportunity to show aspects of a drawing that would otherwise be unclear or not seen. They are used particularly where a component has angular faces. The rules regarding projection of elevations should be applied to auxiliary views wherever possible although it is often the case, particularly with first angle projection, that clarity is best achieved by placing the auxiliary view adjacent to the face in question rather than projecting it through.

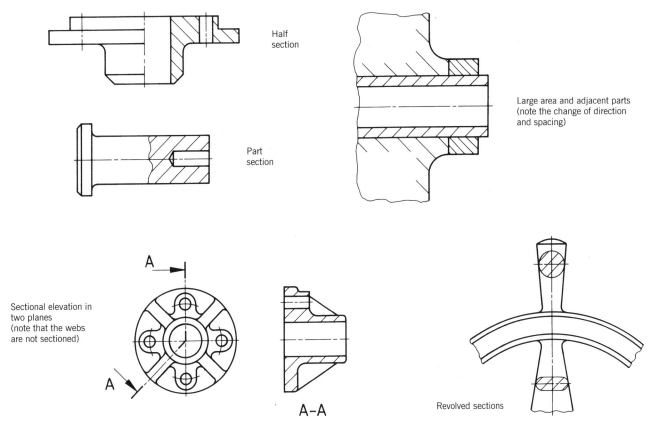

Half
section

Part
section

Large area and adjacent parts
(note the change of direction
and spacing)

Sectional elevation in
two planes
(note that the webs
are not sectioned)

A

A

A–A

Revolved sections

Figure 1.55 Sectional elevations in more than one plane

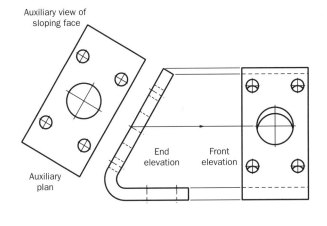

Auxiliary view of
sloping face

Auxiliary
plan

End
elevation

Front
elevation

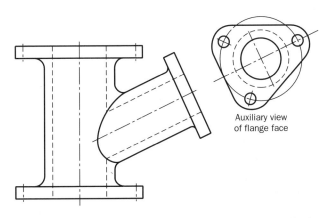

Auxiliary view
of flange face

Figure 1.56 Auxiliary views (after L.C. Mott *Engineering Design
and Construction*, Oxford University Press)

Self-assessment tasks

The diagram below shows a drawing of a block that has been
created using AutoCAD LT.

1. Copy the front and end elevations from the drawing using
   either CAD software or conventional drawing.

2. Add a horizontal cutting plane at mid height and from it project
   a sectional plan view.

3. From your drawing project an auxiliary elevation at right angles
   to the inclined face of the block.

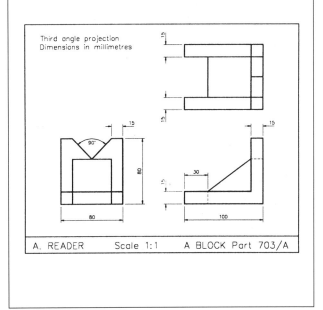

Third angle projection
Dimensions in millimetres

15

15

15

90°

80

15

15

30

15

80

100

A. READER   Scale 1:1   A BLOCK Part 703/A

Engineering features

There are many components and features within engineering drawing that should be represented according to conventions set down in British Standards. This use of common conventions avoids the need for explanation and reduces confusion.

Screw threads

Whenever screw threads are shown, irrespective of the thread type, the conventions shown in Fig. 1.57 should be used. This convention enables drawings to be created more quickly and appear less cluttered. Two views of a hexagonal-headed bolt are shown, a plan view of a threaded hole and a sectional elevation through a bolt in a hole. Notice the differences between the thread (the broken line) in the end elevation of the bolt and in the thread in the plan. Look also at the detail in the sectional elevation: the drilled hole, the threaded portion of the hole and the bolt within it.

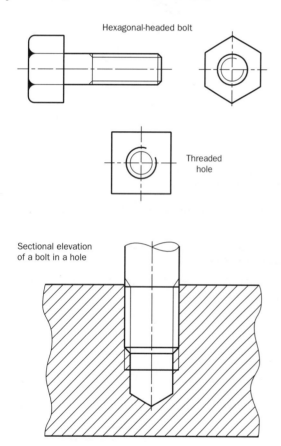

Figure 1.57 Screw threads

Welded joints

A comprehensive range of welding symbols is contained within PP7307. This includes: butt welds; flat, single bevel and double bevel welds; welds with flat, convex or concave surfaces; spot welds and a range of fillet welds. Figure 1.58 shows examples of the symbols used in engineering drawings for welds within fabricated structures. The two examples show an illustration followed by a graphical representation, as it should appear within a drawing, and a symbolic

representation using the recommended symbol for that weld type. Symbolic representations are more likely to be used rather than graphical representations when there are a large number of welded joints on a particular drawing.

Gears and bearings

Like screw threads, gears and bearings are simplified and there is no requirement to show the actual detail. Gears are shown as solids without teeth and the pitch circle, the effective diameter of a gear is shown by a chain line. Gear trains are therefore shown with the meshed gears' pitch circles touching. Figure 1.59 shows examples of spur gears and bevel gears.

Bearings, other than plain bearings, are shown as in Fig. 1.60 irrespective of whether they are ball or roller types of bearings.

Common symbols and abbreviations

Only those symbols and abbreviations specified within BS 308 and PP7308 should be used on engineering drawings. Any other necessary notes and information should be clearly printed in full. Table 1.3 includes the most commonly used abbreviations.

Table 1.3 Symbols and abbreviations

Term	Abbreviation or symbol
Across flats	AF
Centres	CRS
Chamfered	CHAM
Countersunk	CSK
Counterbore	CBORE
Diameter	DIA *or* 1
Drawing	DRG
Equally spaced	EQUI SP
Figure	FIG
Hexagon	HEX
Left hand	LH
Long	LG
Material	MATL
Maximum	MAX
Minimum	MIN
Number	NO
Pitch circle diameter	PCD
Radius (in a note)	RAD
Radius (preceding a dimension)	R
Right hand	RH
Round head	RD HD
Specification	SPEC
Spotface	SFACE
Square	SQ
Standard	STD
Undercut	UCUT

Machining symbols

It is often necessary, particularly with cast components, to indicate those faces that have a critical function or a flatness requirement sufficient for them to require some form of machine finishing. It is the engineering designer's responsibility to make these decisions. Such faces or surfaces that require finishing are indicated by a machining symbol,

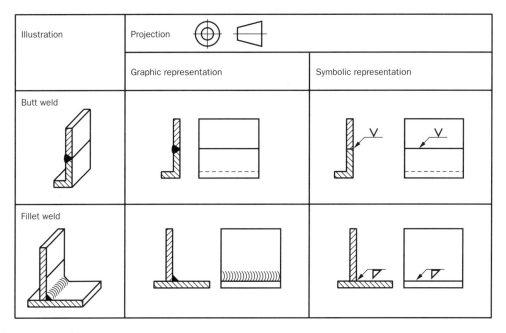

Illustration	Projection ⊕ ◁		
	Graphic representation		Symbolic representation
Butt weld			
Fillet weld			

Figure 1.58 Examples of welds

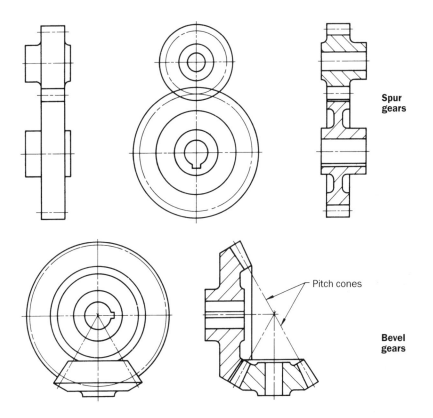

Spur gears

Pitch cones

Bevel gears

Figure 1.59 Gears

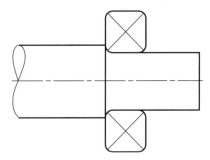

Figure 1.60 A bearing

often including an indication of the acceptable surface finish. This texture or roughness value is a measurement in micrometres (μm) and it is added to the symbol as shown in Fig. 1.61. This value will indicate whether a milled or turned finish is acceptable or if the surface requires further machining such as surface grinding or honing. Where it is necessary to machine finish all over then a general note may be added.

Spotfacing, countersinking and counterboring are other examples of localised surface machining for a particular function (Fig. 1.62). In these instances it is the location or seating of the heads of bolts and screws, and of washers and nuts.

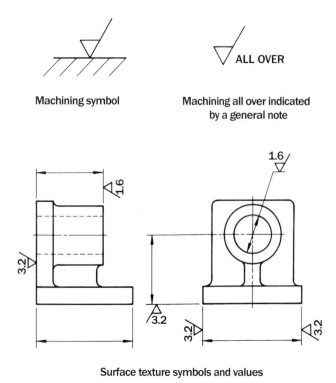

Machining symbol   Machining all over indicated by a general note

Surface texture symbols and values

Figure 1.61 Machining symbols

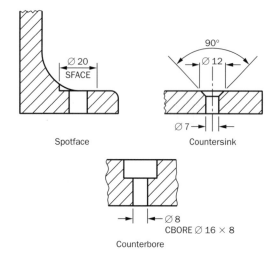

Spotface   Countersink

Counterbore

Figure 1.62 Spotfaces, countersinks and counterbores

Scale drawings

The application of scale to engineering drawings is common practice. This is principally to ensure a correct fit regardless of the size of paper used for the drawing, but is also used for clarity of detail. When using CAD drawings are normally made full size and the plot or print size is then scaled if a 'hardcopy' is required. When drawing using conventional instruments scale rules should be used in preference to carrying out calculations which may be prone to error. In the drawings shown in Fig. 1.66 (p. 34) you can see how scale can also be applied to just a part of a drawing, in this instance enabling the dimensioning of a small detail.

Scale is expressed in the form of a ratio and there are a number of British Standard recommended scales to use. For drawings that are smaller than full size there are the following recommended reduction scales:

1:2   1:5   1:10
1:20   1:50 1:100
1:200 1:500 1:1000

For drawings larger than full size there are the following recommended enlargement scales:

2:1   5:1   10:1
20:1   50:1

Scale, including full size, should never be used with the expectation that during manufacture the drawing can be measured and dimensions extracted in this way. As drawings are copied and reproduced they are liable to distortion, for this reason the words 'DO NOT SCALE' are often added to drawings to prompt the user to read rather than measure the drawing.

Tolerancing

It is not actually possible repeatedly to manufacture components to a precisely identical size, nor is it often cost effective to try. There will always therefore be some small variation. When component parts of an assembly are brought together it is important to know that they will fit as required without selection having to take place. Tolerancing dimensions is concerned with what is acceptable in respect of the ability of components to fit together or to function as the design intends. It regards the permitted variation from the nominal or basic size.

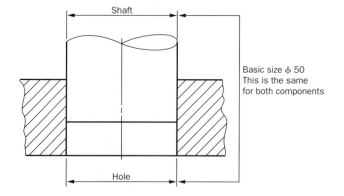

Figure 1.63 Shaft in a hole

Figure 1.63 shows a shaft in a hole. Consider the following in relation to the function of the components and dimensioning them for manufacture (see Fig. 1.64):

- Let us assume that their basic size is 50 mm (diameter) and it is a requirement of the function of these components that clearance exists between them. The hole, therefore, must always be larger than the shaft.
- The design engineer must determine what will be an acceptable functional clearance; this could typically be a minimum of 0.025 mm and a maximum of 0.095 mm: a tolerance band of 0.070 mm.

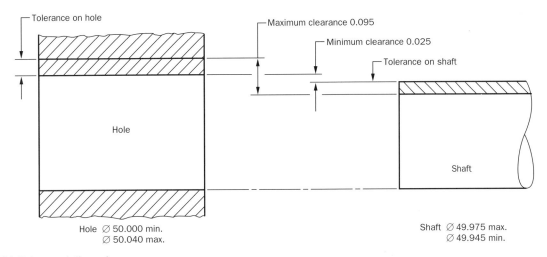

Figure 1.64 Toleranced dimensions

- The task now is to determine the manufacturing tolerances for the two components, i.e. the dimensions for both the shaft and the hole that will ensure that the clearance achieved, with any possible assembly combination, will not go beyond the acceptable tolerance limits.
- By attaching slightly more than half of the tolerance band to the hole (it is always easier to be accurate with a shaft than with a hole), the hole size can be fixed at say 1 50.000 min. and 1 50.040 max. This means that a 1 50.000 hole would be acceptable, as would any size up to a maximum of 1 50.040.
- The largest acceptable size of shaft can be determined by considering the smallest possible hole and the minimum clearance, i.e. 1 50.000 − 0.025 = 1 49.975. The smallest acceptable shaft is therefore the largest hole minus the largest clearance, i.e. 1 50.040 − 0.095 = 1 49.945.

To assist the design engineer in making decisions regarding the amount of tolerance required to achieve specific functions, ranging from large clearance to heavy interference, British Standards publish tables of limits and fits in BS 4500. The BS guide to tolerancing for schools and colleges, PP7309, does not contain limits and fits specifications.

Communicating tolerance

There are two principal methods of expressing toleranced sizes on engineering drawings. Either with the upper and lower limits of size (Fig. 1.65(a)) or with the tolerances expressed as a variation from the nominal size (Fig. 1.65(b)).

Self-assessment tasks

1. The diagram below shows the front elevation of a pressed steel component. Make a fully dimensioned 2:1 scale copy of this drawing. The hole should be dimensioned with a $+/- 0.050$ mm tolerance.

2. The two pieces of 40 × 15 mm mild steel bar shown below are fastened together using a hexagonal headed bolt, a nut and two washers. Draw a full-size sectional elevation through the centre of the hole with all of the components assembled.

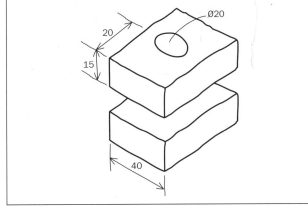

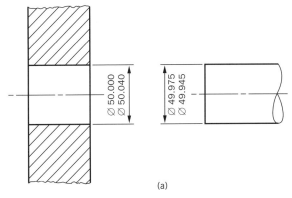

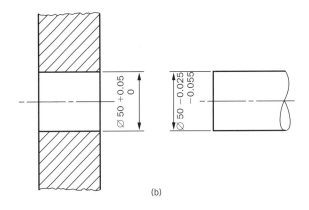

Figure 1.65 Communicating tolerances

Engineering drawing in practice

Title block

All engineering drawings should have a title block that contains the following basic information (Fig. 1.66):

- Name of the draughtsperson
- Date
- Scale
- Title
- Drawing and issue number
- Method of projection used in words or symbol (this may be located elsewhere on the drawing)

The drawing in Fig. 1.66 of a connector is taken from PP7308 as an example of a typical engineering drawing. Study the drawing to locate and note the following:

- From the front elevation is projected, in third angle projection, a part plan and a part sectional elevation. There is also an enlarged scale detail drawing.
- There is tolerance attached to particular dimensions and as a general note within the title block.
- The 165 mm dimension is shown in brackets to show that this is an overall dimension for guidance only. It is possible that this dimension cannot be achieved within the general tolerance of the drawing because it must depend upon the two dimensions (40 mm and 125 mm) that make it up.

- The drawing also shows examples of:
  - chamfers at 458
  - knurling (MEDIUM KNURL)
  - a spherical radii (SR)
  - holes equally spaced around a 65 mm pitch circle diameter (EQUI SP ON 65 PCD)
  - screw threads
  - angular dimensioning
  - flat faces on circular parts, indicated by cross lines on the flat
  - machining symbols and surface texture values

Assembly drawings

Figure 1.67 shows an example of an assembly drawing. It shows a ball bearing race located within a split bearing housing bolted down to a cast bedway. Assembly drawings are often shown sectioned to reveal the inner details. This drawing is part sectioned with the vertical centre line acting as the cutting plane. Dimensions are not normally added to assembly drawings other than a few overall dimensions to indicate the assembled size for packaging, storage, transportation, etc.

The numbers around the drawing are used as reference for the parts list that may be included on the assembly drawing. This will be similar to the electronics parts list example shown earlier in this unit (Fig. 1.47). Part lists should be numbered from the bottom of the drawing going upwards, see Fig. 1.68 of from the top going down. This enables additional parts to be added with subsequent modifications and re-issues.

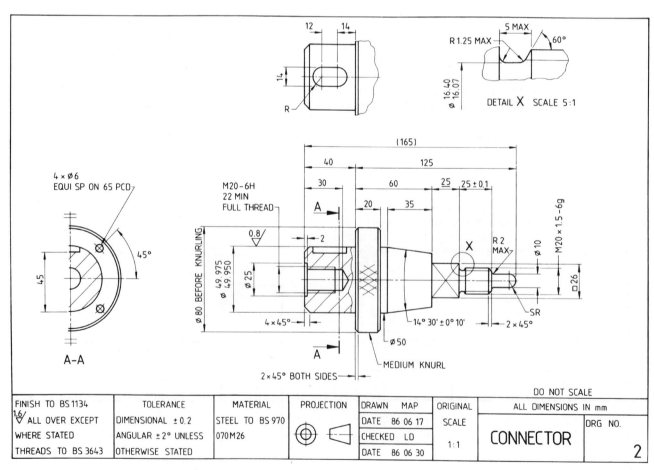

Figure 1.66 Detail drawing

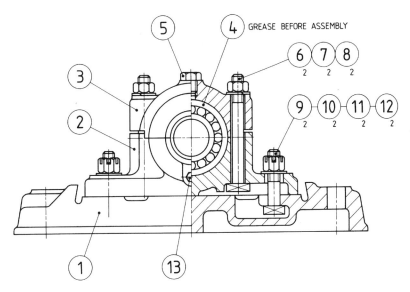

Figure 1.67 Assembly drawing

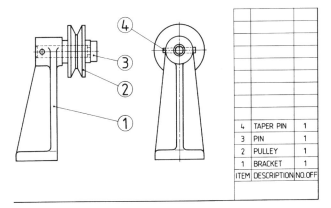

ITEM	DESCRIPTION	NO.OFF
4	TAPER PIN	1
3	PIN	1
2	PULLEY	1
1	BRACKET	1

Figure 1.68 Parts list

Self-assessment tasks

1. Study the drawing of the swivel bracket in Fig. 1.69 and then answer the following questions.
   (i) State the method of projection used.
   (ii) What material and manufacturing process are to be used to make the bracket.
   (iii) With reference to the process by which the bracket has been manufactured explain the note 'FILLET RADII R3 MIN'.
   (iv) With reference to the tolerances and the machining symbols state the maximum and minimum acceptable sizes for the width and the height of the bracket.
   (v) The drawing has two principal views, a plan and a sectional front elevation, from the sectional front elevation draw or sketch two end elevations.
2. From the assembly drawing in Fig 1.67 produce a parts list containing the name of the part, the material from which it is made and the quantity required.
3. Produce detail and assembly drawings of a cassette or CD case.

Engineering drawing case study

This short case study focuses upon an airbox unit that is part of a gas turbine training rig manufactured by TecQuipment Ltd and used by military and civil training establishments. All TecQuipment's drawings are currently carried out using CAD systems but existing conventional drawings of components that are still in use are only converted when a modification or new design takes place. The move from conventional drawing to CAD is expensive but the advantages (outlined on p. 25) soon make the transition worthwhile.

Another advantage of computer integration within engineering is the use of digitised photographic images. Fig. 1.70 shows a digital image of the airbox which is stored along with the drawings as a computer image file. This format enables transmission of the photographs and drawings via land-line or satellite links. This means that discussions can take place with clients and repairs can be undertaken at any distance, including overseas, by the engineer from their desk without the delay involved in waiting for information to be sent and received by post.

The airbox assembly drawing in Fig. 1.71 shows what is essentially a sheet metal fabrication. Sheet materials are drawn as thick lines and you can see that this drawing requires a lot of notes regarding adhesives and sealants.

The part numbered 4 on the assembly drawing, the 'intake diffuser', is shown as a detail drawing in Fig. 1.72. Compare this CAD-generated drawing with Fig. 1.73 which is an older conventional drawing of a similar component. The drawing is showing signs of deterioration after some years of storage and handling and you can see in particular the lack of consistency with the textual information on the drawing.

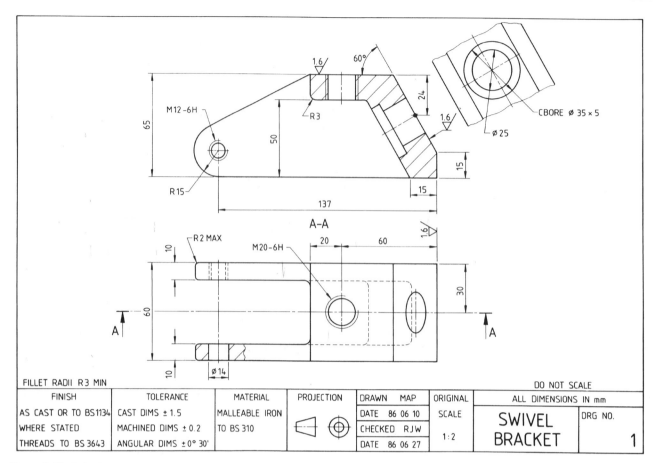

FILLET RADII R3 MIN								DO NOT SCALE	
FINISH	TOLERANCE	MATERIAL	PROJECTION	DRAWN	MAP	ORIGINAL	ALL DIMENSIONS IN mm		
AS CAST OR TO BS1134	CAST DIMS ± 1.5	MALLEABLE IRON		DATE 86 06 10		SCALE	SWIVEL BRACKET	DRG NO.	
WHERE STATED	MACHINED DIMS ± 0.2	TO BS 310		CHECKED RJW		1:2			1
THREADS TO BS 3643	ANGULAR DIMS ± 0° 30'			DATE 86 06 27					

Figure 1.69 Swivel bracket

Figure 1.70 Airbox (*reproduced courtesy of* TecQuipment Limited)

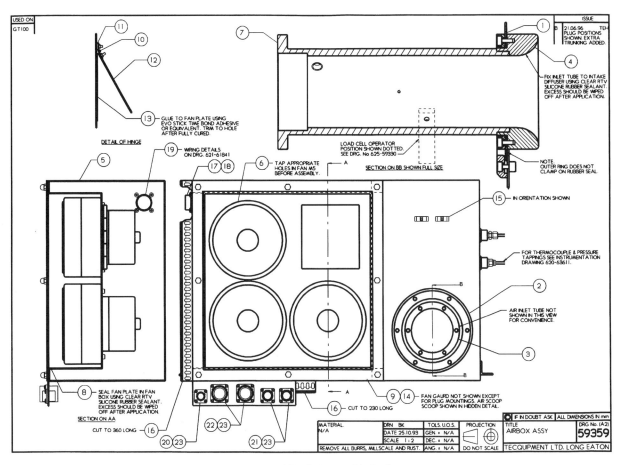

Figure 1.71 Airbox assembly drawing (*reproduced courtesy of* TecQuipment Limited)

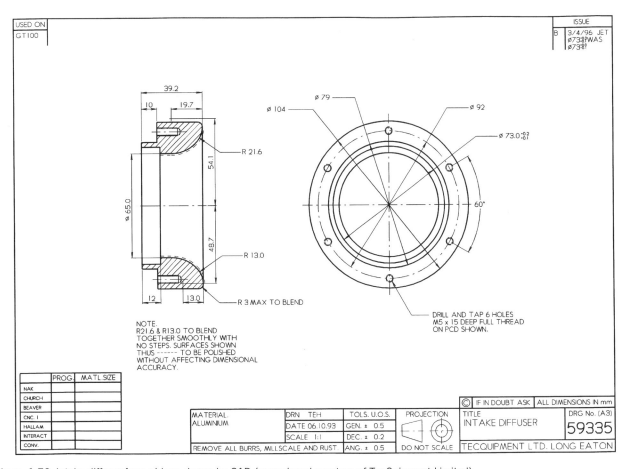

Figure 1.72 Intake diffuser from airbox, drawn by CAD (*reproduced courtesy of* TecQuipment Limited)

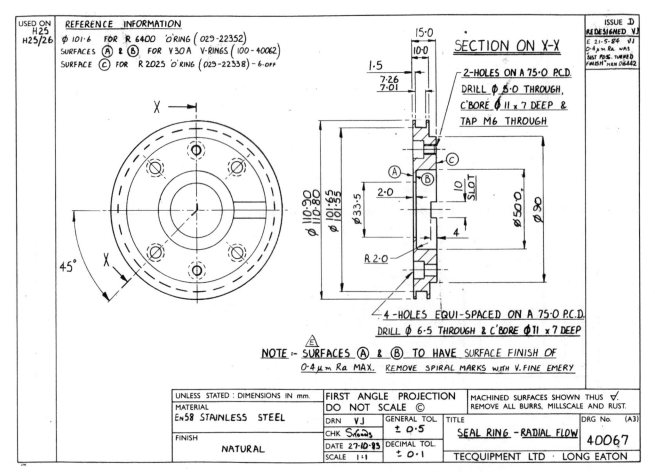

Figure 1.73 Intake diffuser from airbox, drawn conventionally (*reproduced courtesy of* TecQuipment Limited)

Application of New Technology in Engineering

This unit looks at the role of new technology through the investigation of engineered products. It focuses on the development of the product, which uses new technology from the following areas:

- Information technology
- New materials
- Automation.

You are asked to investigate a new technological product by looking at its purpose, form and structure and how new technologies have been used in its production. The unit will also look at how new technology affects society and the impact it has had on the engineering industry as a whole. You will be asked to describe these features with reference to your chosen product.

Two case studies will be explored in this unit:

- All aspect of new technology related to the design and production of a CD-ROM (Fig. 2.1).
- All aspects of new technology related to the design and production of a CD Player (Fig. 2.2).

Case Studies CD-ROM and CD Player

Introduction

Compact disc (CD) technology was developed in the early 1980s. Initially, it was used for digital recording of music.

The digital information in the form of binary code (0 or 1) was imprinted onto the disc, to be read by a laser and decoded by a microprocessor. The decoded signal could then be amplified and relayed to loudspeakers.

The technology advanced very rapidly and it became possible to record more and more digital information enabling the CD to hold computer code and associated data. These CDs were used for permanent storage of data and were given the name Compact Disc Read-Only Memory, or CD-ROM for short. CD-ROMs were identical in form to music CDs, but contained different data.

Both types of disc have their data recorded and read in much the same way, which means that the most up-to-date CDs can have music, computer code, still images, video, etc., all held on the same disc. The delivery of the information is handled by a dedicated microprocessor.

The company

ComLaser is an electronics company that has specialised in the production of CD players since 1984. The basic players are supplied to both audio equipment and computer manufacturers for installation in their own products.

In 1992 ComLaser extended its business to include the production of CD-ROMs, having noticed a rapid increase in the demand for such products. Involvement in both product markets allowed the company to improve its production methods and advance the technology required.

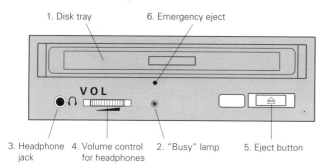

Figure 2.1 CD-ROM drive parts and functions

1. Disk tray
6. Emergency eject
3. Headphone jack
4. Volume control for headphones
2. "Busy" lamp
5. Eject button

Figure 2.2 CD Player

2.1 New technological product assignment

The student should select one, or more than one, technological product from the following product areas and investigate all aspects of the new technology selected.

Communications: The digital cellular telephone

Cellular telephones remove the restrictions normally associated with conventional telephones. They can be carried easily from place to place and be used in any situation. As well as being used for voice communication, they can transmit and receive electronic data such as fax, e-mail and pager messages.

Early cellular phones used analogue radio technology. This suffered from electrical interference called 'noise'. By adding an analogue to digital (A/D) converter the signal could be transmitted as binary data which is noise free and can correct errors. A second advantage is that the signal can also be transmitted at reduced power, which extends battery life.

In order to be successful in the increasingly competitive market, a cellular telephone must be light in weight, and compact. It must also have a number of user-friendly features, and have a long battery life.

Entertainment: The Sony PlayStation

The Sony PlayStation is a computer for playing electronic games. The main unit contains a central processor, RAM, and audio/video card. The game controller is attached to the central unit via a multicore cable. The games are programmed on a CD-ROM which can be inserted into the main unit.

This is an example of fully interactive technology, where user input is used to determine the output from the program.

Transportation: Electronic toll collection

Electronic toll collection (ETC) is a computerised system that automatically collects fees from motorists. Examples are pay-per-use services such as parking, tunnel/bridge entry, etc. (Fig. 2.3) Future uses include restricting or deterring city centre access, and payment for fuel at petrol station forecourts. The system requires:

- Automatic vehicle identification (AVI) using a radio frequency (RF) tag fixed in the vehicle. This identifies the specific vehicle to the computer.
- Automatic vehicle classification (AVC) using sensors in and around the payment zone. This determines the type of vehicle so that the proper toll can be charged.
- Video enforcement systems (VES) which capture images of the licence plates of vehicles that use the facility without a valid AVI device.

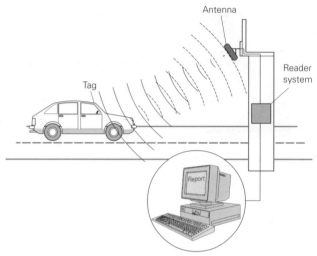

Figure 2.3 Electronic toll collection

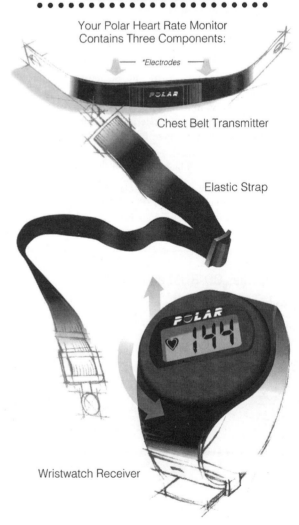

Figure 2.4 Personal heart rate monitor

When a customer signs up to use the system they provide personal details for automatic payment from a bank account. They are then issued with a unique AVI device. The system is secure as its identification code can be altered every time it logs on to the host computer to prevent fraud. When a payment zone is entered, e.g. a car park, the AVI device signals the host computer which records entry and exit times. The payment is then deducted automatically from the user's bank account. A monthly statement of use and payment is also issued to the user.

Medical: personal heart rate monitor

Those who are training for sporting events or wish to improve their fitness level may want to keep a track of their heart rate during exercise.

The personal heart rate monitor (Fig. 2.4) consists of a sensor band which is worn around the chest. This band also contains a short-range radio transmitter which transmits data to a microprocessor and a display device worn on the wrist. The sensor detects the electrical activity of the heart during a beat. The data received by the microprocessor is displayed on an LCD screen as numbers of beats per minute.

Industrial: intelligent sprinkler system

Conventional sprinkler systems are triggered in response to heat. An entire network of sprinklers are triggered at once, and even those areas not affected by the fire will be doused with water.

Computer-controlled alarm and sprinkler systems locate the exact position of a fire and trigger only those sprinklers that will affect the fire directly. This protects unaffected stock and machinery from water damage.

Infrared detection technology is used to locate the fire in three dimensions. A central computer can then activate specific sprinklers and only for the time needed to put out the fire.

2.2 Investigation of new technology products

> *Activity*: For your chosen product research information from manufacturers and suppliers.

Assessment of the products properties

You will need to assess the product's properties in terms of:

- Weight
- Colour
- Surface finish
- Scratch resistance
- Areas likely to be damaged.

Case Study: CD Player

Heaviness

Careful consideration was given to the final location of the CD Player. The device is designed to be installed as part of an audio (Fig 2.5) or computer system and two main factors had to be taken into account:

- **Resistance to resonant vibration** – In operation slight variations in CD mass will set up vibrations as it rotates at high speed. The player had to be heavy enough not to resonate with the vibration. This is particularly critical when playing CD-ROMs.
- **Pressure on other units** – An audio CD player that is too heavy will put strain on the housing of other units should it be placed on top.

Figure 2.5 Pioneer HiFi stacker system

Colour and Surface Finish

CD Players are offered in a variety of colours to suit the taste of the user. The most popular colours are black (associated with high technology products) and off-white (associated with computers). Brushed aluminium units are also available. They cater for the hi-fi market where this new fashionable appearance is favoured.

When choosing a finish, a number of factors are considered:

- Wear resistance – The finish must not rub away if items such as CD boxes, papers, etc., are regularly placed on top of the unit.
- Manufacturing defects – Minor scratches in the metal surface can be concealed with a covering finish.
- Environment in which the unit is to be used – Exposure to sunlight may fade some finishes, dust in the home may be more attracted to some surfaces, etc.

Feel

Although not handled very often, the surface had to be slip resistant and have an attractive appearance. A public survey of several options revealed that a slightly roughened, matt surface was the most acceptable.

Scratch resistance

A testing device was constructed in which an arm rubbed a variety of abrasive surfaces onto the product casing. It was found that an acrylic paint coating was the most abrasion resistant.

Areas likely to be damaged

Apart from the possibility of the complete unit being dropped, there is little risk of user damage. However, damage occurring during mechanical and electrical operation needs to be determined. The product was set up in a mounting jig so that the movements (open/close, spin/brake) and electronic functions could be tested over many thousands of operations. Simple mechanical links pressed the open/close button. The motor of the unit operated automatically on closure. Electronic functions were operated by further mechanical links cycling through the various push-button operations of the player. Testing continued until failure occurred, or until five years use had been simulated. At these times the player was disassembled and its individual components examined for damage. Those parts that had shown unacceptable failure rates need to be redesigned.

Case Study: ComLaser CDs/CD-ROMs

Assessment of the products properties

Heaviness

With the use of new polymers such as acrylic and polycarbonate, CDs are inherently light in weight; they are less than one-quarter of the size and weight of a vinyl disc.

This makes recording, storage and carriage of the product very easy.

As the disc will be spun at high speed, the overall balance of the CD is critical. Any heavy spot on the disc will cause severe vibration in use, which will prevent accurate reading by the laser.

Colour

The data surface of the CD must be highly reflective. The most common material used is aluminium, giving a bright silver finish. Gold and silver may also be used with a corresponding change in colour. As only one side of the CD is used for data reading, the other side may carry graphics and text of any kind.

Feel

The use of clear polymer holders (crystal boxes) for the product was highly favoured to give added weight and enhance product appearance.

Scratch resistance

As CDs carry digital data, minor scratches do not affect the sound obtained from audio products. Minor errors in the data stream caused by these scratches are ignored as CD Players have in-built correction systems. CD-ROMs are more susceptible to scratch failure and so must be handled carefully by the user. During production, testing of the CD data quality is carried out by selecting a sample from the production run. A computer system reads the data, rejecting any that do not fall within tolerance limits.

Areas likely to be damaged

The data surface of CDs is highly sensitive to damage. The use of crystal boxes protects the surface during storage and carriage, but the user of the CD must take appropriate care to ensure product reliability after purchase, and advice for correct handling and cleaning is included with the product.

Some damage, abrasion for example, is likely to occur with regular use. Deterioration in data quality is minimised by breaking the data up into small sections, each containing error correction codes, and mixing it up over one circuit of the disc. This would be similar to cutting up the page of a book into, say, 10 numbered squares and putting them together in the order 1, 6, 2, 7, 3, 8, 4, 9, 5, 10. A misread of a small amount of data is much easier to correct electronically than an entire sequence. The laser reads the data with each revolution of the CD. A microprocessor corrects any errors found in the small sections and puts the data back into sequence. The data can then be used as intended.

The purpose of the product

Case Study: CD Player

A CD Player has the following function: Holding the CD/CD-ROM to be played in the correct position for reading.

A movable tray is built into the player. The tray is recessed to accept the disc and to locate it in the correct position. The user presses a button, operating a motor which extends the tray out of the player. The disc can then be placed on the tray. A second push on the button retracts the tray back into the player (Fig. 2.7).

Figure 2.6 CD Player: LCD

Spinning the disc at the appropriate rotational speed for accurate reading

Once the disc is positioned correctly a second motor locks into the central hole of the disc. The motor then spins the disc. The speed of the rotation depends on the speed of the reading/decoding process. This is under the control of a microprocessor, which varies the speed of the disc accordingly. CD-ROM players often declare the maximum speed at which they can read data in comparison to a predetermined reference speed. For example, a 4× Player can read data 4× faster than the reference.

Reading of the data on the CD/CD-ROM using a focused laser beam

When the player tray is in the correct position a laser device is activated. The laser emits a narrow beam of light which is focused to a point corresponding to the data surface of the CD/CD-ROM. The data surface consists of silvered pits arranged in concentric circles around the disc. The varying quality of the beam reflected from the data surface is detected by a photosensor, which delivers its output to a microprocessor for decoding.

Data processing

The binary signal from the photosensor is analysed by a microprocessor. The microprocessor then delivers its output to several other components within the player unit. For example, sound data will be delivered to a digital / analogue converter which will produce a signal suitable for amplification and transmission to loudspeakers. Other data for use in an audio player may include the number of music tracks on the CD and their timing. This data will be processed and delivered to an illuminated character (LCD) display unit on the front of the player unit (Fig. 2.6).

The front plate of the device is fabricated from plastic and coloured to match that of the computer.

Case Study: CDs/CD-ROMs

The purpose of the product

CDs/CD-ROMs are designed to hold large amounts of data in digital form. Text, graphics, audio, video and computer code

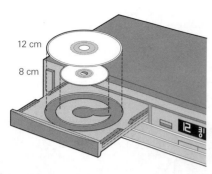

Figure 2.7 CD Player: open tray

can all be stored digitally and retrieved on demand. This allows CDs to be used as low-cost, compact, immediately accessible information systems which do not deteriorate with time.

The form and structure of the product

The agreed standard in the CD industry is for a product made from rigid, distortion resistant polymer, 120 mm diameter and 1.2 mm thick with a central hole 15 mm in diameter. Data is recorded in a spiral from the centre of the disc outwards, beginning at a point 23 mm from the centre of the disc and ending 58.5 mm from the same point. This method allows for future changes in disc size, e.g. a reduction in diameter, yet still allow the CD to be read in a standard player.

The CD carries a single helical track of data about $0.5\ \mu m$ wide with a track circuit separation of about $1.6\ \mu m$. The track itself is approximately 8 km in length.

The use of thermoplastic polycarbonate enables the product to be injection moulded:

- Laser scanning the surface of a glass disc coated in a photosensitive layer (photoresist) makes a master recording (Fig. 2.8). The photoresist sets hard where it has been exposed to the laser beam, the remainder being washed off.

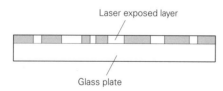

Figure 2.8 Making of a master recording

- A nickel layer is then coated over the photoresist, followed by a layer of silver. This allows the disc to be played to check for errors in the data recorded (Fig. 2.9).

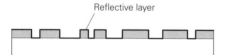

Figure 2.9 Photo resist: layer of nickel

- A layer of metal a few millimetres thick is then deposited over the surface of the master CD (Fig. 2.10). The master is then removed from the metal layer, which is now a 'negative' copy of the master. This plate is now called the 'father' copy.

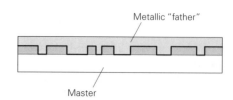

Figure 2.10 Metal deposition layer

- An electroplating process is used to coat the 'father' a number of times to produce several 'positive' or 'mother' copies. In turn the 'mother' copies are used to produce many more 'negative' copies, now called 'sons'. The 'sons' are the copies that are used in injection moulds. Polycarbonate of a precise refractive index is used in the injection process (Fig. 2.11). It is refraction of the laser beam through the polycarbonate that achieves the final precise focus.

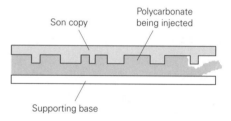

Figure 2.11 Electroplating process

- The polymer copies are then plated with aluminium on the data surface to provide the necessary reflective layer (Figs. 2.12).

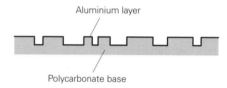

Figure 2.12 Aluminium coating of data surface

- The metallised data surface then receives a protective layer of acrylic (Fig. 2.13), which is cured on exposure to UV light. The label of the disc, or any other text or graphics, can then be screen-printed on top of the acrylic.

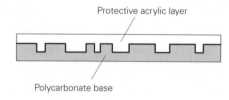

Figure 2.13 Protective layer of acrylic

Case Study: CD Player

The form and structure of the product

Audio CD Player

The traditional shape for a unit of this type is a rectangular box, although the more contemporary microsystems demand a more cubic shape. Fabrication is therefore relatively easy.

The main chassis is made up of pressed steel sheet, onto which is mounted the PCB, CD laser unit, operation/display panel and rear panel input/output connectors for mains and audio. This is then covered over the top and sides with another pressed steel sheet. Steel is used in preference to other materials as it must resist the pressure of other units being placed on top and must be rigid enough to hold vibration-sensitive components in place. The frame into which the CD laser unit is mounted is fabricated from high-carbon steel. This combines strength with great rigidity and vibration resistance. The U-shape of the frame allows the CD laser unit, which is purchased pre-assembled from a manufacturer, to be slid into place and fixed with a single screw. This also allows for easy removal and replacement in the event of failure.

CD-ROM Player

This consists of the CD laser unit, a dedicated control PCB (called a 'card') and the steel frame only, to be mounted within the chassis of a computer

New technologies used in the design of the product

Case Study: CD/CD-ROM Player

The laser

The diode laser used in the ComLaser CD/CD-ROM Player emits an infrared beam when a current passes through it. The beam can be autofocused to a point approximately 1.7 μm in diameter at the data surface of the disc.

The optics

The optics needed to keep the laser beam on the data track of the disc are quite complicated.

At first the beam is split into three parallel beams by a diffraction grating. As the central beam follows the data track, its reflection varies in brightness. The reflection brightness of the two side beams is constant as they follow the flat region (**land**) between data tracks (Fig. 2.14).

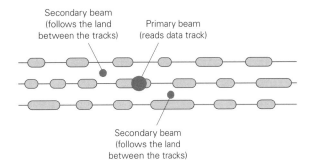

Figure 2.14 Diagram of three beams on data track

If the beams drift off track, the relative brightness of the beams will change. The brightness of the side beams will fall as they cross into the data track; and the brightness of the central beam will rise as it crosses into the land. A microprocessor analyses the drift and activates the tracking motor to realign the beams.

Data is read by analysing the reflected central beam, which may be fully reflected or not reflected at all by the data track, corresponding to a binary 0 or 1 respectively.

Put simply, the presence or absence of the reflected beam is detected by a photosensor, which directs its output to a microprocessor. The data is then analysed and the appropriate output generated.

Activity: Relate any of the above features to the development of your chosen product.

2.3 Information technology

DATA STORAGE: Databases

A database is simply a store from which information can be retrieved easily. A good example of a simple database is the index of this book. A key word is selected and the index database directs you to the information you require.

Before the invention of electronic data storage all information was written on paper. The paper then had to be filed according to an agreed system, such as by date, by subject, by company, etc., usually in a filing cabinet. Problems arose if the same information needed to be filed under a number of categories. In this case an equivalent number of copies of the original information would have to be made. Those copies would then be filed separately. To keep track of all the copies a cross-referencing system would then be needed. In large businesses with many thousands of files this rapidly became extremely difficult to manage and information was lost with alarming regularity.

A computerised database, however, holds all the categorised information in one master file. Depending on the needs of the user, that information can be retrieved and cross-referenced in an infinite number of ways.

Example of a simple database: Engineering records
An engineer may wish to keep track of every product designed for a particular company. Creating a database with a number of categories can do this. These categories are called **fields** (Fig. 2.15). Each field occupies one column in a database table.

Alternatively, data can be entered into boxes laid out on a form. Each box represents one field (Fig. 2.16). Most people find this an easier way of entering the information required. The number of fields in the database design is limited only by the capacity of the software used to build it and the imagination of the user!

The engineer then enters the information (**data**) about each design as it is drafted. The database program automatically allocates to each a unique identification number. This is all that needs to be recorded on the design itself. The order of input does not matter – the entries can be made totally at random.

ID	Supplier	PartCode	Status	Contact Name
10	Woodford Engineering	B12-D	Cancelled	n/a
2	Woodford Engineering	B21-D	In production	John Woodford
16	Woodford Engineering	B17-B	Prototype testing	Bruce Harrison
15	Woodford Engineering	B08-A	In production	John Woodford
6	Woodford Engineering	B27-C	Prototype testing	Darren Livingstone
5	Hi Tech Aero Ltd	A14-B	In production	Helen Stubbs
8	Hi Tech Aero Ltd	A27-B	In production	Helen Stubbs
3	Helix Ltd	F71-B	Ready	Colin Wilson
9	Helix Ltd	E16-B	Prototype testing	Howard Motherwell
20	Helix Ltd	F02-C	In production	Zoe Campbell
12	Helix Ltd	E34-C	Design stage	Kirsty Lodge
13	Helix Ltd	E12-C	Ready	Colin Wilson
1	Dynamic Systems Ltd	C46-A	Ready	Alison Staples
7	Dynamic Systems Ltd	C09-A	Design stage	Jose Lopez
4	Dynamic Systems Ltd	G04-A	Design stage	Adrian Hill
18	Dynamic Systems Ltd	G22-A	Design stage	Adrian Hill
11	Dynamic Systems Ltd	G22-D	Ready	Adam Scott
14	Clayton & Marshall	A35-D	Ready	Roger Clayton
17	Clayton & Marshall	A24-C	Ready	Roger Clayton
19	Clayton & Marshall	A05-D	Ready	Roger Clayton

Figure 2.15 Simple database: data entering by fields

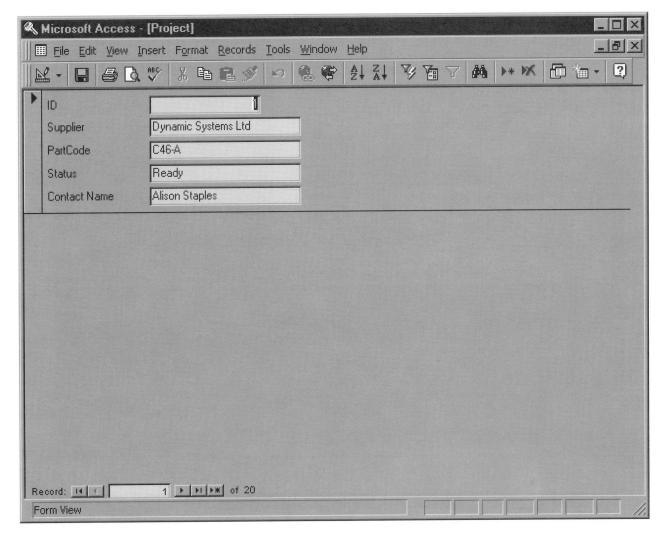

Figure 2.16 Simple database: data entry to boxes

Once all the pieces of data have been entered the engineer can now select and sort the information as required. For example, designs from one supplier can be grouped together in the same table instead of being mixed in together. To do this the database **Sort** command can be used (Fig.2.17).

The computer then sorts and displays the information (Fig. 2.18).

Selected information may also be displayed by creating a set of instructions for the computer to follow. This set of instructions is called a **query**, and informs the computer to select only those components being supplied by Helix Ltd (Fig. 2.19). Additional information required is also included in the instructions:

- The ID number of the design for easy retrieval
- Its content (aircraft wing or boat hull)
- Its description
- Its format (on paper plan or floppy disc).

The computer then displays the information requested (Fig. 2.20).

Alternatively, the engineer may wish to know which of the components are at each stage of the design and production process, sorting the information by status (Fig. 2.21). Another query can be set up to give this result.

In large businesses the number of fields and queries may run into hundreds or even thousands. On paper such records would occupy whole buildings, the information sorting and

selecting taking many weeks to achieve. An electronic database holds all of this information in one place, such as a single floppy disc. The data it holds can be processed in any way imaginable, delivering the result in fractions of a second.

INTERNET WEBSITES

The Internet is a global library of information held on millions of computers around the world. In order to gain access to the information it contains, you must access an Internet service provider (**ISP**). The ISP will then allow you to link your computer to the Internet via a telephone line and modem using its host computer (called a **Web Server**) as a gateway.

The ISP will usually offer you a certain amount of memory space on its web server as part of the account package. This memory space can be used to store files written in a special code called **HTML** (hyper-text markup language). HTML describes the format of the web page. The stored files can then be accessed by anyone else connected to the Internet.

Each HTML file represents one **web page**. Collections of web pages make up a **website** (Fig. 2.22).

In order to view the contents of the Internet – a website, for example – a piece of software called a **Web Browser** is required. A web browser (such as Netscape Navigator and Microsoft Explorer) has two basic functions:

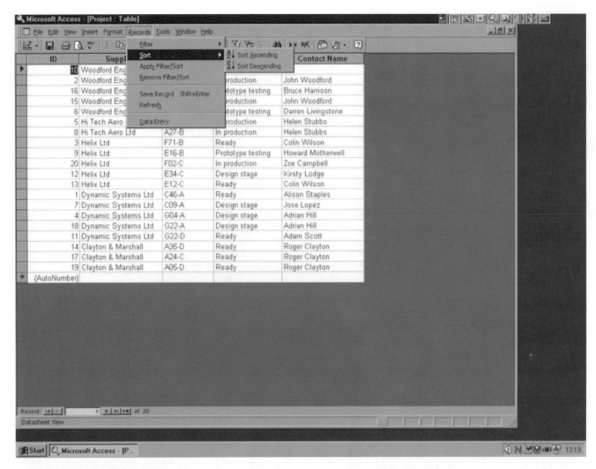

Figure 2.17 Simple database: sort command

ID	Supplier	PartCode	Status	
19	Clayton & Marshall	A05-D	Ready	Roge
17	Clayton & Marshall	A24-C	Ready	Roge
14	Clayton & Marshall	A35-D	Ready	Roge
11	Dynamic Systems Ltd	G22-D	Ready	Adar
18	Dynamic Systems Ltd	G22-A	Design stage	Adria
4	Dynamic Systems Ltd	G04-A	Design stage	Adria
7	Dynamic Systems Ltd	C09-A	Design stage	Jose
1	Dynamic Systems Ltd	C46-A	Ready	Aliso
3	Helix Ltd	F71-B	Ready	Colin
9	Helix Ltd	E16-B	Prototype testing	Howa
20	Helix Ltd	F02-C	In production	Zoe (
12	Helix Ltd	E34-C	Design stage	Kirst
13	Helix Ltd	E12-C	Ready	Colin
8	Hi Tech Aero Ltd	A27-B	In production	Hele
5	Hi Tech Aero Ltd	A14-B	In production	Hele
6	Woodford Engineering	B27-C	Prototype testing	Darre
15	Woodford Engineering	B08-A	In production	John
16	Woodford Engineering	B17-B	Prototype testing	Bruc
2	Woodford Engineering	B21-D	In production	John
10	Woodford Engineering	B12-D	Cancelled	n/a

Figure 2.18 Simple database: sorted information displayed

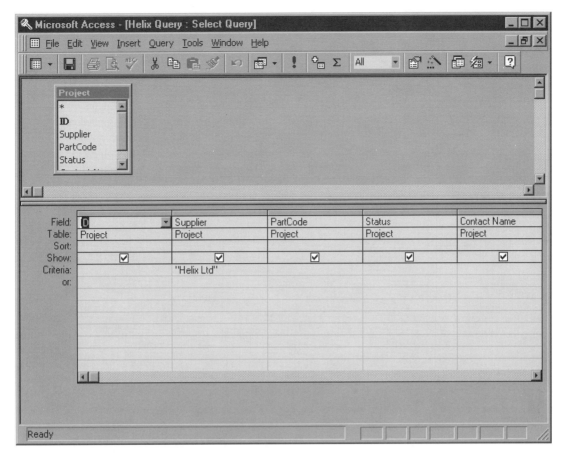

Figure 2.19 Simple database: query instruction

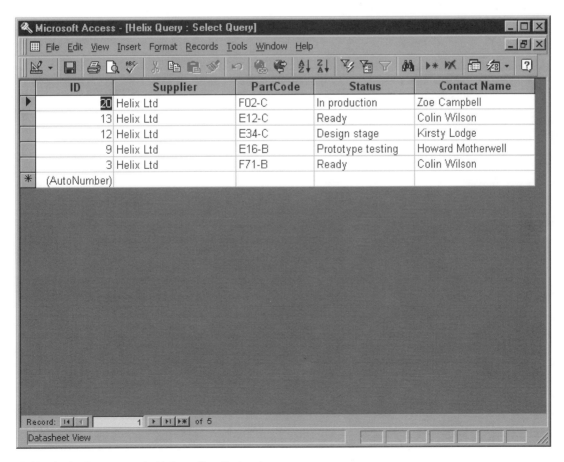

Figure 2.20 Simple database: requested information displayed

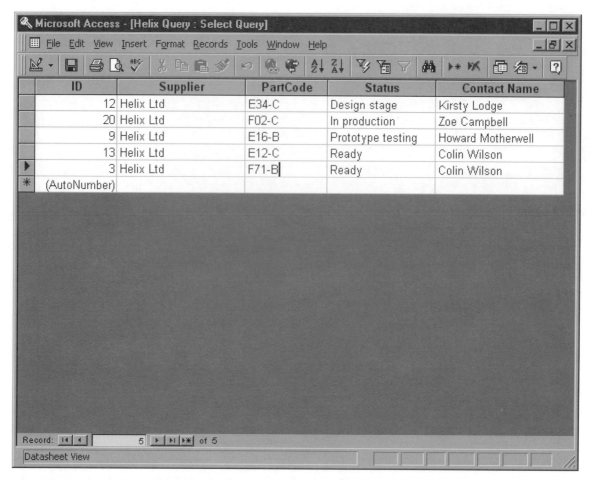

Figure 2.21 Simple database: information sorted by status

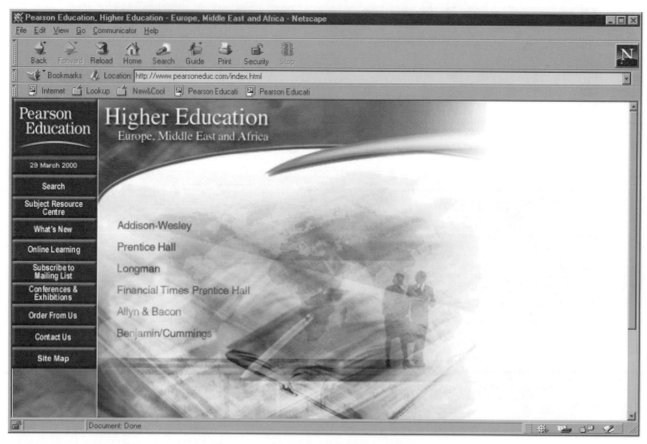

Figure 2.22 Internet website

- It instructs the web server to download a page from a chosen website.
- It decodes the HTML of the page, displaying the page as it was designed.

A typical web page can be designed to contain the following features among many others:

- Text – The written word.
- Images – Photographs, drawings, company logos, push buttons, animations, etc.
- Links – Shortcuts to information within a page, a different page, or a different website.
- Forms – Used to gather information from the reader. The information is automatically delivered to the author of the page by e-mail. These are most often used for ordering items over the Internet.
- Frames – Pages within pages. In Fig. 2.24 a frame is used to separate the site menu from the form.

Web pages are usually produced using software similar to a word processor. As the desired page is designed the software automatically writes the HTML code needed to display the page on the Internet (Fig. 2.23).

Once the page is complete it can be downloaded onto the ISP web server using another piece of software called an **FTP** (file transfer protocol) program. The collection of pages that make up the website are stored together and given a unique location called a **URL** (universal resource locator). The URL is quite simply the address of the website. No other website can have the same address.

The URL for the first page of the Pearson Education website is:

http://www.pearsoneduc.com/

- **http://** = Hypertext Transfer Protocol.
- **www.** = World Wide Web.
- **pearsoneduc.** is the unique identifier Pearson Education have chosen for their site.
- **com** identifies the website as one belonging to a company.
- **/** is the page separator.

The page separator is usually followed by the filename of the page as stored on the host computer, e.g.

http://www.pearsoneduc.com/order.html

In this case this URL will link directly with the page (order.html) containing information on how to order Pearson Education products.

To move between pages on the website only the filename need be changed. To make this easy for the reader the URL is linked to an item on the menu. Clicking the left button on the computer mouse while the screen cursor is over the menu item will activate the link. This linking and movement between pages is called **navigation**. A well-designed website allows the user to navigate easily and quickly.

2. CAD/CAM

Printed circuit board (PCB) design

A typical PCB is made up of a flat composite board onto which copper-conducting tracks have been etched. Electrical

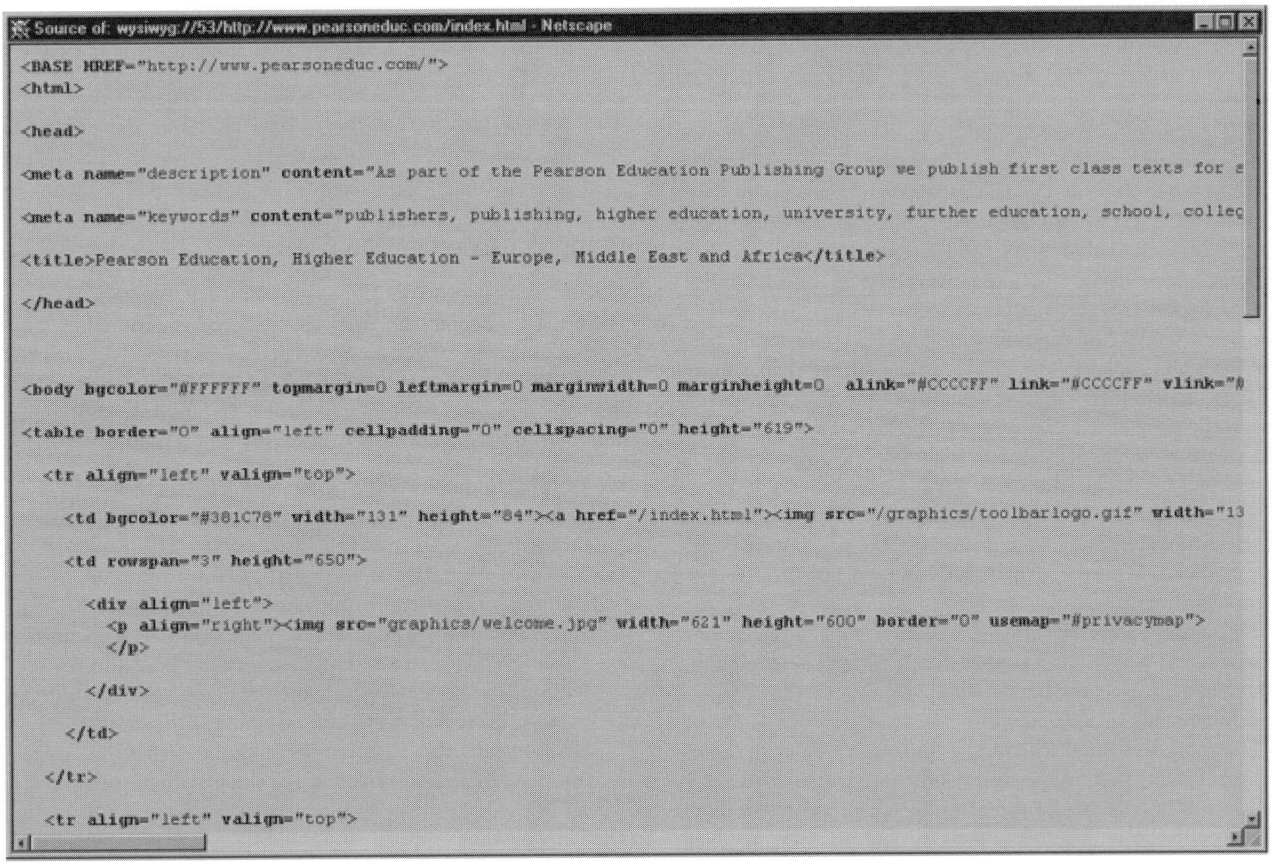

Figure 2.23 Web page design

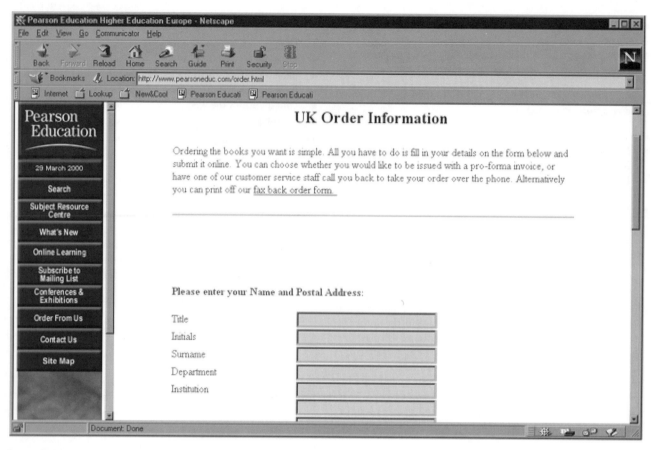

Figure 2.24 Web page display

components are soldered onto those tracks in predetermined positions. The finished board is used as a unit on its own (e.g. in a portable radio) or as a subunit of a much larger system (e.g. a sound card in a personal computer).

The circuits that are required by modern electronic devices are extremely complex. The PCB design for such a device would take even a highly skilled circuit designer many weeks to achieve. Even when completed no one would know if the circuit or PCB would work until the components had been mounted and the entire device powered up.

CAD came to the rescue. All the designer need do is construct the circuit diagram within the CAD program using the accepted symbols. The software then allows virtual testing of the circuit under whatever conditions the designer cares to use in the program.

Once the circuit performs as required, the software can be instructed to design the PCB needed. Within seconds, the program drafts the PCB such that the conducting tracks are as short as possible and the components occupy the minimum space. This saves time, materials and energy in the final manufacturing process.

The final design is usually screen-printed directly onto circuit board which has a copper film surface. The conducting tracks appear as black bands while the rest of the design is unprinted. This is called a **mask**.

The board is then chemically etched to remove excess copper, leaving behind the final conducting tracks of the PCB, which will appear where the printing ink prevented removal of the copper film. The ink is then washed off using a solvent and the circuit components soldered into place. Mounting of the components can be done in one of two ways:

- In holes drilled through the PCB with the solder added to the undersurface.
- Surface mounting, where the components are soldered directly onto the face of the PCB.

The second method is more cost effective, as additional machining of the PCB is not necessary.

Computer-aided design (CAD)

Design plans for anything from a workshop layout to a high-performance engine can now be produced on computer. Not only can the basic design be drawn up in a short space of time but the design can be tested and modified almost immediately. All draughts must also be drawn to British Standards specifications, and this is more readily achievable with CAD as it offers:

- Consistent quality of drawing. Variables such as the draughting skill of the designer no longer affect the final design.
- The use of libraries of approved images. Common components or features such as bolts, nuts, screw threads, valves, etc., can be pasted into the design within seconds.
- On-line editing. Initial designs can be checked and revised without the need to redraw the whole design over and over again. It is also possible to transmit the design electronically to a customer's computer so that the design can be seen and approved as the design progresses.

The CAD process
The designer uses a CAD package to construct the design in a **wireframe** form. The drawing may be initially constructed in

two dimensions on a construction grid. The computer logs the mathematical co-ordinates of the wireframe on the grid. Data obtained is then used in calculations using mathematical formulae and geometrical rules to define each co-ordinate in relation to all the others. The computer will convert the information into three dimensions automatically. As the shape of the object is stored as mathematical codes they can be manipulated as required. If the designer wishes to view the object from a different angle, the computer modifies the data and displays the object in the new position.

The software then analyses the design, allowing correction of any errors. The finished design can then be projected in three dimensions in virtual reality. This is called the **Surface Model** (Fig. 2.25).

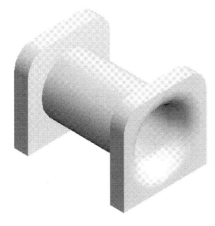

Figure 2.25 CAD process: surface model

The designer can also program data about the volume, mass, material characteristics, etc., of the component, which not only allows the software to generate cross-sectional views at any point or angle on the design, but also to reveal and analyse likely stress and fatigue points within the component. These are called **solid models**.

CAD packages can be used in conjunction with computer-aided manufacture (CAM) packages to test the design under virtual conditions. For example, an aircraft design can be subjected to flight safety testing within the computer program itself. This not only saves time but also the huge costs involved in building a real prototype for testing. The considerable risks involved with test-flying an untried aircraft are also removed.

Finally a program can be used to simulate production requirements for the design. Some examples are given below:

- **Flow modelling** – The casting industry always had the problem of never knowing how the design of a cast would behave during the pouring of the molten metal. Any design faults, which impeded the flow of the metal, would show up as uncast areas in the final casting. Successful casting often relied on the skill of the designer. However, CAD/CAM software programmed with the flow characteristics of the molten metal can design the cast and then simulate the casting process. This will reveal design faults long before the expense of actual casting takes place.
- **Modelling production lines** – If the product requires a number of separate operations in its manufacture, the production line must be designed to minimise time, material, space and energy costs. A CAD/CAM package can simulate the production process many thousands of times in a few minutes and devise the optimum layout and sequence of operations for the production line.

Computer-aided manufacture (CAM)

The manufacturing/engineering industry in the UK has been in decline, while that of other countries, notably those in the Far East, has grown. One of the acknowledged reasons was the failure of British industry to modernise and take advantage of new technology. Traditional industrial practice and trade union influence favoured the low-tech and male-dominated manual labour approach in order to maximise employment.

However, change was forced upon the entire industry, as it became impossible to compete with the productivity, consistent quality and low-cost of goods produced abroad using hi-tech, automated systems. Only those who were prepared to undergo the radical change from old to new technology survived, and only on a much reduced scale.

CAM systems overcame the main problem of traditional methods, that of carrying out repetitive, unsafe or dirty manufacturing processes on a continuous basis. In use, CAM has distinct advantages:

- Production errors are almost eliminated.
- Product quality is high and consistent.
- Design specifications can be changed in an instant allowing for maximum flexibility in production.
- Productivity is highly predictable allowing for accurate costing.
- Tooling costs are reduced as tool life is increased.
- Wastage and spoilage is reduced.
- Labour costs are reduced.

The only disadvantage is the high capital cost of setting up the CAM system. Large mainframe computers are needed to store and process the production programs, and CNC (computer numerical control) machines and robots are needed to carry out the manufacturing process. Only very large production runs make the use of CAM cost-effective.

However, advances in micro-technology are steadily reducing the set-up costs and CAM is now within the financial reach of even the smallest engineering company.

Much attention is now being paid to the development of

- **Computer Integrated Manufacture** (CIM) – Where one or a number of linked machines can be reprogrammed to manufacture a whole range of products without the need for expensive retooling.
- **Flexible Manufacturing Systems** (FMS) – Where the entire process, from raw material delivery to dispatch of end product, is computer controlled (Fig. 2.26).

Both systems interface CAD and CAM directly. Using FMS/CIM it is theoretically possible for one person to design, model, establish and control an entire production process from a single computer station.

Computer numerical control (CNC)

CNC machines rely on a set of coded instructions to carry out the task assigned. In order that a machine in one country could be used in another, an international system of standard control codes was agreed. The CNC system consists of numerical data, which define the exact position of a machine tool, etc. in three planes of movement, X, Y and Z. Coded instructions are also included to define other commands such as *start, stop, move clockwise, move anticlockwise, change tool*, and so on. Table 2.1 shows some of the codes and their action if applied.

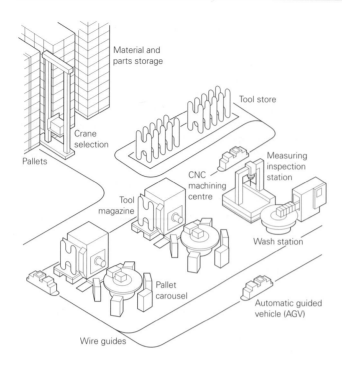

Figure 2.26 Flexible manufacturing system

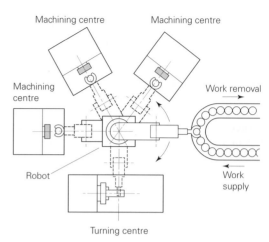

Figure 2.27 Typical CNC manufacturing cell

Table 2.1 CNC machine: International system of control codes

Code	Action
G00	Move rapidly from one point to another
G01	Perform task in a straight line
G02	Perform task in a clockwise direction
G03	Perform task in an anticlockwise direction
G70	Units specified in task are imperial
G71	Units specified in task are metric
M02	End of program
M06	Change tool

Once the optimum production set-up has been devised by CAD/CAM software it can write a CNC program that can then be loaded directly into the required machinery. For example, in a milling machine program data can be used to control tool selection, tool position, speed of cutting, material feed rate, coolant flow rate, and even allow for gradual wear of the tools during use.

A single multi-operation machine can be designed to carry out an entire sequence of operations. If separate machines are required, a robot arm can be used to transfer the component between machines. This group of machines is called a **manufacturing cell** (see, for example, Fig. 2.27).

3. Telecommunications

Cellular phone networks

A cellular phone network consists of a number of radio transmitters (**base stations**) arranged at geographic intervals. Each base station transmits at a low power of around 3–5 watts so that the signal only travels a few miles over a fixed area. These areas are called **cells**. The cells are arranged so

that they just overlap (Fig. 2.28) and each cell can handle a few hundred calls at one time.

Adjacent transmitters operate on different frequencies to ensure that they do not interfere with each other's signal.

When a user makes a call on a cellular telephone, a signal is transmitted from the phone to the nearest base station. The station transmitter then makes the connection. If the user is mobile there is a risk that the phone will go out of range of the first base station and the call will be disconnected. To prevent this a control computer analyses the call signal, continuously checking for a fall in signal strength. If the signal strength falls the computer sends a coded signal to the phone. A similar signal is sent to the base station the user is now approaching, which detects an increase in phone signal strength. The phone and new base station are instructed to co-ordinate their activities by the control computer. At an appropriate time the computer then instructs the phone to switch its transmission frequency to that of the new base station. This is called **handover** and ensures that continuity is never lost (Fig. 2.29).

It is important that the network knows which cell is hosting a phone at any particular time so that it can always receive incoming calls. This is achieved by constant communication between the phone and the control computer at the base station. When a phone is switched on it registers with the nearest base station using unique identification codes programmed into the phone microprocessor. As the phone

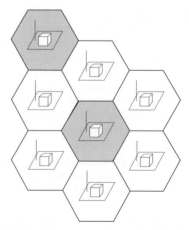

Figure 2.28 Cellular phone network: arrangement of transmitting cell

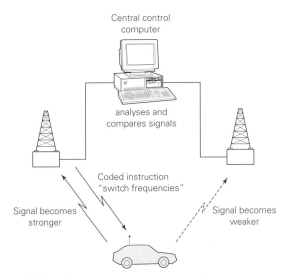

Figure 2.29 Cellular phone handover protocol

moves between cells it is constantly re-registered. The location is then held in a database so that an incoming call is routed to the transmitter nearest to that phone.

Case Study: CD Player

How CAD/CAM or integrated manufacturing techniques have been used

Printed circuit boards (PCBs)

In order to reduce capital costs, ComLaser subcontract the manufacture of PCBs to a dedicated manufacturer.

The PCB is designed by ComLaser to their precise specifications using a CAD package. The circuit diagram of the board is first drawn out using conventional symbols. The design program itself can then carry out testing of the circuit. Once the circuit functions as required, the program then converts the circuit diagram into a diagram of the PCB layout.

The finished PCB diagram is then downloaded via a modem connection from the ComLaser design computer to that of the PCB manufacturer. Final discussion between companies concerning the design also takes place electronically, the link between the two computers allowing for immediate exchange of information with on-line editing and testing. This method alone saves both companies weeks of design time. Paper plans no longer have to be mailed between locations, avoiding the added risk of misunderstood instructions and loss en route.

Fibreglass/epoxy resin mounting boards are used for their heat-resistant properties as temperatures within a mains-powered CD Player can reach 70–80 °C. They are also resistant to vibration damage, a major consideration if the board is to be used in a CD Player for audio playback.

The CAD diagram is first printed out as a plastic mask to be laid over a photosensitive emulsion coated onto the copper-coated board. The mask is produced as a photographic negative with the conducting track layout appearing as transparent paths on a black background.

The board and mask are then exposed to UV light and the board developed in the same way as a photograph. Exposed areas form an etch-resistant layer. The remaining copper is chemically etched away, leaving the desired conducting track layout on the board. The board is then dip coated in solder, which adheres only to the copper tracks. This process ensures

good electrical continuity when components are soldered onto the PCB at a later stage.

Holes for the electronic components must then be drilled through the PCB. This is carried out by a computer numerically controlled (CNC) drilling machine, which receives its instructions from the same CAD program.

Finally, the PCB diagram is used once again to produce a silk screen image, used to print a protective, solder-resistant, polymer coating over all parts of the PCB except the conducting tracks.

Component assembly

CNC programming is again used to mount the electronic components, the correct type and value being placed in the correct position on the PCB. As the process involves a precise sequence of operations carried out by single machines, this is called **line production**.

The PCBs are stacked in a feed system to be mounted on a turntable jig by a robot arm. A light is shone onto the PCB, and only the pre-drilled holes allow light to get through. A video camera positioned below the jig therefore receives an image of bright spots on a black background. The pattern of spots is electronically compared with the data held in the CNC program, and any adjustment to the PCB alignment is carried out automatically. If the video image fails to match the data image the PCB is rejected. The machine operator may then investigate and rectify the fault (a hole blocked by solder, for example) and return the PCB to the production line.

Components may be mounted horizontally (e.g. resistors, diodes), vertically (e.g. capacitors, transistors) or any specially required position (e.g. integrated circuits). Fed from tape reels or cartridges held in the required orientation, robots place the correct components in the correct holes (called 'populating' the board), bend the wire tails in the optimum direction (to avoid short circuiting between components) and trim off the excess wire. Occasionally, some larger components cannot be mounted automatically. In such cases the part-finished board is delivered to a hand-assembly line where the final components are added.

Soldering

The assembled PCB is delivered to another set of machines that solder the components to the conducting tracks.

Firstly, flux is sprayed onto the PCB surface, only adhering to the exposed copper track at the drilled holes. The board is then heated to dry the flux. This stage also limits the thermal shock experienced by the components during soldering.

Secondly, the board is passed over a bath of molten solder held at 184 °C, the solder adhering to those parts of the PCB carrying flux. The PCB is now cooled to set the solder and delivered to the testing area. At this stage components that are particularly heat sensitive and which could not be exposed to the soldering process (e.g. microprocessors) may be hand mounted into special sockets that have been soldered to the PCB.

Testing

Completed boards are placed on a jig that brings the board into contact with projecting metal spikes. The spikes are in precise positions corresponding to conducting terminals on the PCB. The PCB is then powered up and an analysis program run by a computer, which compares its stored data with that being obtained from the PCB. Any faults, such as short circuits, failed or poorly soldered joints, non-functioning components, etc., are reported to the operator for correction.

The finished boards then receive a quality control label to confirm that they meet ComLaser specifications. Packaging and delivery can then take place.

Final assembly

Final assembly of the entire CD player is still a manual process. Production is divided into batches with a definite start and finish. Largely demand-led, the size of a batch can vary considerably. For example, demand is usually highest around October as retailers buy in stock for Christmas.

Market research and actual production data from previous years is held on a computerised database. Just before a production run is started the computer database is analysed and a batch size determined. The computer then calculates and places the necessary order for components, less those held in stock from previous runs.

However, storage of unused stock is costly so ComLaser's system is tied in very closely with the supply of materials. This allows ComLaser to operate using the 'just in time' principle – production rate exactly matches supply rate so that those bought-in components are only delivered as they are needed. With no 'left-overs', costly storage space is not required.

The production run begins with the assembly of kits, which contain all the parts needed to make the finished CD player. The kits are then delivered to the assembly personnel who proceed to build the product, testing its function at various points during manufacture. This is called '**cell production**', in that all the personnel are capable of carrying out any of the assembly functions, and gives two distinct advantages:

- The work is more interesting as more than one assembly stage is involved.
- Assembly personnel become responsible, both personally and as a team, for quality control.

However, unlike machines which work at a constant rate without tiring, the pace of manual assembly can vary considerably. The optimum pace can be determined by the collection of data from the total assembly process, concerning time taken to complete the various operations. Critical path analysis (CPA) software can then be used to determine a production program so that delivery of kits and removal of finished products occurs with the minimum of unproductive time. The assembly personnel are then consulted to take into account individual and team needs such as rest breaks, and a final production plan agreed. Table 2.2 shows the production plan for the ComLaser CD Player.

Product testing

From the production of the first prototype to a sample of each production batch, the following tests are also carried out.

Functional test

The individual performance of every component, e.g. individual resistors, ICs, wiring, connectors, fasteners, display units, chassis, paint finish, etc., is regularly tested. This guarantees consistency between batches and ensures that suppliers are maintaining company specifications. Data is

Table 2.2 Production plan for ComLaser CD Player

Operation Number	Task	Time limit (min.sec)
1	Secure power supply to PCB. Attach warning label	2.30
2	Place PCB on test jig. Run electronic function test	2.50
3	Secure PCB to chassis	1.00
4	Secure CD Laser unit to chassis Attach laser warning label	0.52
5	Attach power and input/output wiring. Run electrical continuity and earthing test. Attach earth warning label	3.35
6	Secure LCD display/control panel to chassis	1.45
7	Attach display/control wiring. Run display/control operation test	3.21
8	*Carry out repairs if required*	*4.00*
9	Secure unit cover onto chassis	1.05
10	Attach CD drawer front plate	1.12
11	Attach batch ID and serial number labels to rear panel	0.20
12	Visual inspection	1.30
13	Insert test CD. Run function test. Remove test CD	3.35
13	Wrap, box and dispatch	0.40
	Total time (inc. repairs if required)	**28.15**

gathered electronically from the testing processes and compared with a database of desired performance characteristics.

The overall performance of the unit as a CD Player is assessed according to the following criteria:

- Data transfer rate – How fast the binary information on the CD is transferred to the microprocessor.
- Access time – How long it takes the laser to locate itself over a particular data track on the CD.
- Sound (CD) and video/graphic (CD-ROM) quality – Assesses stereo separation, accuracy of reproduction, smoothness of video, audio/video synchronisation, etc.
- Error correction – How accurately the microprocessor corrects errors in the data stream. This is an indirect measure of how the unit performs with dirty or damaged CDs.
- Operational noise – How quietly the unit loads, unloads and spins the CD.

Environmental test

The finished unit is exposed to every conceivable condition of use (e.g. variations in ambient temperature, humidity, pressure, light, etc.) and abuse (dropping, scratching, etc.). Sensors mounted inside the unit are linked to a computerised testing system, which monitors performance.

Market test

Consumer tastes and demands are constantly changing. In order to maintain market share, ComLaser carries out an annual market survey of current and proposed designs. The data gathered is stored on a database and used to plan future production.

2.4 New materials and components

Polymers

A polymer is composed of very large molecules (**macromolecules**), made up of identical, repeating, smaller molecules (**monomers**) which have bonded together in a chain. The bonding process is called **polymerisation**.

The vast majority of polymers in industry are man-made, although natural polymers, e.g. latex rubber, may also be used extensively.

Plastics

There are two main types of plastic:

- **Thermoplastics** – Those that can be softened and remoulded by heat.
- **Thermosets** – Those that set hard on production and once set cannot be softened by heat.

Table 2.3 lists some important plastics and their uses.

Adhesives

An adhesive is any substance that is used to stick solid materials together. Most modern industrial adhesives are synthetic polymers and are very strong.

Resin-base adhesives used in the aerospace industry, for example, are stronger than the metals they are used to join. In addition, the joint formed is more resilient and fatigue resistant than a weld. In modern aircraft these are essential characteristics.

Properties of adhesives

- **Wetting** – The liquid adhesive should wet the surface of the material to be joined. This will ensure that total contact is obtained. The wetting characteristics are controlled by choice of solvent. The small molecules of the solvent prevent interaction between the larger adhesive molecules. This reduces the viscosity and allows the adhesive to flow freely.
- **Adhesion** – This depends on strong chemical bonds being formed between the material to be joined and the adhesive. As they set the adhesive molecules form strong bonds with each other. Similarly, they form equally strong bonds with the material to be joined – resulting in adhesion of great strength.
- **Setting** – Setting characteristics are affected by
  - **Choice and proportion of solvent** – The faster the solvent evaporates the faster the adhesive sets.
  - **Catalytic hardeners** – The reaction between adhesive molecules, especially those of a resin, may be accelerated with the use of a catalyst.
  - **Temperature** – As with all other chemical reactions, setting rate is affected by changes in temperature.
- **Solid properties** – The behaviour of adhesives once set may be modified by:

Table 2.3 Important plastics and their uses

Name	Uses
Thermoplastics	
Poly(e)thene (PE)	Low density (LDPE) – electrical cable insulation.
	High density (HDPE)
Polypropylene (PP)	Gas transport pipes
Polystyrene (PS)	Rigid: packaging, refrigerator/freezer linings, shells of domestic appliances.
	Expanded: sound and heat insulation, packaging, protective filling for fragile goods.
Polycarbonate (PC)	Rigid transparent covers, compact discs, safety helmets.
Polyvinyl chloride (PVC)	Plasticised
	Unplasticised (uPVC)
Polyvinyl acetate (PVA)	Adhesive
Polymethyl methacrylate (Acrylic)	Military aircraft canopies
Polytetrafluoroethene (PTFE)	Fire-resistant coatings on safety clothing: low-friction bush bearings; joint sealant for fluid pipes.
Polytheneterephthalate (PET)	Carbonated drink bottles
Acrylonitrile-butadiene-styrene (ABS)	Housings for computers and similar goods
Nylon	Bush bearings; gear wheels; electrical tool casings; hinges
Thermosets	
Polyurethane (PU)	Expanded: insulation foam
Melamine formaldehyde (MF)	Electrical fittings
Urea methanol (UM)	White electrical fittings; appliance fittings; adhesive.
Phenol methanol (PM)	Electrical fittings
Polyester resin (PR)	Castings; embedding of electrical components (tamper and shock proofing); boat hulls; car bodies; large containers
Epoxy resin (ER)	Chemically resistant surface coatings; castings; embedding of electrical components (tamper and shock proofing); adhesives; printed circuit boards; pressure vessels; boat hulls; car bodies.

Table 2.4 Some modern engineering adhesives and their applications

Adhesive type	Chemical nature	Applications
Anaerobic	Acrylic polyester resin which bonds only to metal and in the absence of oxygen	Joint sealing of metal components, especially those with a thread or spline
Cyanoacrylate	Acrylic monomer in liquid form which polymerises on exposure to moisture and air. Bonds most surfaces very strongly in seconds	Rapid fixing of small components to surfaces
Emulsion	Polyvinyl acetate dispersed in water	Fixing of engineered paper or fabric-based goods such as packaging materials, loudspeaker cones, electronic sounders
Resin	Liquid resin (e.g. epoxy) mixed with catalytic hardener. Sets hard by polymerisation	Fixing of components subject to high-impact conditions.
Hot melt	Thermoplastic applied in molten state to the surfaces to be joined. Solidifies on cooling	Rapid fixing of small components to surfaces

Table 2.5 Modern paints and their applications

Paint type	Components	Uses
Oil based	Pigment + polymer, natural oil, e.g. linseed, solvent. May also be emulsified in water.	Decorative and protective finish on most goods. Can be used indoors or outdoors
Enamels	Pigment + polymer resin	Metal work only as the coating must be heated to melting temperature
Catalytic	Pigment + polymer resin, solvent and chemical hardener (catalyst)	Decorative and protective finish on most goods. Can be used indoors or outdoors. Solvent evaporation allows catalytic hardening of the polymer resin. This makes the paint more durable than oil-based paints
Lacquers	Pigment + polymer (cellulose, shellac, polyurethane, etc.), organic solvent	Coating of wire used in motor windings and transformer coils; vehicle body finishes

- **Plasticisers** – These retain a small degree of flexibility within the adhesive. This additional 'give' can help prevent cracks spreading and even out strain across a joint.
- **Fillers** – These alter the thermal expansion of the adhesive to match that of the material to be joined. This prevents the cracking at the joint that would occur if the two expanded/contracted at different rates. They can also be used to strengthen the joint in the form of reinforcing fibres. As fillers are cheaper than the adhesive itself, they help to reduce the overall cost.

Table 2.4 lists some important modern engineering adhesives and their applications.

Coatings

Paints and varnishes

Paints are used to protect, decorate or both. There are many types of paint, each of which is suitable for specific purposes. The finish required determines the choice of paint and the conditions in which the painted item is to be used.

Most modern paints are polymer-based (polyurethane, acrylic), the polymer being dissolved in a solvent (see Table 2.5). Gelling agents may also be added to make the paint semi-solid.

Polymer coating

Wires or wire fabrications (e.g. baskets) are heated and dipped into fluidised thermoplastic polymer powder. The plastic melts and coats the component.

Modern metals and composites

Alloys

An alloy is a mixture of a metal plus one or more other elements in varying proportions. The aim is to alter the crystal structure of the metal on cooling. The end result may be an alloy with enhanced hardness, strength, durability or reduced density.

The most common alloys are a mixture of iron and carbon and are known as **steels**. It is the percentage of carbon (0.1–0.8 per cent) that determines the properties of the steel. The most useful properties of modern steels (see Table 2.6) are their resistance to corrosion and hardness.

These new micro-alloyed steels are used mainly for cutting tools and gears. Although very expensive to produce, the increased benefits of strength and resistance to wear make the products very cost-effective.

- **Aluminium** alloys (Table 2.7) are increasingly used in engineering for their high strength to weight ratio, resistance to corrosion and ease of machining.

Table 2.6 Composition of modern steels

Steel type	Carbon (%)	Other elements
High Speed	0.3–0.8	Tungsten Chromium Vanadium
High strength low alloy (HSLA)	0.3–0.8	Very small amounts of: Aluminium Niobium Zirconium Titanium Vanadium

- **Magnesium** mixed with small amounts of **zinc** and **zirconium** produces alloys of use to nuclear engineering. Their corrosion and fatigue resistance are extremely high.
- **Titanium** mixed with **aluminium, vanadium, molybdenum** and **tin** produces extremely strong alloys with the highest fatigue resistance of all. They are extensively used in aerospace applications, especially for the turbine blades of jet engines.
- **Nimonics**, alloys of **nickel** and **chromium,** have similar properties and applications to titanium alloys.

Coating alloys

Some alloys are best used as thin coatings over a base metal. These are used to produce extremely hard and durable cutting surfaces on machine tools. For example:

- **Titanium aluminium nitride** gives a brown coating whose wear resistance improves the hotter the component becomes. This makes it particularly suitable for cutting or milling tools.
- **Aluminium titanium nitride** gives a dark grey coating that is extremely hard, durable and ductile. It is extremely suitable for tools used in high-speed production such as hot forging and die-casting.

Combinations of coatings may also be used, e.g. a duplex coating of **titanium carbide** (dark grey in colour) followed by a top coating of **titanium nitride** (bright gold in colour). Tool wear patterns may then be recognised by exposure of the grey coat beneath the gold, without sacrificing the overall performance of the component.

Superplastic alloys

Sheet metal fabrications such as vehicle body panels are usually produced in a number of stages. This allows different pressures and temperatures to be used to form more complex shapes without failure of the sheet. It is the plasticity of the sheet metal that is critical – the ease with which the atoms in the metal flow in relation to each other when the metal is put under strain, e.g. when deformed in a press.

If the metal is deformed too quickly, the interatomic forces holding atoms in relation to each other are overcome and failure occurs. This shows up as cracking at the surface or within the sheet. (This can be illustrated with the use of plasticine. Pull a length of the material slowly and it stretches quite far before breaking. Pull it too fast and it snaps immediately – its plastic limit has been exceeded.)

The atoms of metal in a superplastic alloy, however, flow very easily so that the plastic limit of the material is very high. This means that even high strain-forming processes (e.g. acute angle bending) can be carried out at the same time as those involving low strain without failure. This is called **superplastic forming**. The only disadvantage is that the forming pressure must be held for an extended time (20 minutes plus) to allow the atoms of the alloy to flow and rearrange their relationship in the new position.

The most successful superplastic alloy is **aluminium + 6% copper** and **0.5% zirconium**. Many others have been discovered but are seldom used. One of the major problems is that the superplasticity also allows those alloys to 'creep' in use, leading to deformation of the product.

Although a single tool is needed to form a complex panel rather than the several previously needed, the slow processing time is costly. This means that the use of superplastic alloys is usually restricted to high-value products manufactured in small quantities. Aerospace applications (high value-added components) are more likely to be successful. The premium on the product performance is much higher than with general engineering components. This balances the high cost of the material and the low production rates presently achievable.

Composites

Composites are materials that consist of two or more solid components with different properties physically bonded together. The properties of materials used are chosen to complement each other and contribute to the overall properties of the composite.

A good example of a simple composite is glass-reinforced plastic (GRP). Glass fibre (strong in tension and compression, flexible, lightweight but very soft) is bonded within a matrix of epoxy resin (hard but brittle). GRP composite is hard, strong and flexible.

As a substitute for metal, composites have a number of applications.

Body panels for high performance vehicles

In this example, lightness must be combined with great strength. Fibre mats are laid in one side of an injection mould and the other side is laid on top. The gap between the two is then pressure injected with a fluid containing a short-chain-length polymer. This polymer has been treated so that the

Table 2.7 Aluminium alloys and their applications

Alloy	Properties	Uses
Aluminium–lithium	Extremely stiff and lightweight; Fatigue resistant	Aerospace applications
Aluminium–magnesium	Strong and lightweight	Motor vehicle bodies
Duralumin (aluminium–copper–manganese–magnesium)	Strong and lightweight	Aerospace applications
Aluminium–copper–zirconium	Strong and lightweight; high heat conduction	Vehicle engines

chains possess chemically reactive ends. Hence, the short-chain polymer reacts within the mould to form a long-chain polymer. This process is called **Reaction Injection Moulding**, as polymerisation occurs within the mould. Tubular sections may be reinforced further by an injection of polyurethane foam. Similar to animal bone in structure, this greatly enhances resistance to both tension and compression.

Navy minesweepers

Modern high-explosive mines that are used to disable shipping do not rely on physical contact to trigger the explosion. Instead, microelectronic sensors detect any sudden variations in the earth's magnetic field in the immediate area. Such variations occur when a metal object, such as the hull of a ship, moves within the field. Mines can also be programmed to explode only when a characteristic field change occurs, e.g. that caused by a destroyer. This is called the 'magnetic signature' of the ship. Minesweepers are therefore constructed from non-metal composites, wherever possible, to minimise their magnetic signature, allowing them to approach mines closely and render them harmless.

Modern composites include:

- **Carbon fibre composite** – Carbon fibres embedded in a polymer resin matrix. Many hundreds of times stronger in tension and compression than glass fibre, carbon fibre composites are replacing metal alloys in a number of applications where weight is an issue:
- **Metal matrix composite (MMC)** – Ceramic fibres such as alumina and silicon carbide are embedded in a metal matrix. MMCs are extremely tough with very high temperature and wear resistance. An example is tungsten carbide, which is used as the cutting edge of high-speed machine tools.

Ceramics

Ceramics are materials that have been hardened by firing at a very high temperature and allowed to cool slowly. A close-packed crystalline structure is formed which gives the material such properties as extreme hardness, durability and thermal shock resistance. Ceramics are replacing metal alloys in a number of applications and ceramic fibres are increasingly used in modern composites (see above). One of the most novel uses of ceramic material is in the form of replaceable tiles used in the heat shield of the space shuttle.

Table 2.8 shows some of the most useful engineering ceramics.

New computer technology

Memory devices

These are integrated circuits (ICs) dedicated to the storage of binary data. They consist of an array of many millions of transistor circuits that can either be '**ON**' or '**OFF**'. This corresponds to the **1** and **0** of binary code. There are two main types of memory device:

- **Read-only memory (ROM)** – This device has its stored information permanently built or programmed into the IC. In other words, the transistor circuits that are 'ON' or 'OFF' has been decided in advance and designed into the device. A ROM is usually used to store a dedicated program within a device, e.g. the program needed to perform the functions of an electronic calculator.
- **Random Access Memory (RAM)** – This device stores information in the same way as ROM but only temporarily. A RAM is usually used to store variables coming from an input device such as a keyboard or mouse, and from a microprocessor for display. This data is constantly changing and so cannot be stored permanently.

Unlike ROM, the data stored in RAM is lost as soon as its power supply is switched off.

Microprocessors

A microprocessor is defined as a computer designed to perform a single task by running a single program. Made up of many thousands of ICs built onto a single, but larger, silicon chip, a microprocessor is usually built into a device. Its role is to act as a central controller for the activities of the device, e.g. those of a pocket calculator, cellular phone, television, etc.

A microprocessor always contains:

- **Read-only memory (ROM)** – This stores the dedicated program of the microprocessor.
- **Input/output (I/O) devices** – These receive information for processing within the program and display the results, e.g. keypads, LCD display units.
- **Random access memory (RAM)** – This stores the variables coming from the input device so that they can be processed by the program. The logic used by RAM is the same as in truth tables, where an operation gives an output of false or true. In binary code this translates as 0 or 1 respectively.
- **A central processing unit (CPU)** – This is the part of the microprocessor that executes the stored program in the ROM, processes data from the RAM, and delivers the results to the output device. The program instructions

Table 2.8 Some engineering ceramics and their applications

Ceramic	Special properties	Uses
Alumina (Al_2O_3)	High strength; corrosion and wear resistance; electrical insulator	Machine parts; industrial capacitors; sodium vapour light bulb casings
Silicaon nitride (Si_3N_4)	Best thermal shock resistance of all; maintains full strength at very high temperatures	Engine and gas turbine parts such as turbo charger rotors, diesel engine glow plugs, etc.
Silicon carbide (SiC)	Best corrosion resistance of all; retains strength at temperatures up to 1400 °C	Mechanical seals and pump parts
Zirconia (ZrO_2)	Highest strength and durability of all at room temperature	Industrial guillotines; pump parts

usually specify the numerical operations that the processor must carry out (e.g. add, subtract, multiply and divide). The basic program built into the CPU is called its **instruction set**. The number of operations the CPU can carry out in one second is described as its speed and is controlled by a timing circuit. The latest CPUs can run at a speed of 400 MHz – or 400 000 000 operations per second.

A desktop computer uses a number of microprocessors to perform the many functions of the whole machine.

New electronic technology

Integrated circuits

In the early days of transistorised circuits, individual components were soldered onto printed circuit boards. As circuits became more complex the size of the PCB had to be increased. Eventually a solution had to be found to the size and space problem this created.

With the development of silicon semiconductor technology it became possible to create a complete circuit on a piece of silicon wafer a fraction of a millimetre square (a '**chip**'). The chips are manufactured in bulk:

- A single crystal of the semiconducting element silicon is 'grown' in a controlled environment. This crystal is, in fact, a cylinder about 100 mm in diameter.
- The cylinder is then sliced into very thin wafers, each polished to a mirror finish and cleaned with the highest quality distilled water.
- Many hundreds of the micro-miniaturised circuits are then created on the surface of the wafers using complex chemical processing methods. These circuits contain all of the components (transistors, diodes, resistors, etc.) to perform a particular function.
- A computer then tests each of the circuits. Those that fail the test are automatically marked with a spot of coloured dye.
- The wafer is then scored with a diamond knife and broken up into individual chips.
- The chips are then carried on a conveyor to be mounted on a plastic carrier, those marked with the dye spot being rejected.

One chip could take over the role of several PCBs. For example the PCBs needed to receive and amplify an radio signal would need to be mounted in a box with dimensions in the order of several centimetres. A single chip could contain all the same circuitry in a space less than $0.2\,\text{mm}^2$.

A typical chip is mounted onto a plastic base, which also carries a number of metal pins. A robot wiring machine links input and output points on the chip with the appropriate metal pin using extremely fine gold wires. The mounted chip is then totally encapsulated in plastic with only the metal pins exposed. The finished article is now known as an **integrated circuit (IC)**.

Display and other output devices

A display device is any item of hardware that will display the output of a microprocessor for the user to see. Other output devices include **loudspeakers** for sound reproduction, **disc drives** for magnetic data storage and **modems** for transmission of data between computers along telephone lines.

There are several types of display devices:

- **LED** – This uses light emitting diodes in a display matrix. It is most often used in scrolling advertising signs. The LEDs making up the matrix may be 'on' or 'off' to make up the shape of the image to be displayed.
- **LCD** – This uses liquid crystal display technology in a display matrix. The LCD may be simple as in the 7-segment array of a timer, or complex as in those used in the screen of a pocket television. In a similar way to the LED, the LCD may be 'visible' or 'transparent'. When switched on it becomes visible, becoming transparent when switched off.
- **Cathode ray tube (CRT)** – This is the familiar television or monitor screen. The output may be monochrome (black and white) or colour.
- **Dot matrix printers** – Images are printed onto paper in the form of small dots. The print head contains up to 24 metal pins which strike an inked ribbon in the desired pattern.
- **Ink and bubble jet printers** – Images are printed onto paper in the form of microscopically small dots (commonly in a matrix of 360×360 dots, although finer resolution is possible). The print head sprays a jet of ink onto the paper in the desired pattern.
- **Laser printers** – A laser beam scans a metal drum, which becomes electrically charged along the path of the beam. The electrical charge attracts particles of dry polymer ink, called toner, onto the drum. The toner sticks to the drum in the exact pattern scanned by the laser. The toner is then transferred to paper which is passed through heated rollers. The heat melts the polymer ink fixing it permanently onto the paper (Fig. 2.30).

Figure 2.30 Laser printer

Case Study: CD player

New materials

Polymers

The pressed steel sheet making up the top and sides of the CD Player are spray coated with an acrylic paint which is applied as a dry powder. The steel is first electrostatically charged to attract the powder in an even layer, then baked in an oven. The heat melts the acrylic paint, bonding it to the metal surface. On cooling, the acrylic forms an abrasion-resistant matt finish.

The face of the player is made up of a high-impact polystyrene moulding to resist wear and tear.

Modern metals

An aluminium alloy frame is used to house the components of the laser. As well as being light and strong, it resists resonant vibration.

Composites

The PCB used in the CD Player has a base of fabric/resin laminate. This has excellent electrical insulation properties combined with great strength.

New components

The CD Player uses the following new components:

- **Microprocessors** – Used to control the laser and decode the signals from the photosensors. In the audio CD Player, it is also used to program the settings desired by the user.
- **Memory devices** – ROM devices are used to store the programs used by the microprocessors. In the audio CD Player, RAM devices are used to store user preferences such as running order of the tracks on the CD to be played.

- **Integrated circuits** – Amplification and equalisation circuitry, timers and LCD control units are built into ICs on the PCB. Taking up much less room than conventional circuits, they are also lighter and cheaper to produce.
- **Display devices** – LEDs and LCDs are used extensively to provide the information the user requires. LEDs are used to indicate ON/OFF states, while LCDs are used to provide graphical information such as track number, time, volume settings, etc.

Case Study: CD-ROM

New materials

- **Polycarbonate** – Manufactured with a precise refractive index.
- **Acrylic** – Used initially in an uncured form and spin-coated onto the data surface of the CD, this material can be hardened on exposure to UV light.

Activity: **Explain** how your chosen product uses new material and components.

2.5 Automation

Control technology

In order to function at its most efficient, an automated production system must have high precision control. As human input is subject to inaccuracy and error, computerised control technology developed rapidly to keep pace with the demands of new production methods. There are two main types of control system:

- **Open loop control** – This is basically a start-to-finish control system. The controller is programmed to begin and end an operation according to fixed criteria, e.g. speed, coolant flow, depth of cut, etc. If a change occurs, e.g. a tool breaks or the coolant flow stops, the operation continues unchecked to the end point. In other words, there is no feedback to the controller to modify the criteria applied.
- **Closed loop control** – Data obtained from sensors linked to the programmed operation is used to modify the controller action. In other words the system has **feedback control**. There are two forms of feedback control:

    - **On/Off or two-step control** – The feedback data is used to switch an operation ON or OFF. A typical example would be temperature control in an automatic soldering machine. The heater would switch on if the temperature fell below 183 °C and off when the temperature reached 185 °C.
    - **Proportional control** – The feedback data can have a range of values, the operation being varied according to the value at a particular time. For example, the rotation of a CD Master for laser writing must be at an extremely precise and consistent speed. A sensor attached to the drive motor detects any change in rotational speed and feeds that data to the controller. The controller then adjusts the speed of rotation accordingly. Such modifications may occur many thousands of times a second.

        Proportional control depends on negative feedback. The action taken by the controller is in proportion to the size of the detected change. The value of the change is called the **error**. Corrective action is always directed towards reducing the size of the error to zero.

Uses of control technology

Quality monitoring

The likelihood of every product manufactured in a specific process being identical in every respect is very small. The manufacturing/engineering industry usually settles for an acceptable range of quality and works strictly within those boundaries, called **tolerances**. Quality control monitors the success of such an approach in terms of short- and long-term product performance and customer satisfaction.

If the quality of a product falls outside the agreed tolerances there are three possible explanations:

1. Design errors
CAD/CAM and virtual testing have almost eliminated this possibility.

2. Components or raw materials from external suppliers are of unacceptable quality
Solved most easily by changing the source of supply.

3. Faults in the manufacturing process
Errors are most likely to occur in the following instances. Note that quality control is most important and can be achieved easily with the use of control systems.

Checking the dimensions of a component
In a production run of many thousands of small components it is impossible to check the dimensions of each one. Manual examination involved the selection of a small sample, say 1% of the batch, and recording the dimensional data. The rest of the batch was assumed to conform to the sample taken. If a few of the unexamined batch were indeed faulty they would go undetected.

In high-technology industry, it is important to examine each and every component so that those of substandard quality are immediately rejected. This task can only be carried out by machine and the simplest control arrangement involves the use of a displacement sensor. The sensor head is in contact with the component as it passes beneath. If the component is too large, the sensor head is pushed upwards; if it is too small, the sensor head drops downwards (Fig. 2.31). The acceptable range of rise and fall of the sensor head (the **tolerance**) is programmed into a control computer. If the dimensions of a component are within the tolerance level it passes on to the next stage of manufacture. If not, the component is diverted off the production line by a gate that swings into its path, to be dropped into a reject bin.

Component inspection
Inspection of a component for damage is best achieved by a human operator. The item is delivered to the operator on a conveyor belt at a speed suitable for visual inspection (Fig. 2.32). This speed will have been determined in a work study as being the optimum for the task. However, different operators work at different rates and the belt may need to carry different components at different times. All would require variations in belt speed, which can be set by the operator or stopped in an emergency. This would require a simple two-step controller.

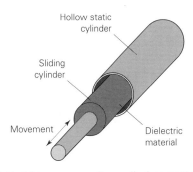

Figure 2.31 Variable area capacitance displacement transducer

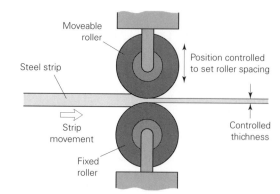

Figure 2.32 Product inspection conveyor belt

In order to ensure that the belt speed is not set to run too slowly by the operator, a visual display of the belt speed is linked into the system via a speed sensor built into the belt roller. Available for inspection at any time, the display can be used to indicate the lower limit for that production run.

Process control

Most production processes involve the movement of a device. Such devices may include tools, presses, rollers, jointed arms, etc. Control of the movement of those devices can be achieved by three systems, either singly or in combination:

- Electrical
- Pneumatic
- Hydraulic

Sensors built into each can be linked into closed loop control to ensure that if a functional combination is used the systems co-ordinate their activities to a high degree of accuracy, for example, in the manufacture of mild steel sheet (Fig. 2.33). The final thickness of the steel sheet depends on the distance between the press rollers, with the upper roller moved hydraulically to vary this distance. In order to measure the thickness of the sheet (Fig. 2.34) a displacement sensor is fixed just beyond the rollers. The steel sheet is fed through the sensor on leaving the press. The system functions as follows:

1. Steel sheet fed into rollers set at the required thickness.
2. Sheet feeds through the displacement sensor.
3. Correct thickness – sheet feeds through to next process.
4. Too thick – error signal generated. Rollers reversed to move sheet back to start.
5. Controller moves rollers closer together in proportion to size of error signal.
6. Sheet fed into repositioned rollers.
7. Sheet feeds through the displacement sensor.
8. Correct thickness – sheet feeds through to next process.
9. Too thick – error signal generated. Rollers reversed to move sheet back to start.

And so on until sheet is the required thickness, the choice of movement control device to use in a given situation depends on a number of factors (see Table 2.9).

Computer Numerical Control (CNC) programming

A CNC machine needs three items of information in order to perform a task:

Figure 2.33 Setting steel strip thickness

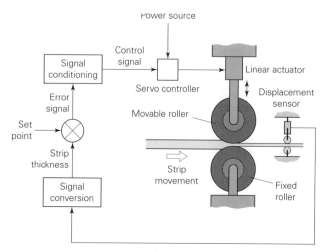

Figure 2.34 Thickness control in a steel mill

Table 2.9 Properties of movement control devices

System	Positive factors	Negative factors
Electrical	Best in rotary applications; low cost easy to obtain and set up	Poor in linear applications; cannot be used where explosive substances are present – risk of sparking
Pneumatic	Best in low force, linear applications; can be used in all hazardous environments	Expensive; can be imprecise
Hydraulic	Best in high force, precision linear applications; can be used in some hazardous environments	Very expensive; high pressure in use can be hazardous

- The operation to be carried out, e.g. start, stop, change tool, coolant on.
- The direction of the action, e.g. forward, reverse, clockwise, anticlockwise.
- The dimensions of that action, e.g. 50 mm, 45°.

The International Standardisation Organisation (ISO) has defined a set of codes, which are used to describe machining operations. Tables 2.10 and 2.11, respectively, show those suitable for milling and turning operations, in which 'G' refers to *preparatory* functions and 'M' refers to *miscellaneous* functions. The direction and dimensions of the action are programmed using the ISO codes together with a set of co-ordinates which define start and stop points, and movement to any datum points in between.

Table 2.10 Selected codes used to describe milling operations

Code	Operation
G00	Rapid movement
G01	Linear interpolation (straight line cutting)
G02	Circular interpolation, clockwise
G03	Circular interpolation, counterclockwise
G04	Time dwell
G25	Jump to block number
G26	Return from jump
G28	Mirror image
G53	Cancel change of datum
G57	Set new datum position
G70	Imperial units
G71	Metric units
G79	Point-to-point milling
G81	Drilling cycle
G84	Tapping cycle
G85	Boring cycle
G86	PCD drilling cycle
G87	Dish milling cycle
G88	Rectangle milling cycle
G89	Circle milliing cycle
G90	Absolute programming
G91	Incremental programming
M02	End of program (single quantity)
M03	Start spindle forward
M04	Start spindle reverse
M05	Stop spindle
M06	Tool change
M08	Coolant on
M09	Coolant off
M30	End of program (repeat)
M39	Close automatic chuck
M40	Open automatic chuck
M43	Subroutine create
M44	Subroutine terminate
M45	Subroutine call

Table 2.11 Selected codes used to describe turning operations

Code	Operation
G00	Rapid movement, point-to-point
G01	Linear movement
G02	Circular interpolation, clockwise
G03	Circular interpolation, counterclockwise
G70	Imperial units selected
G71	Metric units selected
G81	Outside diameter (parallel) turning cycle
G82	Facing/grooving cycle
G83	Peak drill cycle
G84	Thread cycle
G90	Absolute programming selected
G91	Incremental programming selected
M02	End of program
M03	Start spindle forwards
M04	Start spindle reverse
M05	Spindle stop
M06	Tool change
M08	Coolant on
M09	Coolant off
M39	Close air chuck
M40	Open air chuck

- The z axis should be regarded as the axis of rotation of the workpiece or of the tool carrying out the action.
- Movement in the negative (−) direction will reduce the size of the workpiece.

A computer usually writes the final program after it obtains responses from the machine operator. In order to keep things as simple as possible the computer is programmed to ask simple questions, such as:

'Which tool is to be used?'; 'In which direction is the cut to be made?'; or 'What are the finished dimensions of the workpiece?'.

From the responses obtained the operation code, direction and co-ordinates are written into a program, which can be copied onto floppy disc. That disc is then inserted into the machine and the operation started. All the operator need do is load and unload raw and finished components respectively.

Figure 2.36 shows an example for a component to be turned out on a CNC lathe.

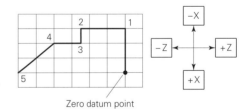

Figure 2.36 A component to be turned out on a CNC lathe

The co-ordinates defining the start, finish and waypoints are laid out in the table. The cutting tool will move from the start ($Z = 0$) to the first waypoint. It will then move from there to the next, and so on.

X	Z
−3	0
−3	−2.5
−2	−2.5
−2	−4
0	−6

Absolute programming

The ISO and British Standard BS 3635 have also standardised the co-ordinate system used. Three axes of movement are defined, **X**, **Y** and **Z**, according to the '**Right-handed Cartesian co-ordinate system**' (Fig. 2.35). Positive (+) and negative (−) directions are also indicated. A fourth axis, **W** or **W′**, may be used if a third movable unit is present, e.g. the table of a rotary milling machine.

The axes are further defined as **X**, **Y** and **Z** to specify tool movement and **X′**, **Y′** and **Z′** to specify workpiece movement. BS 3635 also states that:

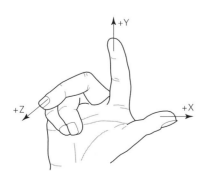

Figure 2.35 The right-handed Cartesian co-ordinate system

Table 2.12 Control of a sheet metal press

Safety guard	Press	Sheet in place	Controller output
0 = open	0 = lowered	0 = no	0 = wait
1 = closed	1 = raised	1 = yes	1 = begin
0	0	0	0
1	0	0	0
0	1	0	0
0	0	1	0
1	0	1	0
1	1	0	0
0	1	1	0
1	**1**	**1**	1

Programmable logic controllers

Sequential control, a combination of two-step and proportional control, is used where a specific operation only occurs after a preceding operation has been completed. For example, in automated assembly those components that are to be covered by other components must be placed first. Only when sensors detect the presence of the first component is the second put in place, and so on.

In multi-state sequential operations (i.e. a number of criteria must be met before the next operation occurs) a **programmable logic controller** is used:

- Completion of an operation is logged by the controller as 'TRUE' or '1' in a truth table. Non-completion is recorded as 'FALSE' or '0'.
- Only when the controller logs all operations in the set as 'TRUE' does the next operation set begin.

For example, the control of a sheet metal press is shown in Table 2.12.

In this case the operation which will press the steel sheet 1 will only occur when the safety guard is closed, the press is raised and the sheet metal is in place.

Put more simply, a PLC controls a system by an instruction set which says 'when this, this and this happens, do this.'

Activity: Write a simple program for a component part.

Robotics

Although there are probably as many definitions of the word 'robot' as there are robots, the most up to date would be *'a reprogrammable, multifunctional machine designed to move materials, parts, tools, specialised devices or itself for the performance of a variety of tasks, and which, if required, can modify its program according to the data received from sensory devices'*.

Manufacturing/engineering industry has been revolutionised by the use of robotics. Production rates are higher than they have ever been, with levels of product quality and consistency that were previously impossible to achieve. Robots can now be equipped with sensors to mimic sight, hearing, touch and even smell to sensitivity far beyond the capability of a human worker.

However, the new industrial revolution has had a high social cost in the form of rising unemployment. Robots have all but replaced unskilled or semi-skilled labour in many areas of engineering, and further advances in robotics may even lead to a similar loss of skilled labour. There are a number of reasons why robotic technology has been so successful.

Adaptability and flexibility

Robots can perform any tasks that are very repetitive, too boring, too precise, too dangerous or beyond the physical or mental capability of humans. Most industrial robots are also multifunctional and reprogrammable. For example:

- The Milacron T^3 robot can accurately machine the edges of over 250 different engineering components in any sequence, retooling itself automatically.
- Warehousing robots can load, lift and stack items that are too heavy for humans to lift without risk of injury.
- The Pragma A3000 robot can assemble the 12 components of an industrial valve unit at a rate of 320 units per hour. This is equivalent to the output of 10 human workers.
- One vehicle body-welding robot can perform the task of four human workers, and is 20% faster.

Continuous operation

Robots can perform their assigned task 24 hours a day, every day of the year. They do not require breaks, holidays or time off for illness, etc. For example:

- The writing of master files onto floppy discs involves the insertion of a single floppy disc into a disc drive and its removal and packaging after the download is complete. A robot can repeat this action continuously and fatigue-free for an entire production run lasting many months.
- Back injuries resulting from the handling of heavy goods are the greatest cause of lost production in manufacturing industry. Robots are unaffected by the handling of loads many times heavier than would cause injury to a human.

Improved reproducibility

Humans have a tendency to vary the way they perform a task to reduce boredom. This increases the risk of error. However, robots follow a precise series of instructions according to their programming. This means that single or multiple tasks are repeated in exactly the same way every time and within very narrow tolerance limits. The closed loop control systems used by robots also allow for extremely high accuracy. For example:

- In the assembly of PCBs for computers, testing of the board cannot take place until the assembly is complete. A single misplaced component can prevent the board from working correctly. Locating and rectifying such errors is very costly in terms of time and money. Unlike a human, a pre-programmed robot assembles the board in the exactly the same way every time, and will never place a component in the wrong location or orientation.

Speed

When a human performs, say, an assembly operation, the movements will vary every time the operation is carried out. However, that of robots will be identical every time in a specific operation. Although the time saving is small, it becomes very significant in a large production run. An additional problem for humans is fatigue which slows down production even further. Again robots are unaffected by this. For example:

- A 2-minute unit assembly process may take a human 2 seconds longer on average to perform than a robot simply because arm movements follow a longer curved path rather than a straight one.
- In a production run of 100,000 units this additional time adds up to 200,000 seconds or about 3333 minutes. This is the equivalent to the lost production of almost 1667 units.
- A robot will move the minimum distance possible between assembly operations, saving those 2 seconds and thereby increasing production rates.

Use in hazardous environments

Some environments are simply too dangerous for humans to work within even with the use of protective clothing. Robots suffer no ill effects from exposure to such things as excess heat, toxic gas, radiation, etc. For example:

- The spray-painting process on a vehicle production line is very hazardous for human workers. Robots, however, are unaffected by spray drift, solvent fumes, etc. As humans are no longer exposed to the hazards this also allows cost savings in terms of the provision of safety equipment.
- Weld examination involves the use of high-energy x-rays. The x-rays are shone through a weld onto photographic film, any flaws showing up as overexposed areas on the film. Long-term exposure can cause serious burns and cancer in humans. However, robots are largely unaffected by radiation exposure and so can work continuously.

Case Study: CD-ROM

Automation

ComLaser produce very high quality products and wish to maintain the reputation they have for product reliability. Quality control is highly automated from the testing of PCB function to the final testing of the complete CD Players and CDs. Computers have been programmed with the minimum specification to which the products should perform. Any product that fails to meet the specified criteria is rejected.

Quality targets are met by the use of process control. Robots that do not tire or make mistakes in repetitive procedures are used extensively, mainly in the assembly of the PCBs and chassis, and the many CD replication stages. Reproducibility is enhanced and production rates can be faster. Computers using CNC programs strictly control the rate of manufacture.

> *Activity*: **Explain** how automation is used in the production of your chosen product.

2.6 Impact of new technology on people

Both case studies are used to illustrate the following section.

Impact of new products on people

Up to the 1980s sound recordings were only available on vinyl disc and magnetic tape. Played by a needlepoint stylus riding in a groove pressed into the surface of the vinyl, such discs were prone to noise and damage. Magnetic tape was less susceptible to noise and damage but sound quality fell with time.

In the early days of CD players the discs were very expensive compared with the existing vinyl disc and magnetic tape technologies. Mass production, advances in integrated circuitry and the falling cost of microchips led to the availability of cheaper and cheaper models and public demand increased rapidly. This, and the superior quality of digital recordings, eventually led to retail units terminating the sale of vinyl discs and concentrating on CDs and magnetic tapes only.

The cost of the products steadily fell for two main reasons:

- *Miniaturisation* – A cheaper and more compact product style became an important selling point. More extensive use of low-cost integrated circuitry and microprocessors reduced material and production costs. This allowed the development of portable, battery-operated CD Players for everyday use, increasing demand further.

- *Mass production* – The very high demand for more compact CD Players required faster production methods. This in turn allowed for a reduction in per unit costs and refinement of the product. With the new availability of mass production systems, more companies began producing CD Players and competition forced prices down still further.

Improved performance and ease of use promoted further advances:

- Application of CD technology to the field of data storage led to the use of CDs to store computerised data. Prior to this, standard 90 mm floppy discs could store a maximum of 1.44 megabytes (Mb) of data. A standard 120 mm CD-ROM can store around 780 Mb.

- The CD Players required to read the CD-ROMs were installed directly into computers, the data read by the laser interfacing directly with the central processing unit of the computer.

- The term 'multimedia' is now used to describe the CD-ROM technology. Audio, video, photographic, text and software data could be packaged together on one CD-ROM. Now the general public had complete access to as much information as they required on demand and in any format.

2.7 Impact of new technology on companies

Impact of new products and technology on industry

Advances in electronic and communications technology opened up manufacturing industry to a wider market. No longer tied to one country, competition became intense as large engineering companies relocated to where raw materials were readily obtainable and distribution was easy. Automation reduced the number and nature of the workforce. Energy also became more and more expensive so energy efficiency became a major market force. Many companies went out of business as they failed to adapt to the change. Traditional practices eventually gave way to new (see Table 2.13), the entire industry becoming streamlined, energy efficient and less labour intensive. Modern industry is now compact, flexible and adaptable.

New products

When one product is invented it is not long before advances are made and new uses are determined. For example, advances in CD Player technology led to the production of CD-ROM Players, which required more accurate tracking and data processing control. It became important to design systems that were immediately adaptable to the production of new items. CAD, CAM, CNC and integrated manufacturing allowed this to happen. Using such systems a company can be tooled up to produce a certain type of product, yet it is not that costly or difficult to make slight alterations to produce similar, more advanced products.

One acknowledged problem was that home users could not record onto CDs. Increasing demand for this led to the production of player/recorders which could produce permanent CD recordings. Soon to follow was the recordable/erasable CD which could be re-used many times. Still relatively expensive when compared with magnetic tape, this new recording technology should become cheaper as time progresses. However, the likely outcome is the decline of the magnetic tape industry.

Changes in the workforce

The introduction of automation to manufacturing industry led to a massive reduction in the size of the workforce required for the production process. In addition, the use of new technologies such as CNC and robotics to carry out low-skilled, repetitive tasks meant that assembly lines no longer needed manual labour but a workforce of supporting technicians. Their job is to ensure that the computers and robots perform the assembly function at the optimum rate and efficiency. This led to the employment of an increasing number of women in the electronics industry and opened work opportunities for the disabled.

In addition, manufacturing companies are now demanding a minimum level of education for assembly line work, previously regarded as suitable for unqualified, unskilled labour. This education must also continue beyond traditional schooling as advances in technology demand advances in skills and knowledge, especially computer literacy.

It is also necessary for workers to become multi-skilled so that they can move between operations. As well as allowing for changes in production demands, worker boredom is reduced as the task is constantly changing. Most large companies now heavily promote the idea of adaptability and flexibility through lifelong learning.

At management and highly skilled (e.g. design engineer) level the changes have also been profound. Electronic communication in the form of fax, e-mail, modem transmission of data and video conferencing allows co-operative working over great distances. Many employees at these levels can now work from home or in regional offices, and at a time to suit their particular circumstances. In turn, this has led to a reduction in the number of management and highly-skilled personnel employed as computers take over the tasks normally performed by other staff, e.g. draughting, accounting, stock control, administrative and secretarial work, etc.

Automation has led generally to a reduced workforce in the manufacturing/engineering sector while it has also led to an increase in that of the microtechnology industry which supplies the needs of automatic manufacture.

Table 2.13 Comparison of traditional and new engineering practices

Traditional engineering	New engineering
Employed mainly male and large labour force	Employ often a female, small labour force
Heavy industries needing large tonnage of raw materials	Light industries, needing electricity but not usually coal. Raw materials and components often from other factories
Mainly on older inner city sites or located near to raw materials	Mainly on new industrial estates on the edge of towns and cities, often called footloose industries, with a freer choice of location. The locations are market orientated
End product often bulky and both difficult and expensive to move	End product often small and so easier and cheaper to move
Often created air and noise pollution making local residential areas unhealthy	Little noise or air pollution and so built nearer to residential areas
Found near to early canals and railways for bulk movement	Built near to main roads for more flexible transport

New materials used

In order to exploit mass production methods, increasing use of modern materials is vital. Such materials include advanced polymers for cases and covers, new alloys for lightness and strength, and composites to reduce costs.

New technology

CAD, CAM and CNC technologies substantially reduce design, development and production times. Production methods and assembly line operations can also be changed within hours to produce a modified or completely new product. In the past this would require investment in new equipment and the retraining of the entire workforce. Now a simple change in the programming of assembly robots may be all that is required.

Increasing cost benefits of the 'just-in-time' principle have also led to the development of automated stock control and warehousing. Computerised databases keep track of stock issue and production rates, both current and predicted. At a predetermined level, the database generates an electronic order, which is transmitted directly to a supplier. New stock is delivered at the exact time that old stock is about to be exhausted.

In the warehouse stacking and picking up is carried out by Automatic Guided Vehicles (AGVs), again under the control of a production computer. Following magnetic tracks embedded in floor of the warehouse, the AGVs are guided by a transmitter/receiver system to an exact location. Laser bar-code readers or video component recognition systems identify specific items, which can then be delivered or picked for dispatch. Human involvement is limited to the unloading and loading of the AGVs at delivery points.

New markets

World communications increasingly rely on electronics and computerised data transmission. The technology is available in all walks of life with information storage capability of CDs and CD-ROMs used in education, entertainment, administration systems, advertising and more. For example, advances in laser read/write technology has opened up the possibility of recording home video on CD rather than on magnetic tape. Computerised editing of those recordings will then be possible allowing the general public to produce cinema quality images complete with special effects.

Changes in the working environment

In general terms, an environment in which workers feel safe and comfortable will also be efficient and productive. Particular concern is directed at this as human efficiency is now the weakest link in the productivity chain. It is well known that a comfortable, happy and satisfied workforce enhances production, the profits from which exceed the cost of providing employee services. The overall cost savings can be passed on in the form of cheaper goods, or go towards increasing investment or company profits.

In brief, efficient and productive workers will:

- Have been well trained in all aspects of the job, including what to do if things go wrong.
- Be supported by supervisory staff.
- Know how their role fits into the total quality of the product.
- Be kept warm and dry.
- Be protected from hazards such as pollutants, noise and physical injury.
- Enjoy rest, recreation and healthcare facilities in the workplace.

A safe production environment must also be maintained with the end product in mind. For example, tolerances in the production of microchips, CD lasers and CDs can be as low as a fraction of a micron μm or 10^{-6} m). A speck of dust is many hundreds of times this size. The production environment must therefore be dust-free.

Such 'clean-rooms' have their air filtered many times, the staff wearing special body-cover suits and face masks. All surfaces must be specially cleaned and be coated in antistatic materials – a single static discharge could destroy an entire batch of microchips.

Consideration of the production environment has also led to general improvement in health and safety at work as individuals are no longer exposed to hazardous materials or procedures. An additional benefit is that such working environments are light and spacious and at the same time totally practical. Designed by architects with specific purposes in mind, they are generally environments in which people enjoy working. Surveys of such workplaces indicated that staff absenteeism and turnover is much reduced. Both bring considerable savings to the company as production rates are higher and the cost of training of incoming workers is lower.

Cost considerations in a competitive environment also means that it is cheaper for companies to carry out comprehensive risk assessment and work studies in advance of production. This is a relatively new approach in manufacturing industry, essentially forced upon it by legislation, increasingly competitive markets and the consequent need for cost reduction. It has been determined that unsafe and inefficient working practices cost UK manufacturing around £15 billion a year.

- *Risk assessment* – All manufacturing processes carry risk in the operation of machinery or in the use of certain materials. In the past, an educated guess of how to protect the workforce had to be taken based on previous experience. Only incidents occurring during actual production revealed specific hazards. This was costly in terms of re-tooling, addition of safety systems and possible worker compensation for injury. Data gathered from previous and predicted practice can determine almost all risks so that manufacturing systems can be made totally safe.
- *Work study* – This is a close examination of the production environment, e.g. the movements the workers need to make, the time they take, and the effort required. It can determine where automation can be used and where human worker input is essential. One development

that has arisen from work study is the ergonomic workstation. All controls, materials, etc. are within arm's reach of the operator. Unproductive movement is considerably reduced and productivity rises. There are also health and safety benefits as the risk of repetitive strain or back injury is much reduced.

Efficiency

Productivity and efficiency are very closely related in that improvements in one usually lead to improvements in the other.

Automation, robotics and the use of computer control systems has ensured that maximum product output is achieved with minimum energy and time input. Unlike a human workforce, such systems work at a constant rate for 24 hours a day; they do not require time off because of illness and do not take holidays. Wastage is also reduced and any material that can be recycled is recycled.

Energy costs are largely made up of the cost of electricity and that of heating the environment. Automated systems can be designed to make maximum use of cheaper off-peak supply, which is usually available overnight. Production areas that generate heat (e.g. soldering plant) can have the hot air drawn away, filtered and delivered to areas that require heating.

Modern technology can also be used in the form of 'occupation sensors'. When a room is empty, heating is reduced to a minimum. When the room is occupied the sensor detects this and turns the heating up. Increasingly sophisticated, such sensors can not only determine how many people are in a room but also how much body heat is being generated. Direct heating can be adjusted accordingly.

Activity: identify the sector from which your chosen product originates and, using the above features, carry out a cost–benefit analysis for the development of your product within that sector.

UNIT 3 Making Engineered Products

This is a very practical chapter, which develops your understanding of the process of production planning and product engineering. It looks at

- The use of product specifications
- Selection of materials and components
- Creating a production plan.

You are asked to engineer a product from a specification. You should be able to select appropriate components and materials for your product, develop and work to a production plan in producing the product, and finally compare your finished product to the original specification. As part of the production process you should develop a range of practical engineering skills which are used in engineering industries.

One case study is used in this chapter, and will illustrate some of the principles discussed in the text: *The making of an industrial electromechanical engineered product – 'the power screwdriver'*.

3.1 Product specification

Specifications are developed from a design brief and can give information about how a product should perform. These are called performance characteristics and this type of specification is known as a performance specification. It will always:

- Describe what the product has to do
- Describe what the product should look like
- State any other requirements that need to be met.

In the engineering industry, when a design is finalised, it is then passed on to those involved in its manufacture.

A different type of specification is developed called a 'manufacturing specification', which contains specific information about processes and materials to be used.

When you are developing an engineered product, it will be necessary to work from information from both types of specification, the most important of which are:

- Quality of the product, which describes the standards to be met in all areas.
- Size or dimensions of the product.
- Material and component properties required by the product.
- Process to be used to manufacture the product.
- Time scales for the production of the product.

Quality

This refers to the level of quality and reliability expected by the market and the customer/client that is necessary to ensure the product's success.

Quality standards

Standards are the foundations to all product designs. They give the levels that must be achieved in all areas and, because of this, form a framework in which to develop the design. They originate from various organisations which may set different levels for a similar standard. The organisations include:

- BSI (British Standards Institution) who develops national standards.
- CEN (Comité Européen de Normalisation) who develops European standards.
- ISO (International Standards Organisation) who develops Universal standards.

Legislation

One of the most important pieces of legislation of which the design engineer has to be aware is the Health and Safety at Work Act, etc. Section 6 of the Act says that designed and constructed products should be safe and without risk to health at all times when being set, cleaned, used or maintained by a person at work. Also that steps should be taken to ensure that any person supplied with a product has adequate information about the use for which it was designed.

Aesthetics

The appearance of a product is often very important to the customer and in some cases is more important than how the product functions. Think about the design of watches for example. When you purchase a watch from a shop, what is your main consideration? How well it works, or the variety of different functions it performs or how good it looks or whether it is fashionable?

Aesthetics relates to the appearance of a product and includes the product's:

- Shape
- Colour
- Form
- Style

Texture/pattern/decoration and surface finish

The surface finish or texture of a product will be given in the specification and then drawn in an engineering drawing. They are represented by the symbols shown in Fig. 3.1. The number gives the level of surface roughness (a). This is measured in micrometres μm) which are thousandths of a millimetre. This number shows the limits of roughness that are allowable when manufacturing the surface (b). Sometimes additional information is included which states the finishing process to be used (b).

When selecting the most appropriate technique or process to achieve the finish or surface roughness required, Fig. 3.2 should give a valuable guide.

Size and tolerances

The dimensions needed to make a product are first given in the specification and then drawn in an engineering drawing. To construct an engineering drawing, a datum or reference

Lay symbol	Meaning
=	Lay approximately parallel to the line representing the surface to which the symbol is applied
⊥	Lay approximately perpendicular to the line representing the surface to which the symbol is applied
X	Lay angular in both directions to line representing the surface to which the symbol is applied
M	Lay multidirectional
C	Lay approximately circular relative to the centre of the surface to which the symbol is applied
R	Lay approximately radial relative to the centre of the surface to which the symbol is applied
P	Lay particulate, non-directional, or protuberant

Figure 3.1 Symbols for surface texture

Typical textures produced by various processes

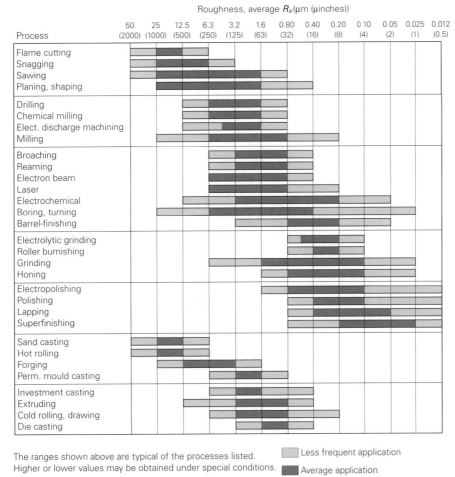

Figure 3.2 Typical texture produced by various processes

surface, line or point is found and the dimensions are given as measurements from this datum point (Fig. 3.3).

A tolerance dimension (Fig. 3.4) states the allowable limits of size of a part of the product or, in other words, the accuracy to which the product must be produced. A tolerance of 45 ±0.2 means that the final measurement can be 45.2 to 44.8 allowing a total of 0.4 variation in dimensional accuracy.

The tolerances often influence the choice of production technique used to manufacture the product, as some processes are much more accurate or work to tighter tolerances than other processes. If no tolerance is given next to a dimension, this is known as an open dimension and usually information about all the open dimensions on a drawing may be given on the title block, for instance: 'All dimensions to be ±0.55 unless otherwise stated.'

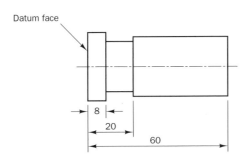

Figure 3.3 Dimensioning from a datum face

Materials and components

A specification will outline the material requirements of a product and will include a description of the material and component properties including: strength, toughness, elasticity, plasticity, ductility, malleability, hardness, brittleness, electrical conductivity, electrical resistivity, permittivity, magnetic conductivity, thermal conductivity, thermal expansivity and chemical stability. It will also include the quantity of materials and components required and possibly the form in which they are supplied.

Process methods

The specification should describe the requirements and features of a process or processes, e.g. quantity to be produced, tolerances required by the product, surface finish, material properties and the time available to produce the product. The product specification you will be working from should not at this stage specify the actual processes that will be used. However, in industry a manufacturing specification should give exact details of all the processes used to manufacture the product.

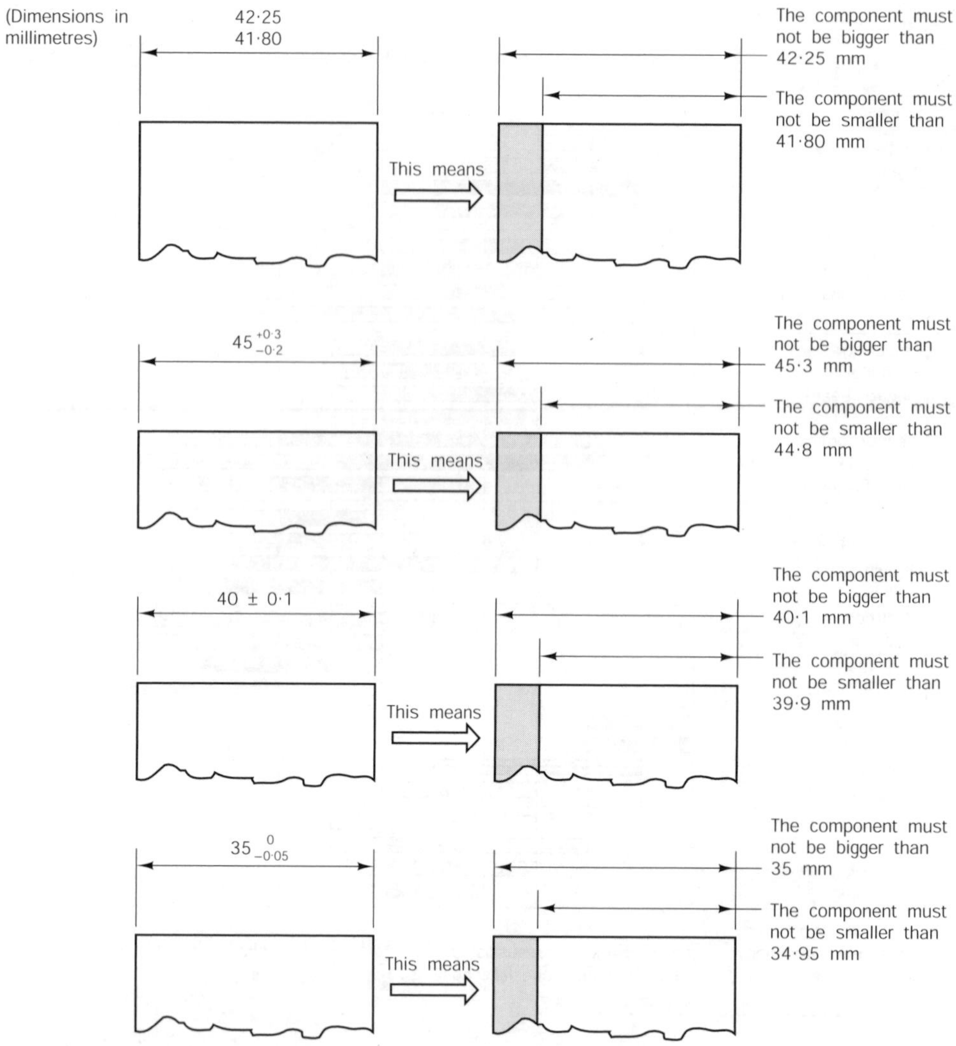

(Dimensions in millimetres)
42·25
41·80
This means
The component must not be bigger than 42·25 mm
The component must not be smaller than 41·80 mm
$45^{+0.3}_{-0.2}$
This means
The component must not be bigger than 45·3 mm
The component must not be smaller than 44·8 mm
40 ± 0·1
This means
The component must not be bigger than 40·1 mm
The component must not be smaller than 39·9 mm
$35^{0}_{-0.05}$
This means
The component must not be bigger than 35 mm
The component must not be smaller than 34·95 mm

Figure 3.4 Toleranced dimensions

Time scales

The processes involved in manufacturing a product have to be organised into a smooth flow. Planning starts from the time the product is due to be delivered to the customer. The amount of time it takes to lead up to the product being delivered is known as the lead time (Fig. 3.5). Because some processes take longer than others it is important that they are arranged so that each is completed in the time allowed. This ensures that there are no delays or build-ups that would disturb the flow or exceed the delivery deadline.

INPUTS
(need for a product)
Routing and scheduling
Part A
Part B
Part C
Part D
Part E
Material delivery
Parts manufacture
Subassembly No. 1
Subassembly No. 2
Sub-assembly
Product
Final assembly
OUTPUT
(Product for delivery)
Sales forecast or customer order
Order materials and purchased parts
Materials needed
All parts needed
Assemblies needed
Shipping date
LEAD TIME

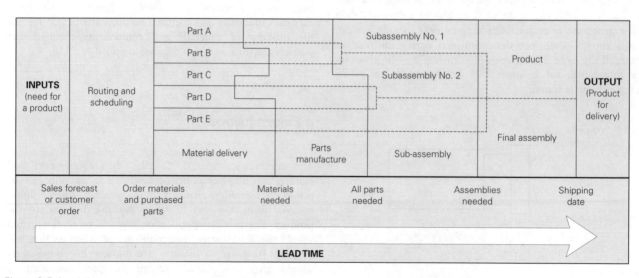

Figure 3.5 Lead time

3.2 Select materials and components

You should be able to recognise and select materials and components to meet a product specification.

Materials

You should be able to **recognise** and **select** materials with suitable properties to meet a product specification and, where appropriate, suggest alternatives

Selecting materials to make products is not easy. To make good choices requires an understanding of a wide range of materials. To help you to make your choices think about the following topics.

Material availability

The availability of material depends on several factors:

- How rare or common is the material?
- Is the material natural or man-made? If the material is man-made, how simple, easy or safe is the manufacturing process?
- How easy is the material to obtain or to extract? Does the extraction process involve work in hazardous conditions?
- Does the material have to be brought in from elsewhere? Technologists generally receive materials in what are called standard forms and standard preferred sizes. These have come about by the traditional requirements of manufacturing.

Environmental issues

- Depletion of natural resources, such as using hardwood (which takes such a long time to grow) occurs faster than it can be replaced; or the extraction and use of a very rare mineral.
- Pollution caused by the extraction and use of materials. There are all kinds of pollution, such as noise, visual, and vibrational, as well as the more obvious ones such as air pollution, water pollution and ground pollution.
- Destruction or disturbance of the environment, such as those caused by open-cast mining and also the need for landfill sites to dispose of waste materials or products after they have been used.

Social and moral issues

A moral decision may have to be made about a material which is well known to be very harmful to work with or use, but has some other very useful properties. Should you take the risk and use the material or not?

Another social and moral issue is one called *exploitation*. This can mean overworking or underpaying labourers in order to make money for yourself.

Cost

Cost is a vital part in the manufacture of any product. There are all sorts of costs that occur when making a product, the main ones being:

- Original cost of the material.
- Delivery costs of the material.
- Processing costs – are the processes cheap or expensive to run?
- Storage costs – are the products or materials cheap or expensive to store?
- Waste or recycling costs – if the material can be recycled, money can be saved.

All the costs need to be added together to find the total cost of the product.

Methods of production

The main material production categories are:

- Preparation of materials
- Material removal
- Material addition
- Forming with materials
- Casting and moulding
- Finishing processes.

When choosing materials, the properties of that material have to be appropriate to the chosen production methods. The ease with which a material can be machined and the quality of the finish obtained are also very important. It is also important to think about scale of manufacture – in other words, how many products need to be made. The aim of a engineer would be to choose a material and production method that would together produce a high-quality product.

Product design detail

The choice of a material for a product is also influenced by the product design detail, which includes:

- *Aesthetics* – How it looks or is required to look. This is determined by various properties:
  - optical properties such as colour, reflection, transparency and surface pattern.
  - textural properties – roughness or smoothness (can include surface detail and finish)
  - form – 3D shape and size.
- Function How the product is required to work.
- Purpose What the product is required to do. This can include durability or life span.

Experimental testing

Engineers have some difficult decisions to make when selecting the right material for the job, especially when new materials are appearing all the time!

In order for a material to be successful it must possess the right properties, i.e. strength, weight, ductility, hardness, toughness, elasticity, rigidity, malleability, etc. In addition, certain other properties such as electrical, magnetic or thermal properties and fatigue or creep resistance may be required. Corrosion resistance must usually be as high as possible or, alternatively, the material must respond to corrosion treatment.

A good way to make decisions about material properties is to use the most appropriate property test.

Selection conclusion

The final choice is often a compromise, which means that it partly satisfies all the product requirements, but does not completely satisfy them all!

In certain cases, some requirements are more important than others, e.g. cost may be more important than function. It is only when all the information is collected that a decision can be made. There is rarely one correct answer or one absolute best material. Usually there are several materials that will do the job (Fig. 3.6).

You will have a basic understanding of the following materials:

- Polymers
- Ceramics
- Composites
- Metals and alloys.

Polymers

Selection polymers

Tables 3.1 and 3.2 are designed to help you to make your initial general selection of polymers, which you think might be suitable to meet a given product specification.

Polymer databank

Once you have made a rough selection, look in the databank for more specific information about your chosen polymers. Available forms are shown in Fig. 3.7.

Thermoplastics

The polymer is produced in a chemical reaction (Fig. 3.8) as individual chains. As cross-linking of the chains occurs, they can flow over each other on heating. This means that the polymer can be softened and remoulded on heating. The polymer can also be recycled as lower-grade products.

Polythene

Low density (LDPE)
   Cheap and readily available.
   Soft and flexible with smooth, polished surface appearance.
   Transparent or coloured opaque.
   Weak with poor wear resistance.
   Resistant to corrosion and chemical attack.
   Used mainly in the form of thin sheet, films or injection mouldings
   Uses: Low-cost packaging ('Squeezy' bottles, food storage), moulded toys, electrical cable insulation, damp-proof membrane in building construction.

High density (HDPE)
   Cheap and readily available.
   Stiff and hard with smooth, waxy surface appearance.
   Brittle below 0 °C.

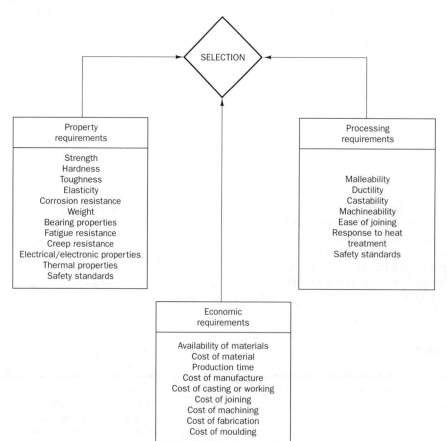

Figure 3.6 Selection of materials

Table 3.1 Thermoplastic polymers (Property *Key*: * = very low – ***** = very high)

	Density	Durability	Wear resistance	Fracture resistance	Plasticity	Most suitable process	Cost	Availability
Acrylic (e.g. Polymethyl methacrylate)	***	****	****	***	**	Line bending	***	****
uPVC (Unplasticised polyvinylchloride)	**	****	**	***	***	Vacuum forming	**	****
Polyamide (e.g. Nylon)	***	*****	***	*****	*	Turning; injection moulding	**	**
Low-density polythene	***	****	**	*****	*****	Injection moulding	**	*****
High-density polythene	****	*****	***	***	*****	Injection moulding	***	*****
Polypropylene	***	*****	***	***	*****	Injection moulding	**	*****
Polystyrene	****	*****	****	**	*	Turning; vacuum forming; line bending	**	***
Expanded polystyrene	*	*	*	*	*	Hot wire cutting	*	*****
Fluoroplastics (e.g. PTFE)	***	*****	**	*****	*****	Spray coating	*****	*
Polyester (e.g. Polyethylene tetraphthalate)	****	*****	***	*****	**	Fibre drawing	**	***
ABS (Acrylonitrile–butadiene–styrene)	***	*****	*****	*****	**	Injection moulding	**	***

Table 3.2 Thermosetting polymers (Property *Key*: * = very low – ***** = very high)

	Density	Durability	Wear Resistance	Fracture resistance	Plasticity	Ease of Working	Most suitable process	Cost	Availability
Melamine formaldehyde	*****	*****	*****	**	*	**	Moulding and cutting	****	*****
Amino resins (e.g. Urea methanal)	*****	*****	*****	**	*	**	Moulding and cutting	****	*****
Phenolic resins (e.g. Phenol methanal)	*****	*****	*****	*	*	**	Moulding and cutting	****	**
Polyester resin	*****	*****	*****	***** (reinforced)	*	**	Moulding and cutting	*****.	****
Epoxy resin	*****	*****	*****	***** (reinforced)	*	**	Moulding and cutting	*****	****

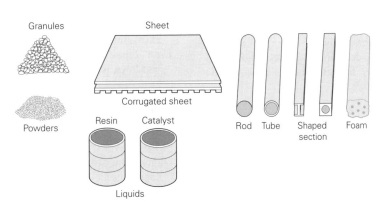

Figure 3.7

Coloured opaque.
Strong with good wear and impact resistance, but breaks on bending.
Heat resistant up to 130 °C.

Resistant to corrosion and chemical attack. (To find out more look up Corrosion in the Fact File.)
Used mainly in the form of injection mouldings.
Uses: Crates, bottles, pipes, kitchenware.

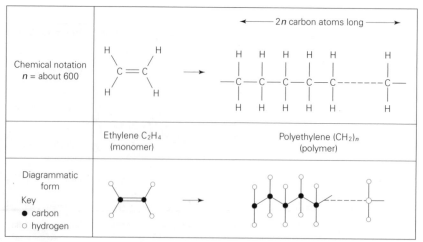

Figure 3.8 Polymerisation of ethylene

Polypropylene (PP)

Slightly more costly than polythene. Readily available.

Flexible but hard with smooth, waxy surface appearance. Brittle below 0 °C.

Coloured opaque.

Strong with good wear and impact resistance. Can be bent without breaking.

Fibre form is stretch resistant.

Heat resistant up to 130 °C.

Resistant to corrosion and chemical attack.

Used mainly in the form of injection mouldings.

Can be welded.

Uses: Gas transport pipes, kitchenware, medical equipment, food containers with moulded hinges, string, rope.

Polystyrene (PS)

Rigid

Cheap and readily available.

Hard and rigid with smooth, polished surface appearance.

Transparent or coloured opaque.

Strong. Poor wear and impact resistance. Shatters on bending.

Cold resistant and heat resistant up to 130 °C.

Resistant to corrosion and chemical attack, except from organic solvents.

Used mainly in the form of sheet or injection mouldings.

Easily joined using solvent-based glues.

Uses: Packaging, disposable domestic ware, toys and model kits, refrigerator/freezer linings, shells of domestic appliances.

Expanded

Cheap and readily available.

Very lightweight, buoyant and soft with dull surface appearance.

Coloured opaque.

Very weak. Poor wear and impact resistance. Crumbles easily. Breaks on bending.

Cold resistant and heat resistant up to 130 °C.

Resistant to corrosion and chemical attack, except from organic solvents.

Used mainly in the form of sheet or injection mouldings.

Cannot be joined.

Excellent sound and heat insulator.

Uses: Sound and heat insulation, packaging, protective filling for fragile goods, model construction.

Polyvinylchloride

Plasticised (PVC) – chemicals added to make the polymer flexible

Moderately priced and readily available.

Soft and flexible with smooth, polished surface appearance.

Transparent or coloured opaque.

Weak but with good wear resistance.

Resistant to corrosion and chemical attack.

Used mainly in the form of thin sheet, or films.

Uses: Waterproof clothing, undersealing of vehicles, water hoses, wall covering.

Unplasticised (uPVC)

Moderately priced and readily available.

Lightweight, stiff and hard with smooth, polished surface appearance.

Transparent or coloured opaque.

Strong with good wear and impact resistance, but breaks on bending.

Heat resistant.

Resistant to corrosion and chemical attack but requires addition of stabilising chemicals when exposed to sunlight.

Used mainly in the form of sheet for heat forming, or extrusions.

Uses: Pipes, gutters, bottles, corrugated roofing panels, windows, window frames.

Acrylic

Moderately priced and readily available, e.g. 'Perspex' and 'Plexiglas'.

Lightweight, stiff and hard with smooth, polished surface appearance.

Transparent or coloured opaque.

Strong with good impact resistance. Scratches easily. Does not shatter on bending.

Can be machined easily.

Resistant to corrosion and chemical attack.

Used mainly in the form of sheet for heat forming.

Uses: Lighting covers, military aircraft canopies, windows, furniture.

Fluoroplastic (polytetrafluoroethene – PTFE)

Expensive. Limited availability.
Flexible but with exceptionally smooth, friction-free and waxy surface.
Excellent heat resistance, does not burn.
Excellent resistance to corrosion and chemical attack.
Used mainly in the form of sprayed coatings, tape and fibre, but can be moulded with difficulty.
Uses: Fire-resistant coatings on fabrics, clothing (Gore-Tex), non-stick cookware, low-friction bush bearings, joint sealant for water pipes.

Polyamide (e.g. Nylon)

Moderate cost. Readily available.
Flexible but hard with smooth, waxy surface appearance.
Translucent or coloured opaque.
Strong with good wear and impact resistance. Can be bent without breaking.
Machines well but absorbs moisture - size may vary. Self-lubricating.
Moisture absorption makes nylon a poor electrical insulator.
Fibre form is stretch resistant.
Very good heat resistance.
Resistant to corrosion and chemical attack.
Used mainly in the form of fibres, injection mouldings and extrusions.
Can only be joined mechanically.
Uses: Clothing, bush bearings, gear wheels, electrical tool casings, hinges, kitchen implements, brushes.

Polyester (e.g. Terylene – polythenetetraphthalate)

Moderate cost. Readily available.
Drawn as fibres or films so flexible with smooth, waxy surface appearance.
Translucent or coloured opaque.
Light and strong with good wear and impact resistance.
Fibre form is slightly elastic.
Films are excellent electrical insulators.
Resistant to corrosion and chemical attack.
Uses: Clothing, ropes, circuit board coating, reinforcement in drive belts and tyres.

Thermosets

The polymer is produced in a chemical reaction which irreversibly cross-links the polymer chains (Fig. 3.9). It cannot be softened or remoulded on heating.

Filler materials are often used to modify the properties of the thermoset. Common fillers include glass fibre, wood dust, cloth and paper.

Melamine formaldehyde (MF)

Moderate cost and readily available.
Hard and rigid with smooth, polished surface appearance.
Strong but snaps on bending.
Excellent wear and impact resistance.
Excellent electrical insulator.
Cold resistant and heat resistant.

Figure 3.9 Covalent cross-links

Resistant to corrosion and attack from most chemicals.
Used mainly in the form of laminated sheet (Fig. 3.10).
Easily joined using most glues.
Uses: Domestic work surfaces, buttons, electrical fittings.

Amino resins (e.g. urea methanal – UM)

Moderate cost and readily available.
Hard and rigid with smooth, polished surface appearance.
Strong but brittle on bending.
Excellent wear resistance.
Excellent electrical insulator.
Cold resistant and heat resistant.
Resistant to corrosion and attack from most chemicals.
Used mainly in the form of sheets and mouldings.
Can be used as an adhesive.
Uses: Domestic work surfaces ('Formica'), white electrical fittings, appliance fittings, adhesive.

Phenolic resins (e.g. phenol methanal – PM)

Moderate cost. Low availability, usually as black or brown products ('Bakelite').
Hard and rigid with smooth, polished surface appearance.
Strong but brittle on bending. Filler is usually wood dust.
Excellent wear and impact resistance.
Excellent electrical and heat insulator.
Cold resistant and heat resistant.
Resistant to corrosion and attack from most chemicals.
Used mainly in the form of laminated sheet and mouldings.
Uses: Buttons, handles, electrical fittings (see Fig. 3.11).

Polyester resin (PR)

Moderate cost and readily available.
Shrinks on curing.
Hard and rigid with smooth, polished surface appearance.
Strong but brittle on bending so sheet products usually reinforced with glass fibre.

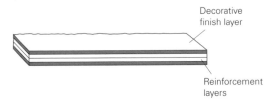

Figure 3.10 Laminated sheet

Figure 3.11 Buttons, handles, electrical fittings

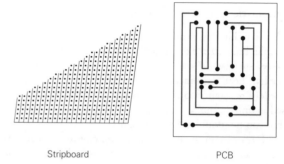

Figure 3.12 PCB: use of epoxy resin (ER)

Excellent wear and impact resistance when reinforced.
Excellent electrical and heat insulator.
Cold resistant and heat resistant.
Resistant to corrosion and attack from most chemicals.
Used mainly in the form of sheet and mouldings.
Uses: Castings, embedding of electrical components (tamper and shock proofing), boat hulls, car bodies, large containers.

Epoxy Resin (ER)

High cost. Readily available.
Extremely hard and rigid with smooth, polished surface appearance.
Strong but brittle on bending so sheet products usually reinforced with fibre, cloth or paper.
Excellent wear and impact resistance.
Excellent electrical and heat insulator.
Cold resistant and heat resistant up to 250 °C.
Resistant to corrosion and attack from most chemicals.
Used mainly in the form of laminated sheet and mouldings.
Can be used as exceptionally strong adhesive.
Uses: Chemically resistant surface coatings, castings, embedding of electrical components (tamper and shock proofing), adhesives, printed circuit boards, pressure vessels, boat hulls, car bodies (see Fig. 3.12).

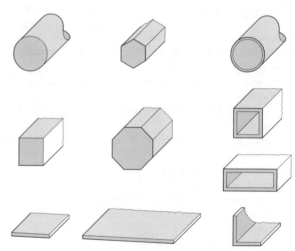

Figure 3.13 Metals and alloy databank: available forms

Forging or bending not possible as the metal will break into fragments along crystal boundaries (Fig. 3.15).
Exposed surfaces must be painted or treated to limit corrosion.
Cost of the metal is low but final cost is determined by the complexity and finish of the cast components.
Uses: Vehicle brake discs and drums, metalworking vices, machine beds and frames.

Metals and Alloys

Selection metals

Tables 3.3 and 3.4 are designed to help you make your initial general selection of metals and alloys that you think might be suitable to meet a given product specification.

Metal and alloy databank

Once you have made a rough selection, look in Table 3.3 or 3.4 for more specific information about your chosen metals and alloys. Available forms are shown in Fig. 3.13.

Grey cast iron

Iron + 3.2 to 3.5% carbon in the form of microscopic graphite flakes.
Hard, resilient outer layer with brittle, crystalline core (Fig. 3.14).
Very fluid on melting and so can be cast into finely detailed components. Usually supplied in the rough cast form.
Machine finishing to a high polish is easy as the high graphite content acts as a lubricant.

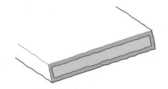

Figure 3.14 Cross section of cast iron

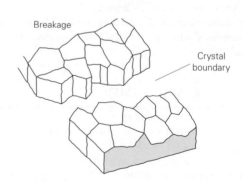

Figure 3.15 Breakage-crystal boundary

Table 3.3 Ferrous metal/Alloy (*Key*: * = very low – ***** = very high)

	Malleable or Ductile	Tensile strength	Compression strength	Hardness/ wear resistance	Corrosion resistance	Ease of working	Cost	Availability
Grey cast iron	N	*	*****	**	*	*	*	*****
Dead mild steel	Y	**	**	*	*	******	*	*****
Mild steel	Y	***	**	*	*	******	*	*****
Plain carbon steel	Y	***	**	**	*	****	*	*****
Medium carbon steel	N	***	***	***	**	***	*	*****
High-carbon steel	N	****	****	****	***	**	**	****
Stainless steel	Y	****	****	***	*****	*	***	***
High-speed steel	N	*****	*****	*****	*****	*	*****	*
High-tensile steel	N	*****	*****	*****	*****	*	*****	*
Manganese steel	N	*****	*****	*****	*****	*	*****	*

Table 3.4 Non-ferrous metal/Alloy (*Key*: * = very low – ***** = very high)

	Malleable or Ductile	Tensile strength	Compression strength	Hardness/ wear resistance	Corrosion resistance	Ease of working	Cost	Availability
Copper	Y	*	*	*	****	*****	*****	*****
Zinc	Y	*	*	*	*****	**	***	****
Tin	Y	*	*	*	*****	****	*****	***
Aluminium	Y	***	***	*	*****	*****	*	*****
Brass	N	****	****	****	*****	*****	***	*****
Tin bronze	N	****	****	****	*****	*****	***	***
Aluminium bronze	N	****	****	****	*****	*****	***	*****
Cupro-nickel	Y	****	****	*****	*****	*****	**	*****
Casting alloy	N	*****	*****	*****	*****	*****	***	*****
Duralumin	Y	*****	*****	*****	*****	*****	*****	**

Plain carbon steels:

Dead mild steel

Iron + 0.1 to 0.15% carbon.

Ductile and malleable when cold so can be pressed, bent, cut and drawn easily into required components (Fig. 3.16).

Soft, easy to machine to a high polish.

Exposed surfaces must be painted or treated to limit corrosion. May be galvanised.

Low cost.

Uses: Vehicle body panels, rivets, nails, screws, fence wire.

Mild steel

Iron + 0.15 to 0.3% carbon.

Ductile and malleable when hot so can be forged, rolled and drawn easily into required components.

Medium soft, so reasonably easy to machine to a high polish. May then be heat treated to increase surface hardness (case hardening).

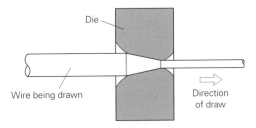

Die

Wire being drawn

Direction of draw

Figure 3.16 Wire being drawn through a die

Exposed surfaces must be painted or treated to limit corrosion. May be galvanised.

Low cost.

Uses: Building construction, vehicle body panels, rivets, nails, screws, fence wire.

Medium carbon steel

Iron + 0.3 to 0.8% carbon.

Malleable when hot so can be forged and rolled into required components.

Stronger and tougher than mild steel so more difficult to machine to a high polish. May be heat treated to increase surface hardness (case hardening).

High impact resistance.

Exposed surfaces must be painted or treated to limit corrosion. May be chromium plated.

Medium cost.

Uses: Low-impact tools (e.g. garden implements), crankshafts, axles, vehicle leaf springs.

High-carbon steel

Iron + 0.8 to 1.4% carbon.

Malleable when very hot so can be forged into required components.

Very hard and wear resistant so very difficult to machine to a high polish. May be heat treated to increase surface hardness (case hardening).

Very high impact resistance.
Corrosion is slow so oiling is sufficient to retard rusting.
High cost.
Uses: High-impact tools (e.g. hammers, chisels, screwdrivers, screw-cutting dies), vehicle coil springs.

Other steels

Stainless steel

Iron + 18% chromium, 8% nickel, 8% magnesium.
Malleable when very hot so can be forged or rolled into required components.
Very hard and wear resistant, so very difficult to machine, cut or file. Can be polished to a mirror finish.
Very high impact resistance.
High corrosion resistance. No surface treatment needed.
High cost.
Uses: Cutlery, medical equipment, storage tank linings, food preparation surfaces.

High-speed steels

Medium carbon steel + varying amounts of tungsten, chromium and vanadium.
Malleable when very hot, so can be forged into required components.
Extremely hard and wear resistant so extremely difficult to machine, cut or file. Can only be ground to a smooth finish.
Very high frictional heat resistance.
High corrosion resistance. No surface treatment needed.
Very high cost.
Uses: Metalworking tools (lathe tools, drills, milling cutters).

Non-ferrous metals

Copper

High-conductivity copper (99.9%)
Very ductile and malleable when cold so can be pressed, bent, cut and drawn easily into required components. May be softened further by annealing to increase workability. Low strength to weight ratio.
Too soft for mechanical applications and may tear when machined.
Corrosion resistant but tarnishes easily. Can be polished to a mirror finish.
High electrical and heat conductivity. Easily joined by soldering or brazing.
High cost.
Uses: Electrical wiring, conductor bars, switchgear.

Tough pitch copper (Copper + copper oxide)
Harder and stronger than pure copper.
Tear resistant during machining.
Slightly lower electrical and heat conductivity.
Slightly lower cost than pure copper.
Uses: Roofing, chemical plant, architectural and decorative metalwork, lightning conductors, kitchenware, water pipes, domestic hot water tanks.

Zinc

Very malleable when cold so can be pressed, bent and cut easily into required components. Ductile but difficult to work as it snaps easily when drawn.
Too soft for mechanical applications and may tear when machined. Low strength to weight ratio.
Extremely resistant to atmospheric corrosion but tarnishes very easily. Can be polished to a mirror finish.
High cost.
Uses: Zinc/carbon battery casings, coated onto iron and steel to increase corrosion resistance (galvanisation), e.g. corrugated iron roofing, dustbins. Also used in alloys such as brass, and rustproof paints.

Tin

Very ductile and malleable when cold so can be pressed, bent, cut and drawn easily into required components.
Too soft and weak for mechanical applications and may tear when machined.
Corrosion resistant. Becomes very brittle and powdery in low temperatures and has a low melting point. Can be polished to a mirror finish.
High cost.
Uses: Plating of mild steel to increase corrosion resistance (tin cans). Also used in alloys such as bearing metals and solder.

Aluminium

Commercially pure (contains up to 1% silicon)
Very light with a high strength to weight ratio.
Ductile so can be drawn, extruded or rolled easily into required components. Malleable but work hardens when cold – may be softened further by annealing to increase workability. May be die-cast and forged.
Machines easily to very fine finish.
Corrosion resistant. Can be polished to a mirror finish.
High electrical and heat conductivity.
Difficult to join.
Low cost.
Uses: Kitchenware, packaging, foil, cans.

Pure aluminium (99.9%)
As above but more difficult to machine as it tears easily.
Higher electrical and heat conductivity and slightly higher corrosion resistance.
Uses: Electrical conductors, especially high-tension transmission cables.

Non-ferrous alloys

Brasses

Moderately expensive alloys of copper and zinc. Properties vary according to the exact composition of the alloy (see Table 3.5). In general, those with a high copper content are more ductile than those with a high zinc content. The high zinc content strengthens the alloy and makes it more suitable for hot forming. All brasses are corrosion resistant, except on exposure to sea water which selectively corrodes the zinc content, weakening and increasing the porosity of the component.

Table 3.5 Composition of brasses

Type of Brass	Mixture	General properties and uses
Cartridge	Copper 70% Zinc 30%	Very malleable and ductile. Used for sheet metal pressings and drawings. *Uses*: Cartridge cases, decorative metalwork, musical instruments
Standard	Copper 65% Zinc 35%	Moderately malleable and ductile. Easily machined to a fine finish. *Uses*: Decorative metalwork, pipe fittings, engineering components
Basis	Copper 63% Zinc 37%	Malleable but poorly ductile. The cheapest of the brasses. Can still be cold-worked and formed. *Uses*: Decorative metalwork
Munzt Metal	Copper 60% Zinc 40%	Malleable and ductile when hot. Cannot be cold-worked. Machines poorly. Best used for hot-stamped and extruded products. *Uses*: Pipe fittings, engineering components
Free-cutting	Copper 58% Zinc 39% Lead 3%	The easiest to machine of the brasses. Malleable when hot. Cannot be cold-worked. *Uses*: Engineering components
Admiralty	Copper 70% Zinc 29% Tin 1%	Resistant to sea water corrosion. Properties the same as cartridge brass. High cost.
Naval	Copper 62% Zinc 37% Tin 1%	Resistant to sea water corrosion. Properties the same as Munzt metal. High cost

Bronzes

Moderately expensive alloys of copper and tin. Properties vary according to the exact composition of the alloy (see Table 3.6). Aluminium bronzes (copper with small amounts of aluminium, nickel and manganese) are also available. They have the similar properties to tin bronzes but corrosion resistance is much greater, and they are more expensive.

Zinc and phosphorus are often added to the alloy mixture to prevent oxidisation of the tin during casting or hot working. Without this protection the bronze would become weak, hard and unworkable.

Cupro-nickel

Copper + varying amounts of nickel, iron and manganese.
Malleable when hot or cold so can be rolled, forged and stamped into required components. Can be cold worked to increase strength.
Strong and hard but easy to machine to a high polish.
High impact resistance.
Corrosion and fatigue resistant.
Medium cost.
Uses: 'Silver' coinage, fine engineering components.

Casting alloy

Aluminium + 5, 12% silicon, 3% copper.
Very fluid when molten so can be sand and die cast successfully.
Easily machined or turned to a very fine finish.
Stronger and tougher than aluminium.
High corrosion and fatigue resistance.
Medium cost.
Uses: Engine cylinder heads, engine blocks.

Duralumin

Aluminium + 4% copper, 1% manganese, variable % magnesium.
Same strength as mild steel but only 30% of the weight.

Hard but malleable when first prepared. Hardens further with age but can be resoftened by annealing. Once annealed is easily machined to give a very fine finish.
High corrosion and fatigue resistance.
High cost.
Uses: Structural components of aircraft.

Ceramics

Ceramic databank

Look in the databank for specific information about ceramics.

Available forms

Amorphous: glass
Crystalline: abrasives
Bonded: china, porcelain, etc.
Cements: mortar, fireclays, etc.
Semiconductors: silicon, germanium

General properties of all ceramics

Very strong in compression.
Very weak in tension and shear.
Extremely hard and wear resistant but brittle. Need to be handled and worked with care.
Fatigue failure common if care not taken in production.
High temperature tolerance.
Excellent electrical insulators.

Specific properties

Amorphous (non-crystalline)

A basic mixture of sodium carbonate (soda), silicon dioxide (sand) is heated until molten. Other chemicals may be

Table 3.6 Composition of bronzes

Type of bronze	Mixture	General properties and uses
Low tin	Copper 96% Tin 3.75% Phosphorus 0.25%	Very malleable and ductile. Can be rolled and cold work-hardened. Fatigue resistant. High electrical conductivity. *Uses*: Leaf springs in electrical switches
Drawn phosphor	Copper 94% Tin 5.5% Phosphorus 0.5%	Very malleable and ductile. Can be cold work-hardened for easy machining or turning. Strong and fatigue resistant. *Uses*: Valve spindles
Cast phosphor	Copper 89.75% Tin 10% Phosphorus 0.25%	Very fluid when molten so casts well into rods and tubes for cutting or machining. Self-lubricating. Fatigue resistant. *Uses*: Bearing bushes, gear wheels and worms
Admiralty gun-metal	Copper 85% Tin 10% Zinc 2%	Very fluid when molten. Usually sand-cast into large components for machining or turning. *Uses*: Pressure-tight pump and valve bodies
Free-cutting gun-metal	Copper 85% Tin 5% Zinc 5% Lead 5%	As for admiralty brass but slightly softer and easier to machine or turn
Leaded	Copper 74% Tin 2% Lead 24%	Very soft, malleable and ductile. Difficult to machine. Uses: Coated onto steel to make shell bearings

added at the time of melting to vary the properties of the glass. The mixture may then be cast into a wide variety of products.

Soda glass

Transparent and colourless. May be coloured with the addition of other chemicals.
Corrosion resistant.
May crack if exposed to extremes of temperature.
Uses: General purpose glassware, decorative glass, glass fibre.

Lead glass

Transparent and colourless. May be coloured with the addition of other chemicals.
Heavy to handle.
Corrosion resistant.
May crack if exposed to extremes of temperature.
High refractive index.
Uses: Luxury glassware, decorative glass, electrical insulators, optical lenses.

Borosilicate glass

Transparent and colourless. May be coloured with the addition of other chemicals.
Heavy to handle.
Corrosion resistant.
Expands very little on heating.
Crack resistant at extremes of temperature.
High refractive index.
Bonds easily to metal surfaces.
Uses: Kitchen glassware ('Pyrex'), electrical insulators, hermetic sealant, chemical tank linings.

Crystalline

Almost all used as abrasives. Some may be used as packing and insulating agents around electrical cables, e.g. magnesium oxide. The most common are described below.

Boron nitride

Hardness the equivalent of diamond.
Uses: Industrial cutting and grinding tools. Diamond cutting and polishing.

Boron carbide

Uses: Industrial cutting, grinding and polishing tools.

Silicon carbide

Uses: Industrial cutting, grinding and polishing tools. 'wet and dry' abrasive papers.

Alumina

Uses: Industrial grinding and polishing tools, 'Emery' abrasive papers.

Beryllium carbide

Uses: Industrial grinding and polishing tools.

Bonded (part amorphous/part crystalline)

Crystalline materials are bonded within a vitreous (glass-like) matrix. All clay-based products are included in this category.

Most clays are a mixture of silicon dioxide and a number of crystalline materials such as feldspar, quartz, calcium carbonate, etc. On firing, the silicon dioxide melts to form the glassy matrix with the crystalline material evenly distributed within it. This is called vitrification.

Properties vary very widely depending on the specific product.

Uses: Refractory linings for furnaces and kilns, high-tension electrical insulators, sanitary ware, domestic crockery and cookware, wall and floor tiles.

Cements

These are chemical mixtures which react together and crystallise on cold curing. The crystallisation process

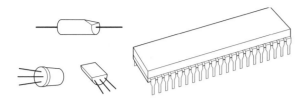

Figure 3.17 Uses of electronic devices: diodes, transistors, microscopes etc.

continues slowly throughout the life of the final product, steadily increasing the strength of the material.

Portland cement
Extremely strong in compression.
Bonds strongly to most other ceramics.
Uses: Construction mortar, concrete.

Fireclays
Extremely heat resistant.
Excellent electrical and heat insulators.
Shrink resistant.
Uses: Mouldings for investment casting, furnace and chimney linings, insulating formers for wire-wound electrical resistors.

Semiconductors

Single crystals of silicon or germanium grown under strictly controlled conditions, or crystalline compounds such as gallium arsenide. Germanium is seldom used nowadays as it is extremely expensive and not readily available. Silicon, however, is very cheap and readily available, and gallium arsenide has valuable electrical properties which, though expensive, make it cost effective. The crystals are usually grown as a cylindrical rod of the material to be cut into thin wafers.

Silicon wafers are treated (doped) with small amounts of other elements to alter the electrical properties of the material. For example:

- *n-Type semiconductors* – Silicon provided with an excess of free electrons by doping with arsenic. The silicon is therefore made electrically negative.
- *p-Type semiconductors* – Silicon depleted of free electrons by doping with gallium. The silicon is therefore made electrically positive.

Apart from the general properties of ceramics, doped semiconductors will electrically insulate or conduct depending on the polarity of a voltage across their surface. In other words, electrical conduction can be in one direction only.

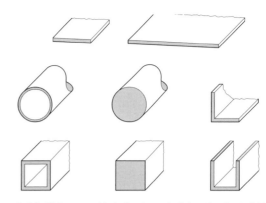

Figure 3.18 Flat or moulded sheets ,rods,tubes,laminated blocks

Uses: Electronic devices such as diodes, transistors, microchips, etc. (Fig. 3.17).

Composites

Composite selection

Table 3.7 is designed to help you to make your initial general selection of composites that you think might be suitable to meet a given product specification.

Composite databank

Once you have made a rough selection, look in Table 3.7 for more specific information about your chosen composite.

Available forms

Plastic based: flat or moulded sheets, rods, tubes, laminated blocks (Fig. 3.18).

Fibre-reinforced plastics

General properties

Very strong in compression and tension but may snap suddenly on bending.
Extremely hard. Impact and wear resistant.
Cuts easily but cannot be machined. Can be manufactured with a very fine finish.

Table 3.7 Composite materials (*Property Key*: * = very low – ***** = very high)

	Durability	Compression Strength	Tensile Strength	Ease of Working	Cost	Availability
Fibre-reinforced plastics						
Glass (GRP)	*****	*****	*****	*****	***	*****
Carbon fibre (CFRP)	*****	*****	*****	*****	*****	**
Laminated plastics						
Wood composites						
Plywood	****	*****	*****	*****	***	*****
Blockboard	***	*****	***	*****	**	*****
Chipboard	***	***	**	*****	*	*****
Medium density fibreboard (MDF)	***	***	*	*****	*	*****

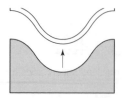

Figure 3.19 Former

Figure 3.20 Finished product lifted off former

Fatigue failure common if care is not taken in production. Tolerant to extremes of temperature.

Glass fibre/carbon fibre
Chopped strand or woven mats of fibre are embedded in a plastic matrix, usually thermosetting polyester or epoxy resin. The fibre is laid over a plaster or wooden former which has been coated with a release agent (Fig. 3.19). The fibre is then soaked in the liquid resin. A hardener added to the resin mix sets the plastic, making a solid moulded sheet (Fig. 3.20).
Overall the layout of the fibre and the number of reinforcing layers determine strength. Carbon fibre is more expensive but gives much more strength to the finished product than glass fibre.

- Glass fibre-reinforced plastics are excellent electrical insulators.
- Carbon fibre-reinforced plastics conduct electricity.

Uses: Canoe and boat hulls, vehicle body panels, protective helmets, fishing rods, heavy duty containers.

Laminate ('Tufnol')
Sheets of fibre (glass, cloth, paper) are soaked with a thermoset resin and then hydraulically compressed and heated until set.
Strong in compression and tension. Does not break when bent.
Can be machined easily to a fine finish.
Moderately high cost compared to other reinforced plastics.
Uses: Electrical insulators (e.g. high-quality printed circuit board), gear wheels, bush bearings.

> *Activity*: From a given product specification, select appropriate materials to produce the product and justify your choices.

Components

You should be able to **recognise**, **select** and **use** the most appropriate components in the development of an engineered product.

Component selection

There are many reasons for selecting appropriate components to make a product. These include:

- The features and function of the component.
- How the component is used.
- Cost.
- Availability.

Mechanical components

Mechanical component selection

There are many reasons for selecting appropriate mechanical components to make a product. These include:

- The features and function of the component.
- How the component is used.
- Cost.
- Availability.

In this section you will be looking at a variety of different mechanical components:

- Nuts
- Bolts
- Screws
- Rivets

In Table 3.8 you have been provided with simplified information about the mechanical components which is designed to help you to select the correct component from a product to specification.

> *Exercise*: Compare and contrast different rivets and their use. Construct a table.

Electrical components

Electrical component selection

There are many reasons for selecting appropriate electrical components to make a product. These include:

- The features and function of the component.
- How the component is used.
- Cost.
- Availability.

In this section you will be looking at a variety of different electrical components:

- Resistors
- Capacitors
- Diodes
- Thermistors
- Transistors
- Bulbs
- Cables
- Insulators
- Batteries
- Motors
- Sounders

Table 3.8 Features of mechanical components (*Key*: * = very low – ***** = very high)

	Appearance	Features and uses	Relative cost
Nuts			
Hexagon		For spanner (wrench) tightening. Used where regular dismantling takes place, e.g. fixing interior components of machines	**
Square		For spanner (wrench) tightening. Greater surface area so used where load must be spread, e.g. fixing of inspection panels	**
Flat square		For spanner (wrench) tightening. Very cheap to produce. Suitable for small low cost items, e.g. metal toys and fixing printed circuit boards	*
Dome		For spanner (wrench) tightening. Used where decorative finish is a consideration, e.g. exterior components of vehicles. Often chromium plated	***
Locknut		For spanner (wrench) tightening. Used where vibration may lead to loosening of the nut, e.g. power tools. Plastic insert compresses and locks the nut in place	****
Castle		For spanner (wrench) tightening. Used where vibration may lead to loosening of the nut, e.g. machine tools. Rotation prevented by pin inserted through drilled bolt	****
Wingnut		For finger tightening. Used where regular dismantling takes place, e.g. hinged inspection panels, storage containers	**
Bolts and machine screws			
Hexagon		For spanner (wrench) tightening. Used for fixing metal panels, components, etc.	**
Coachbolt		For spanner (wrench) tightening. Used for fixing wooden beams, etc.	**
Cheesehead		For screwdriver tightening. Used for fixing small metal panels, printed circuit boards, etc.	*
Stud		Threaded at both ends. One end screwed into the component, the other accepting a nut. Used where regular dismantling takes place, e.g. Inspection panels, Engine cylinder heads. Easy and cheap to replace when worn	*
Screws			
Countersunk		Can be recessed into the material. Head may then be covered with a decorative cap or filler	*
Raised head		Can be recessed into the material. Head usually chromium plated for decorative purposes	*
Round head		Head usually chromium plated for decorative purposes	*
Grub		Used to lock fine cylindrical or extendible components in place to prevent slipping	**

Table 3.8 Continued

	Appearance	Features and uses	Relative cost
Self-tapping screws			
Thread forming		Cuts thread on fixing by displacing the softer material. Used for fixing plastic or aluminium panels	*
Thread cutting		Cuts thread on fixing by cutting material away. Can be used on harder materials such as steel	**
Drive		Hammered into place. Removal not possible. Has multiple large pitch spiral grooves so that it turns as it is driven into its pilot hole. Often used where tamper-proofing is required	**
Screwheads			
Straight		Not slip resistant so used in low torque, simple applications	*
Phillips		Cross shaped grooves increase surface area contact with the screwdriver. Limits slip	**
Posidriv		Additional grooves further increase surface area contact with the screwdriver. Limits slip	**
Allen or socket		Surface area contact with the screwdriver bit maximised. Used in fine engineering applications	***
Tamper resistant	Triangular socket Raised portion 'One-way' slot Specialised tool	Variable design so that conventional tools will not fit the screwhead, or will only work in one direction. Discourages tampering by user but allows repair by manufacturer or repair agent	***
Rivet heads			
Snap or round head		For general engineering applications where appearance is not a major concern	*
Pan head		For general engineering applications where appearance is not a major concern	*

Table 3.8 Continued

	Appearance	Features and uses	Relative cost
Rivet heads *continued*			
Mushroom head		For decorative work	*
Flat head		For decorative work	*
Countersunk		For applications where a flush finish is required, e.g. aircraft body panels	**
Rivet types			
Solid		Shaped and finished with a rivet set and snap. Used for general engineering applications	*
Tubular or eyelet		Rivet snap outwardly rolls the end of the rivet. Used to fix light metal or plastic panels. Also used to bind paper and leather. Central hole allows for passage of ties or laces	**
Semi-tubular		Rivet snap outwardly rolls the end of the rivet. Used to fix light metal or plastic panels. Also used to bind paper and leather	**
Bifurcated		Allows for very rapid fixing where appearance is not important	*
Pop rivet		Allows for an extremely quick fix where appearance is important	***

In Table 3.9 you have been provided with simplified information about the electrical components which is designed to help you select the correct component from a product to specification.

Electrical conductors and conductivity

An electrical conductor is any substance that allows movement of electrons through it. The conductor must have free electrons within its structure for this to happen. It is for this reason that most conductors are metals. However, carbon and silicon are conducting non-metals, but only because they too have free electrons in their structure.

Conductivity is a measure of how easily electrons will flow through a conductor. As a general rule, the greater the number of free electrons in a unit volume the higher the conductivity.

Insulators

An electrical insulator is any substance that does not allow movement of electrons through it. An insulator does not have free electrons within its structure and so no current can flow. It is for this reason that most insulators are non-metals.

Care must be taken when choosing as some insulators, e.g. porous non-metals, polymers and wood, can absorb water from the environment and become conductors. This is an important safety consideration.

*Table 3.9 Features of electrical components (Key: * = very low – ***** = very high)*

Component	Appearance	Circuit symbol	Specific features	Typical use	Relative cost
Resistors					
Carbon rod			Made by mixing graphite powder and clay. The lower the carbon content the higher the resistance. Resistance varies by up to 2% in manufacture and with temperature change so only suitable for general applications	Mass produced, low-cost electrical items	*
High stability			Made by cutting a spiral track in a film of carbon, metal or conducting oxide on the surface of an insulating former. The narrower the pitch of the spiral the higher the resistance. Resistance varies little with changes in temperature so used in precision applications	Computers, measuring devices, telecommunications.	**
Wire wound			Made by coiling fine enamelled wire round an insulating former. The greater the number of turns of wire the higher the resistance. Resistance varies with changes in temperature. Used in high power circuits	Power supply circuits, mains powered devices, power tools	***
Variable			Made by laying a circular track of carbon on an insulating former. A metal contact touches the surface and can be rotated to change the conducting length of the carbon track. The longer the conducting length the higher the resistance. Used where variation of voltage is required	Volume, treble, bass and balance controls on radios and stereos	***
Capacitors					
Ceramic			Small circular metal plates separated by a layer of ceramic material of variable thickness. Capacitance varies with type and thickness of the ceramic	General applications, telecommunications, computers	*
Silvered mica			Sheets of mica are surfaced with silver and stacked together. Capacitance varies with the number of sheets used	High-stability radio-frequency generators	***
Polyester			Rectangular metal plates separated by a layer of polyester resin of variable thickness. Capacitance varies with thickness of the polyester. More stable and have higher capacitance than ceramic type of similar size	Higher quality mass-produced electrical items	*
Polystyrene foil			A film of polystyrene is sandwiched between two sheets of metal foil. The metal/plastic/metal sandwich is then rolled tightly into a cylinder. This offers maximum surface area of metal in minimum space allowing for a very high capacitance. Extremely stable and long-lasting	Telecommunications, computers, televisions	**
Electrolytic			The insulating dielectric is an oxide film coating one of the metal plates. Can be made with a very large capacitance. Must be connected with the correct polarity or they are irreversibly damaged on use. Therefore can only be used in direct current applications	Telecommunications, DC power supply circuits	****
Variable leaf			Uses air as the dielectric. Movable metal plates overlap on a common axis with fixed plates. The more overlap the higher the capacitance	Tuning circuits in radios and televisions. Seldom used in modern equipment	*****
Variable pressure			The surface screw acts against one of the metal plates of the capacitor pushing it closer to the other metal plate. Capacitance increases the tighter the screw	Tuning of radio-frequency circuits prior to permanent sealing	***

Table 3.9 continued (Key: * = very low – ***** = very high)

Component	Appearance	Circuit symbol	Specific features	Typical use	Relative cost
Diodes Junction			Consists of a small chip of silicon based *n*-type semiconductor bonded to a small chip of *p*-type semiconductor	Rectification of alternating current	*
Photodiode			Device contains a transparent window to allow entry of light. If light falls on the reverse-biased diode it becomes fully conducting allowing current to flow in the circuit	Light-sensitive switches	***
Zener			The reverse-biased diode becomes fully conducting when the voltage across it exceeds a predetermined level	Voltage sensitive switch in a recharging circuit	**
Light emitting (LED)	Flat = negative		Contain gallium based *n*- and *p*-type semiconductors. When forward biased a current flows and the diode emits light. Act as visual current flow indicators	On/off indicators. Seven-segment digital displays	***
Thermistors Rod			Resistance to current steadily falls as their temperature increases	Thermal protection circuits in electrical items	**
Bead			Resistance to current steadily falls as their temperature increases	Temperature sensors	**
Transistors			Act as switching devices, allowing a small current in the base/emitter circuit to control a larger current in the collector/emitter circuit. Variations in the small current can therefore be amplified in the larger current. Destroyed if overheated so must be protected with a heat-sink when soldered onto circuit boards	Switching circuits, logic gates, amplification circuits	
Bulbs	Holder		Act as visual current flow indicators	On/off indicators. Illumination	* to *****
Wire Enamelled	Enamel coat Wire		Single strand copper wire coated in a thin insulating ceramic film	Coil windings in motors, transformers, etc.	*
Sheathed	PVC coat Strands of wire		Single or multi-strand copper wire sheathed in a coloured plastic coating	Linking individual components over long distances	**
Cable Mains feed			Live and neutral wires are single strand and sheathed, earthing strand is not. The three wires are then sheathed in a PVC covering	High current feed from street mains supply	***
Two-core mains			Multi-strand live and neutral wires are sheathed. The two wires are then sheathed in a PVC covering	Low current feed from domestic mains supply to double insulated devices	*
Three-core mains			Multi-strand live, neutral and earth wires are sheathed. The three wires are then sheathed in a PVC covering	Low current feed from domestic mains supply to earthed devices	**
Audio			Multi-strand live and neutral wires are sheathed in a PVC covering	Audio signal from amplifiers, etc.	*
Coaxial signal			Central positive single or multi-strand wire is sheathed in an insulating plastic. Earthed braided wire is wrapped around the insulator as a conducting sheath. The cable is then sheathed in a PVC covering. The braided wire shields the central signal wire from outside electrical interference	Telecommunications cables, aerial cables	***

*Table 3.9 continued (Key: * = very low – ***** = very high)*

Component	Appearance	Circuit symbol	Specific features	Typical use	Relative cost
Cable (continued Ribbon			Parallel sheathed multi-strand wire	Linking computers, printers, etc.	***
Insulators Plastic			May be thermoplastic or thermoset. Can be moulded or cut to any shape. Used in low to moderate voltage applications	Printed circuit boards, surface mounting of components	*
Ceramic			May be glass or porcelain. Used in high-voltage applications	Power transmission lines	***
Batteries Zinc carbon			Not rechargeable. Low current. Voltage falls steadily. Short life	Toys	*
Zinc chloride			Not rechargeable. Medium current. Voltage falls steadily. Medium life	Torches, toys	**
Alkaline			Not rechargeable. High current. Voltage steady then falls suddenly. Long life	Torches, toys, portable stereos, calculators	***
Lead acid			Rechargeable. High current. Voltage steady then falls suddenly. Very long life. Hazardous. Explosion risk	Vehicle starting	****
NiCad			Rechargeable. High current. Voltage steady then falls suddenly. Long life	Portable computers, radio-controlled models, portable power tools	*****
Motors Light duty			Wound with thin copper wire. Usually low voltage battery operated (1.5 – 9 V). Overheats and burns out easily under high demand	Toys, small power tools	*
Medium duty			Wound with medium gauge copper wire. Usually medium voltage or transformer operated (9 – 24 V). Overheats easily so usually thermally protected.	Larger toys (e.g. train sets), medium size power tools	***
Heavy duty			Wound with thick gauge copper wire or a rigid copper 'cage'. Usually mains voltage or transformer operated (12V – 240 V). Difficult to overheat but often fan cooled	Vehicle starter motors. Heavy power tools	*****
Sounders Bells			Rely on electromagnetic attraction of the bell hammer so need a high current flow. Polarity of connection not important. Sounding component is made of metal		***
Buzzers			As for a bell but the sounding component is a plastic sheet		**
Beepers			A metal sheet is induced to vibrate by an alternating current generated by an oscillator circuit. Must be connected in the correct polarity		** to *****
Sirens			May be similar to beepers but the current is varied to give a variable sound, or may operate a motor which rotates an air vane which then generates the sound		** to *****

Resistance

The opposite of conductivity, this is a measure of how difficult it is for electrons to pass through a conductor as an electric current. As a general rule, the fewer the free electrons in a unit volume the higher the resistance. Electrons must also travel around and between the atoms of the substance. The longer and more difficult this is the greater the resistance to current flow. If the electron flow is slowed down, the material will be said to increase in resistance.

- **Resistance and temperature** – If the temperature in a conductor/resistor changes, so does the resistance. By looking at thermal conduction, we know that when a material is heated the particles vibrate. We also know that a current is a flow of electrons through a material. However, all this vibration makes it very difficult for electrons to flow easily through the material. If the electron flow is slowed down, the material will be said to increase in resistance.
- **Resistance and length of conductor/resistor** – If the length of a conductor/resistor (e.g. a copper wire) changes, so does its resistance. For example, the longer a conducting wire the more atoms it contains along its length. The increased number of atoms makes it more difficult for electrons to flow easily through the material.

Resistors

Resistors are circuit components that are used to alter current flow in different parts of a circuit. By altering current flow, the voltage across those parts of a circuit can also be altered.

The relationship between resistance (R), current flow (I) and voltage (V) is given by:

$$R = \frac{V}{I}$$

Some resistors may be made by varying the amount of conducting material in a clay matrix, e.g. carbon rod resistors. The lower the percentage of carbon the lower the number of free electrons in a unit volume - and so the higher the resistance. Such resistors cannot be made with great accuracy and so are said to have a wide tolerance. In other words, their resistance can vary from the stated value by up to 20%.

Some resistors may be made of helically wound wire or have a helix of conducting material laid over a cylindrical former. In both, the longer the helix the greater the resistance. Such resistors can be made with great accuracy and high stability. They can have a tolerance of up to 0.1%.

Resistor coding

Resistors are often so small that it is impossible to print their value onto their surface. To overcome this difficulty a system of coloured bands was developed and agreed upon world wide. The agreed code can be seen in Table 3.10.

The tolerance value (Table 3.11) indicates the upper and lower limits of the resistance value, e.g. $10\,000\,\Omega \pm 5\%$ gives a lower limit of $9500\,\Omega$ and an upper limit of $10\,500\,\Omega$. In other words the value states that the resistance of the resistor is anywhere between the upper and lower value. For precision circuitry, tolerances of 0.1% are essential. However, the better the tolerance the more costly the resistor.

Table 3.10 4-Band resistor coding system

Resistance band colour	Numerical value
Black	0
Brown	1
Red	2
Orange	3
Yellow	4
Green	5
Blue	6
Violet	7
Grey	8
White	9

Table 3.11 5-Band resistor coding system

Tolerance band colour	Percentage variation
None	±20%
Silver	±10%
Gold	±5%
Red	±2%
Brown	±1%
Green	±0.5%
Blue	±0.25%
Violet	±0.1%

Coding system

Two systems are in use, the newer 5-band system is gradually overtaking the older 4-band system as more accurate values of resistance are required.

4-Band system

1st band	= First number
2nd band	= Second number
3rd band	= Number of zeros to follow
4th band	= Tolerance value

e.g.   BROWN – RED – ORANGE – GOLD

=   1   2   000   5%

= $12\,000\,\Omega$ ($12\,k\Omega$) with a tolerance of ±5%

5-Band system

1st band	= First number
2nd band	= Second number
3rd band	= Third number
4th band	= Number of zeros to follow
5th band	= Tolerance value

e.g.   BROWN – RED – BLUE – RED – VIOLET

=   1   2   6   00   ±0.1%

= $12\,600\,\Omega$ ($12.6\,k\Omega$) with a tolerance of ±0.1%

On printed circuit boards and larger high-stability resistors, a further code is printed onto the component to indicate resistor values (see Table 3.12).

Table 3.12 Further resistor codes for PCBs and high stability resistors

Example values	Printed code
0.35 Ω	R35
3.5 Ω	3R5
35 Ω	35R
350 Ω	R350
3500 Ω	3k5
35 000 Ω (35 k Ω)	35k
35 000 000 Ω (35 M Ω)	35M

Capacitors and capacitance

Capacitors are devices which store electric charge. All capacitors, no matter what size or shape, share the same basic construction, that is, two conducting plates separated by a thin layer of insulating material called the dielectric.

The size of a capacitor is measured in farads (F) and this size depends on the area of the plates, the distance between them, and the nature of the dielectric.

As a general rule:

- The greater the plate area the **larger** the capacitance.
- The thicker the dielectric the **smaller** the capacitance.
- The stronger the dielectric the **larger** the capacitance.

In fact, capacitors are usually specified in units of microfarads (μF) or smaller as the farad is a very large unit.

Construction of capacitors

In order to reduce the size of capacitors while maintaining a large capacitance the plates and dielectric are often wound into a cylinder. The dielectric material can be ceramic, mica or even paper. Capacitors of this type have no polarity.

Electrolytic capacitors

Some larger capacitors use a piece of gauze soaked in electrolyte (conducting solution) as one plate, aluminium as the other, and the dielectric is a film of oxide just a few molecules thick. These are known as electrolytic capacitors and they have the best capacitance to size ratio, up to about 1000 μF. Care must be taken when connecting this type as they have a definite polarity, i.e. a positive and a negative connection. If connected incorrectly they can explode!

Charging and discharging a capacitor

When a d.c. voltage is connected across a capacitor the positive battery terminal attracts electrons from the plate to

which it is connected leaving it positively charged. Similarly the negative terminal supplies electrons to the plate to which it is connected leaving it negatively charged.

When a capacitor is fully charged the voltage across the plates will be the same as that across the battery terminals. Once this situation is reached no more charge (electrons) can flow.

Because the dielectric is an insulator, no current flows when the battery is connected. When the battery is disconnected the capacitor remains electrostatically charged.

If the capacitor is now connected into a circuit the capacitor will discharge.

Batteries

Batteries store chemical energy. When a battery is connected in a circuit, energy is transferred as electrical energy. Six of the common types of battery are described in Table 3.13. Batteries can be connected together to provide high voltages and currents.

Diodes

A diode is an electronic component which allows current to flow in one direction only under normal operating conditions, a sort of electronic one-way valve.

Bulbs

The main types are tungsten filament bulbs and fluorescent bulbs which come in a very wide variety of shapes and sizes. Filament bulbs rely on the heating of a coil of tungsten wire until it glows white hot. As so much electrical energy is converted into heat rather than light, only low-voltage bulbs are suitable for use in enclosed spaces such as torches, illuminated panels, etc.

Fluorescent bulbs rely on the ionisation of a gas in a strong electric field. The electrons freed in the ionisation then collide with a coating on the glass wall of the bulb. The coating absorbs the electron's energy and converts it into light energy, which is given off by the bulb. Very little energy is wasted as heat so these bulbs do not get hot during use. They also give off more light for less power.

Audio-alarm devices

These include bells, buzzers, beepers, sirens, etc. Bells and buzzers have a high current demand as an electromagnet must

Table 3.13 Common types of batteries

Battery type	Good points	Bad points	Uses
Zinc–carbon	Inexpensive	Not rechargeable; low power	Torches, radios
Alkaline	Inexpensive	Not rechargeable	Watches, hearing aids
Mercuric oxide	Small; long life	Not rechargeable; environmentally unfriendly	Watches, hearing aids
Lithium	Small; long life	Not rechargeable; environmentally unfriendly	Computer backup
NiCad (nickel-cadmium)	High power; rechargeable	Expensive; environmentally unfriendly	Aircraft, radio-controlled cars
Lead-acid	Rechargeable; inexpensive	Contains liquid (acid); environmentally unfriendly	Cars

Unit 3: Making Engineered Products **97**

be energised to operate the hammer, which hits the bell or flat plate. Motor-operated sirens have a similar high demand. Electronic beepers have a low current demand and so can sound for longer. The flat surface area of the sounding device can also be made large to increase the amplitude of the sound.

Typical alarm devices have a sound level of 100–120 decibels – about the same as a passenger jet taking off. The pitch of the sound is also selected to be that to which the ear is most sensitive to – about 3000 Hz.

Power supply

Electrical power can be supplied from

- Mains electricity
- Batteries

Mains electricity

If mains electricity were to be used for the power screwdriver the motor would need to be able to operate at a voltage of 110–240 V. This would require a motor much larger than could be housed in the screwdriver body. An alternative would be to use a step-down transformer to reduce the voltage from mains level to 2.4 V and use the existing motor.

The electrical transformer

A step-down transformer (Fig. 3.21) consists of a laminated iron core wound with two coils of copper wire. The primary (input) coil is in a circuit with the mains a.c. (alternating current) electricity supply. The secondary (output) coil is in a circuit with the device, e.g. the screwdriver motor. Note that the two circuits are completely separate.

The primary coil a.c. supply generates a magnetic field in the iron core. The polarity of the field is constantly changing at the same frequency as the mains supply. This is 50 Hz in the UK and 60 Hz in the USA. The constantly changing magnetic field, in turn, generates a current in the secondary coil, the voltage of which is in proportion to the number of coil turns on primary and secondary coils, i.e. more coils, higher voltage; less coils, lower voltage.

Number of turns on primary (input) coil = 24 000
Number of turns on secondary (output) coil = 240
Ratio of primary:secondary = 100:1

Therefore an input voltage of 100 V across the primary coil would induce an output voltage of 1 V across the secondary coil, a reduction in voltage of 100 ×.

To calculate the output voltage of any transformer use this formula:

$$\text{Output voltage} = \frac{\text{Number of turns on secondary coil}}{\text{Number of turns on primary coil}}$$
$$\times \text{ Input voltage}$$

The problem is that transformers tend to be very large to cope with the number of coils of wire wound round the iron core. They are also very heavy due to the amount of high-density material they contain. If such an arrangement was used in the Black & Decker 2.4 V power screwdriver it would be too heavy for balanced, comfortable use and would be too large to use in confined spaces. Industrial versions (the size and shape of a conventional power drill) do use such an arrangement but they cannot be used in confined spaces.

The most convenient option is to use batteries that are portable, convenient to use and have a long operating life. A number of choices are given in Table 3.14 and their graphs are shown in Fig. 3.22.

The low current capacity of lead–acid rechargeable and ordinary rechargeable batteries is due to their reliance on complex chemical reactions to generate current. The more complex the reaction, the more energy goes into powering the reactions and the less into what is required – electrical energy.

In addition, the products of the reaction slow down the current flow. The products block the free flow of electrons. If a high current demand is placed on the battery, this resistance causes a loss of electrical energy as the electrons use up their energy overcoming the resistance. This electrical energy becomes transformed into heat. After a while the battery becomes too hot to touch and may even explode as pressure builds up inside.

NiCad batteries, however, rely on a very simple chemical reaction with end products that do not resist current flow. Therefore this current can be as high as is demanded with minimum risk of heating or explosion.

Table 3.14 Comparison of battery features

Battery Type	Advantages	Disadvantages
Dry cell (1.5 V per cell)	Very cheap	Short life Low current capacity Not rechargeable Voltage drop during use
Lead–acid rechargeable (1.5 V per cell)	Cheap Rechargeable Long life (if recharged regularly)	Low current capacity Voltage drop during use Contain corrosive acid If left discharged will not accept recharge again Heavy Give off hydrogen during recharge – explosion risk
Ordinary rechargeable (1.5 V per cell)	Moderately priced Rechargeable Medium life	Low current capacity Voltage drop during use
NiCad rechargeable (1.2 V per cell)	Rechargeable High current capacity Constant voltage Long life	Expensive

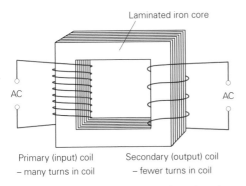

Figure 3.21 Simplified diagram of a step-down transformer

Laminated iron core

AC AC

Primary (input) coil – many turns in coil Secondary (output) coil – fewer turns in coil

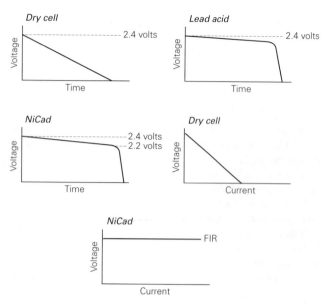

Figure 3.22 Simple graphs:time/voltage,current/voltage

The discharged lead plates in a lead–acid battery are corroded by the sulphuric acid within the cell. An insulating layer forms on the surface preventing a flow of current. This prevents the occurrence of the charging reaction if an attempt is made to recharge the battery.

Activity: From a given product specification, select appropriate components to produce the product, and justify your choices.

3.3 Processes

You should be able to **recognise**, and **use** the most suitable processes in the development of an engineered product.

Process selection

The selection of the correct process for manufacture of a product requires a substantial amount of knowledge about a large range of different processes. Some of the first questions to ask yourself about the different processes are:

- Material removal – Just how much material can be removed in one cut?
- Shaping materials – Can the product be moulded into a shape?
- Joining and assembling – Are the products parts to be permanently joined?
- Heat treatment – How can the hardness be increased?
- Chemical treatment – Will the product require corrosion protection?
- Surface finish – How is consistent quality obtained?

When you have answered these questions you may have refined your choice to two or three different processes. To arrive at the final process choice you must find solutions to the following:

- The properties of the materials to be used.
- Ease of working the material.
- Shape and forms required.
- Tolerances required.
- Cost of process.
- Availability of process.
- Quantity of products required – mass, batch, one off.
- Time factors involved.

A good way to make a decision is to make a matrix, listing all the features required by a process and awarding marks to various features. For instance, the best method for a particular feature is awarded 5 marks and the poorest method is awarded 1 mark, e.g. when fixing the metal back panel of a CD Player into the main chassis you may want to consider the items mentioned in Table 3.15.

Processes

There are many processes, which may be used in the development of an engineered product. You should be able to **recognise** and **use** the most suitable of these for a particular task. Figure 3.23 sets out the main processes and should help you to follow the route to enable you to choose the appropriate processes for your task.

We are going to look at each of these types of process, in turn. The first of these are concerned with material removal.

Table 3.15 Comparison of different methods to achieve process features

Features required by the process	Screws	Moulded clips	Adhesive	Weld	Rivets
Security of fit	3	1	4	5	4
Ease of attachment	3	5	4	1	3
Ease of detachment for maintenance	4	5	1	1	1
Process time	5	5	4	1	2
Process cost	5	4	4	3	3
Overall weight of attachment	2	3	5	3	4
Appearance	1	4	5	1	2
Other miscellaneous requirements	4	4	3	2	2
Total	27	31	30	17	21

Material removal processes

Some of the most common of these processes are:

- Drilling
- Turning
- Milling

We will then look at other processes, such as crimping, soldering, welding, etc.

Drilling

What is it?
This is the process for producing circular holes. These may be cut into a solid piece or may be enlarging an existing hole.

How is it done?
Drilling is carried out by a **drilling machine**! At home, this is commonly in the form of a hand-held electric power drill. In the industrial workplace, it is more common to use a **pillar drill** (Fig. 3.24).

The pillar drill

This comprises a base and pillar. The pillar supports a head unit, containing the motor and drill spindle, and a flat drilling table on which the work to be drilled is secured.

The spindle holds the chuck and the drill bit and is fitted with a simple depth stop. The motor drives the spindle at a range of drilling speeds, typically from 80 to 3000 rpm (revolutions per minute). The spindle is hollow and contains an internal taper known as a 'morse taper'.

The choice of type of drill bit (confusingly also called a drill) and drilling speed depend on the nature of the job to be done and the type of material to be worked with.

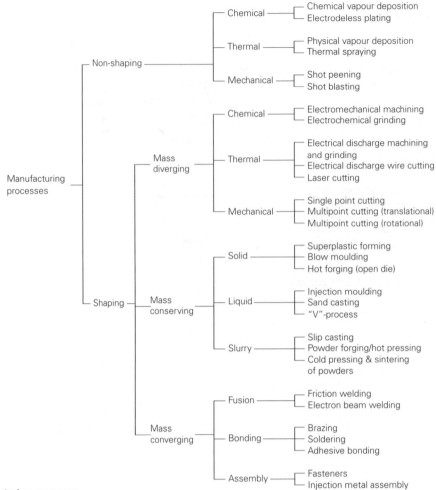

Figure 3.23 Manufacturing processes

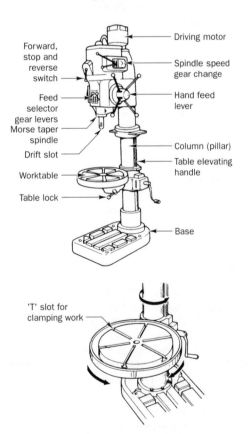

Figure 3.24 Pillar drill (circular work table)

The purpose of the drilling machine is to:

- Rotate the drill at a suitable speed for the material being cut and the diameter of the drill.
- Feed the drill into the workpiece.
- Support the workpiece being drilled (usually at right angles to the drill, although some machines allow you to choose a pre-set angle for drilling).

Drills

Most holes in metal are cut with twist drills, made from high-speed steel (HSS). They have two cutting edges or lips and two helical flutes cut along their length. Each flute has a thin raised land running along it to reduce friction between the body of the drill and the workpiece. A twist drill with a parallel shank is called a jobber and is held in place by a chuck, which is tightened with a chuck key. The drill is held by the three jaws of the chuck, which slide up and down when the chuck key is turned (Fig. 3.25).

Hint: Ensure that the chuck grips as much of the drill shank as possible; that the drill is securely gripped by turning the chuck key as tightly as possible by hand; then remember to remove the chuck key!

Larger drills have tapered shanks and are inserted directly into the spindle of a pillar drill. They are held in the spindle and driven through frictional contact alone (Fig. 3.26).

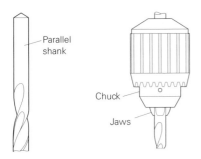

Figure 3.25 Twist drill with parallel shank in chuck

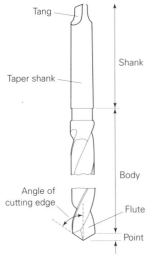

Figure 3.26 Taper shank

The tang of the drill is for extraction purposes only. The drill is removed by locating the drift in an elongated hole at the top of the spindle taper and tapping it with a hammer.

When a smaller drill is to be used in the pillar drill, a chuck must first be fitted. The chuck also has a morse- tapered shank and is located in, and removed from, the spindle in the same way as a large drill.

Choosing the right drill

There are three different types of spiral in a drill, enabling the drill to be slow, normal or fast, depending on the helix angle

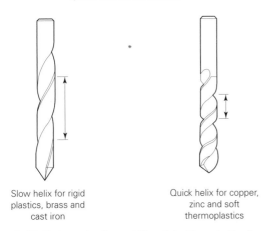

Figure 3.27 Fast and slow drills: (a) Slow helix for rigid plastics, brass and cast iron; (b) Quick helix for copper, zinc and soft thermoplastics

or rake of the drill (Fig. 3.27). Typically, different drills would be chosen for different materials.

- *Slow* – Rigid plastics, brass, bronze, cast iron
- *Normal* – Most steels
- *Fast* – Copper, zinc, aluminium, soft thermo-plastics

Different drills may be used when working with wood, or when producing a countersink. Figure 3.28 illustrates a few from a wide range available.

Choosing the right spindle speed

This will vary according to:

- The type of material – from fast for aluminium to slow for thermo-setting plastic.
- The diameter of the drill – the bigger the diameter, the slower its rotational speed will need to be to give the recommended cutting speed.

Required spindle speeds can be worked out given the following desired cutting speeds for high-speed steel twist drill:

- Aluminium 70–100 m/min
- Brass 35–50 m/min
- Copper 35–45 m/min
- Steel (mild) 30–40 m/min
- Cast iron (grey) 25–45 m/min
- Bronze (phosphor) 20–35 m/min
- Steel (medium carbon) 20–30 m/min
- Thermo-setting plastic 20–30 m/min

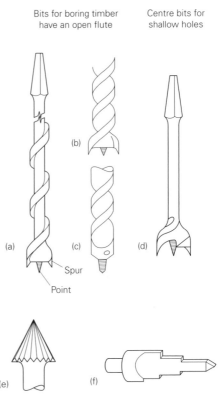

Figure 3.28 Other types of drill: (a) Auger bit-deep holes in green timber; (b) Jennings pattern-dowel holes; (c) Solid nosed-heavy work and drilling at an angle; (d) Screw pointed; (e) Countersink–rosehead for metal, hardwood, plastics; (f) Combination-stepped holes for wood screws

And using the following formula:

$$N = \frac{1000.S}{\pi.d}$$

Where N = spindle speed in revolutions per minute
  S = cutting speed in metres per minute
  $\pi = 3.142$
  d = drill diameter in millimetres

Having calculated the correct speed, choose the speed closest to it on your machine, either by using the speed change lever, or, if none is fitted, by isolating the machine, and then altering the position of the drive belt on its cone pulleys.

Work holding when drilling

Work should always be securely fastened to the machine table. Small work is usually held in a machine vice, which is securely bolted to the machine table (Fig. 3.29(a)). Cylindrical work is held in place using vee-blocks (Fig. 3.29(b)). Larger work can be clamped directly to the machine table, using at least two clamps and positioning clamp bolts as close as possible to the work to exert maximum force. Wherever possible, work should be supported on parallel blocks so that the work table and drill are not damaged as the drill breaks through the workpiece.

Further hints for safe operation

- Care should be taken when hand feeding a drill. Too much pressure can cause breakage of small diameter drills, and overheating of large – a coolant may be needed when drilling deep holes.
- Pressure should be eased off as the drill is about to break through, as there is often a tendency for it to damage the surface. Use of the depth gauge will indicate when the drill is about to break through.
- A correctly ground drill will often produce a continuous length of swarf, especially with mild steel or aluminium. This can cause injury. Drilling pressure should be eased off and the swarf broken off.

(a)

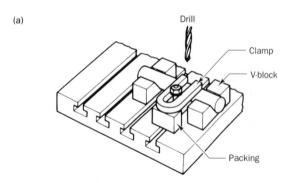

(b)

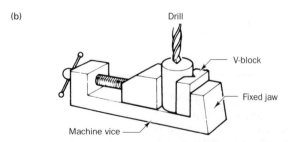

Figure 3.29 (a) Methods of work holding; (b) Use of machine vice

- Safety guards should be in operation at all times.
- After completing drilling operations, the machine table should be carefully cleaned down.

Turning

What is it?
At its simplest, a single point cutting tool or a twist drill removes material from a rotating workpiece. Turning can be used to produce cylindrical and tapered workpieces and can produce flat pieces by machining across the end faces of a component.

How is it done?
Using a **centre lathe** (Fig. 3.30), work is held firmly and rotated while a cutting tool held in a tool post cuts the work using a simple wedge cutting action.

Centre lathe

The centre lathe spindle is driven through a gearbox, giving a selection of cutting speeds and tool feed rates. The spindle can carry a chuck, a faceplate, or a catch plate and centre for gripping or supporting the workpiece. The tailstock, with its centre, is used to support the free end of the workpiece. It can also be used to carry a chuck for drills, screwcutting taps or a die holder for cutting external threads.

The lathe bed contains surface-hardened, V-shaped slideways along which the tail stock and carriage assembly can be moved. The carriage assembly (saddle) contains the cross-slide, which is at right-angles to the spindle axis and the compound slide which can be set at different angles for tapering work. The tool post is mounted on top of the compound slide. The front of the carriage assembly, the apron, contains the feed control hand wheel for moving the carriage along the bed to cut cylindrical surfaces. It also contains the cross-slide feed control wheel, which moves the cutting tool at right angles to the spindle axis to increase the depth of cut and for facing operations. Most centre lathes have automatic carriage and cross-slide feeds, operated by levers on the front of the carriage assembly. These actions are summarised in Table 3.16.

Work holding in the lathe

There are a number of options for holding work, depending on the size and shape of the workpiece. It is important to remember that your piece of work is going to rotate at high speed and may be subjected to large cutting forces. Therefore it must be held firmly and securely.

1. **Between centres** – long pieces of work should be held between centres (Fig. 3.31). Work should be prepared by facing and centre drilling both ends and it is then located on centres in the headstock spindle and tailstock barrel. Work can be removed from the lathe and replaced later, safe in the knowledge that it is returning to precisely the same position. However, one disadvantage of this method is that only limited end facing can be carried out on the component. When the work is located in the lathe, the carrier is clamped to it, and the work is rotated by the catch pin, which drives the carrier.

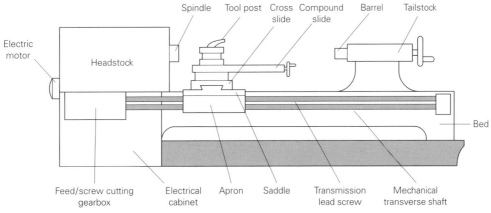

Figure 3.30 Centre lathe

2. **Three-jaw self-centring chuck** – This is suitable for short cylindrical work, but also capable of holding hexagonal workpieces. Turning the chuck key causes all three jaws to close together at the same rate, thus ensuring that the centre line of the work remains on the rotational axis of the machine. Internal jaws for smaller work and external jaws for larger work, can be fitted to the chuck. Work to be turned between centres is usually held in a three-jaw chuck while the ends of the bar are faced flat and then centre drilled. *Remember*:
   - Always remove the chuck key before starting the lathe.
   - This chuck should not be used if the work is not truly cylindrical, as unequal load will be placed on the jaws and the work may not be secure (Fig. 3.32).
3. **Four-jaw independent chuck** – This is designed for holding square, rectangular and irregularly shaped

workpieces. Each jaw is tightened independently, which enables more force to be exerted and greater holding achieved (Fig. 3.33). The work can be set to run concentrically with a high degree of accuracy or can be deliberately set off-centre to produce eccentric components. More versatile than the three-jaw chuck, it can be more time-consuming to set up.

4. **Face plate** – This is used for irregularly shaped work, which may be too large for a four-jaw chuck. For

Table 3.16 Cutting movements of a Centre Lathe

Cutting Movement	How movement is achieved	Work produced
Tool parallel to spindle centre	The saddle moves along the bed slideways	Parallel cylinder
Tool at 90° to the spindle centre	The cross-slide moves along a slideway machined on top of the saddle	A flat face square to the spindle centre line
Tool at an angle relative to the spindle centre line	The compound slide is rotated and set at the desired angle relative to the centre line	A tapered cone

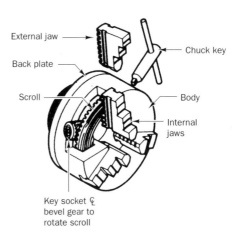

Figure 3.32 Three-jaw self-centring chuck for centring work

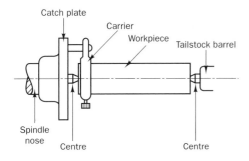

Figure 3.31 Work holding between centres

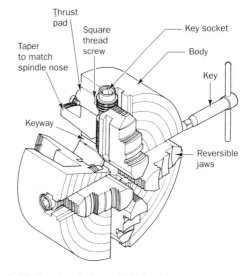

Figure 3.33 Four-jaw independent chuck

irregularly shaped work, or eccentrically mounted work, a counter-balance is required to be fitted to the face plate, to prevent vibration, poor surface finish or harm to the machine bearings. Balance weights are attached to the face plate by trial and error until the plate can be set in any position without swinging round (Fig. 3.34).

All longer pieces of work will need supporting at the tailstock end, regardless of the method of holding used. Remember that they must first be centre drilled.

Holding, using, choosing tools

Holding

The tool post – Single-point cutting tools are held in the **tool post** of the centre lathe (Fig. 3.35). Small centre lathes may have a pillar-type tool post, holding a single tool. Larger machines often have a four-way tool post, capable of bringing different tools into operation by rotating it.

The tailstock – This is used when drilling in the centre lathe. Its spindle contains an internal morse-taper, which can hold a chuck or taper-shank drills. The tailstock is clamped to the lathe bed, while the drill is fed into the rotating workpiece using the spindle feed handwheel.

The tailstock is also used when cutting screw threads with taps and dies. Screw-cutting threads are held in the chuck. Dies are held in a diestock with morse-tapered shank, which locates in the tailstock spindle. The unclamped tailstock is fed by hand to the workpiece, which is rotated backwards and forwards by hand with the lathe isolated.

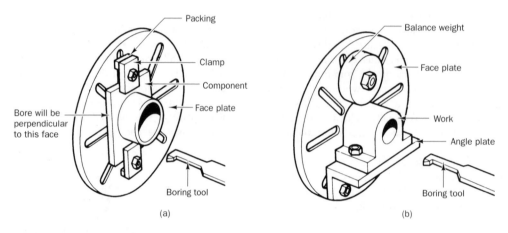

Figure 3.34 Use of face plate:(a) balanced work; (b) unbalanced work

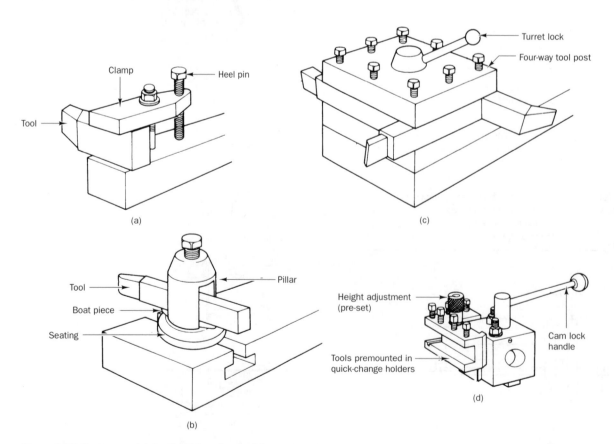

Figure 3.35 Tool posts; (a) English (clamp) type; (b) American (pillar) type; (c) turret (four-way) type; (d) quick-release type

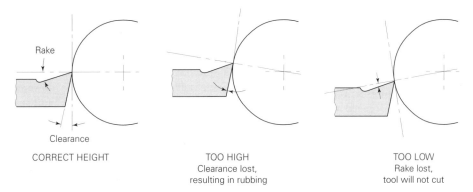

Figure 3.36 Correct height of tool

Using

Tool geometry – all cutting tools are ground to a characteristic wedge shape, with what are known as **rake** and **clearance** angles. The rake is the term used for the top angle of the tool measured along the line of cut (Alpha). The clearance angle (Beta) enables only the cutting edge to be in contact with the work. For efficient cutting, these angles must be correct for the material used – a low rake for hard and brittle materials, and a high rake for ductile metals. The tool must be set at the correct height, which is centre height with the tool located as far back in the tool post as possible, to prevent excessive vibration (Fig. 3.36).

Hint: As a check of correct height, the tool can be run up to the stationary workpiece against an upright steel rule. If the rule will stand vertically, the tool will be close to correct height.

Turning speed

We use the same formula as we used to calculate drill spindle speed, to give us the correct speed for the lathe to rotate:

$$N = \frac{1000.S}{\pi.d}$$

where N = speed of the lathe in revolutions per minute
S = cutting speed
D = diameter of work in millimetres
π = 3.142

Once again, the greater the diameter of workpiece, the slower the rotation required.

Lubricants and coolants

These are used to:

- Keep work cool
- Reduce tool wear

- Give a better finish
- Prevent chip particles from welding themselves to the tool face
- Wash away chips
- Prevent corrosion

There are many types of coolant – most common are emulsified or soluble oils, which contain a mixture of oil, detergent and disinfectant, and when mixed with water are milky in appearance.

Most machines are fitted with a coolant reservoir and delivery pump, supplying coolant to the workpiece through an adjustable pipe and control tap. So, in using our lathe, we have to consider the variables listed in Table 3.17.

Removing material

To remove material as quickly as possible, the depth of cut should be as large as the machine can handle. A deep cut with a slow feed rate is a good combination for fast removal, long tool life and good finish. Feed can be controlled by hand or using the automatic carriage feed, which should guarantee a more uniform action.

Health and safety: The guard should be used whenever the lathe is being operated and should not be removed until the workpiece is stationary and the operation complete. Remember to remove the chuck key after you have used it, before the lathe is operated.

Choosing tools

Lathe tools must be hard and tough and are made from high-speed steel or other alloys where the cutting edge will not distort when temperatures are raised. Many different tools can be used – selection depends on the job to be done! Roughing down to within 1 mm of finished size is carried out with a roughing tool. Fine finishing cuts are best done using a tool with a curved tip. Knife tools enable the cutting of sharp

Table 3.17

Material	Rake angle	Cutting speed in metres/minute with HSS tool	Cutting lubricant
Acrylic	1°	35–60	Soluble oil or paraffin
Aluminium	40°	70–100	Paraffin
Brass	2°	70–100	None
Cast iron	2°	25–40	None
Hard steel	6°	30–35	Soluble oil
Mild steel	20°	35–50	Soluble oil

corners. A parting tool is used to produce undercuts and grooves and to cut your work off from material remaining in the chuck.

Internal turning requires the use of boring tools, which may have any of the range of profiles.

Knurling is the process that presses a pattern into the surface of cylindrical work. The hardened wheels that make up the knurling tool are pressed into the slowly rotating work and then moved slowly along the surface (Fig. 3.37).

Tapers

A chamfer tool is used to produce a taper (Fig. 3.38). This is produced by the tool being ground or set to the appropriate angle (usually 45°) and fed into the workpiece. The work takes on the form of the tool. Turning the compound slide through the required angle may produce longer tapers. The compound slide hand wheel is used to carry out the cutting.

Screw-cutting

A single point tool ground to the profile of the thread being cut is mounted accurately in the tool post. The appropriate gearing is selected to provide the correct pitch of the thread and, using a very slow speed, the tool is traversed repeatedly along the work to cut the thread.

Milling

What is it?
Milling is a process that uses rotating multi-toothed cutters to shape metals and plastics.

How is it done?
Milling is carried out by a milling machine – either a horizontal milling machine (Fig. 3.39(a)) or a vertical milling machine. In both types of machine, the workpiece is secured to a movable table, which is adjusted so that the work passes the rotating cutters and the waste material is removed.

Diamond knurling

Figure 3.37 Diamond knurling

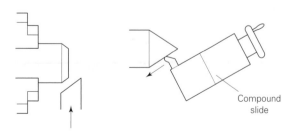

Compound slide

Figure 3.38 Taper turning: chamfering

Milling machines

The lower halves of the horizontal and vertical milling machines are identical, consisting of a flat worktable, cut with T-slots on to which a machine vice may be clamped. The work table can be raised or lowered and will move horizontally, either lengthwise (often automatically) or crosswise.

The horizontal milling machine has its cutter in the horizontal plane, held on a horizontal shaft or arbor (Fig. 3.39(a)).

The vertical milling machine has its cutter in the vertical plane, located at the end of a vertical spindle (Fig. 3.39(b)), supported within the body of the machine at one end and by a support bracket at the other end.

The spindle, which holds the cutter, is driven by a variable speed motor or through a gearbox, for selecting correct cutting speeds.

Work holding

Milling machines are fitted with powerful motors and exert large cutting forces on the workpiece, therefore all work must be held securely to prevent any movement. Methods of work holding are similar to those for drilling.

- Large or irregular work is clamped directly to the T-slots in the worktable, or to an angle plate, which is bolted down itself. At least two clamps should be used. V-blocks can be used to support cylindrical work.
- Clamping in a heavy duty machine vice. This may have a swivel base, which can be set at any angle in the plane of the worktable.

Holding the cutter

Horizontal milling machines
The cutter is mounted on an arbor. The arbor locates in a taper in the machine spindle. It is screwed into position on a draw bar and driven by two blocks of metal (dogs) on the spindle nose, which fit into slots on the end of the arbor. The horizontal milling machine has a long arbor with a keyway running along it (Fig. 3.40). The cutter is keyed to the arbor with spacing collars on both sides. A nut on the end of the arbor holds cutter and collars tightly together.

To prevent the arbor from bending during operation, the cutter and the overarm steady should be positioned to allow as little overhang as possible. Figure 3.41 illustrates the right and wrong way to do this!

Vertical milling machines
The cutter can be held in a number of ways. Large face mills can be fitted **directly to the spindle nose** (Fig. 3.42). They have a stub-arbor, which fits in the taper of the spindle nose and is held by a draw bolt passing through the spindle. Again, dogs on the spindle provide the driving force.

Other cutters may be **fitted into a chuck**. Fig. 3.43 shows an end mill with a parallel shank and screw thread. This locates in an antilock collet chuck, which is so designed that the cutting forces tend to increase the grip of the chuck on the cutter. The chuck has a taper shank, which is mounted in the spindle nose and is retained by draw bolt and driven by dogs as above.

(a)

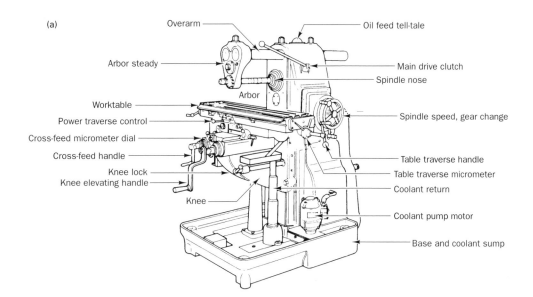

(b)

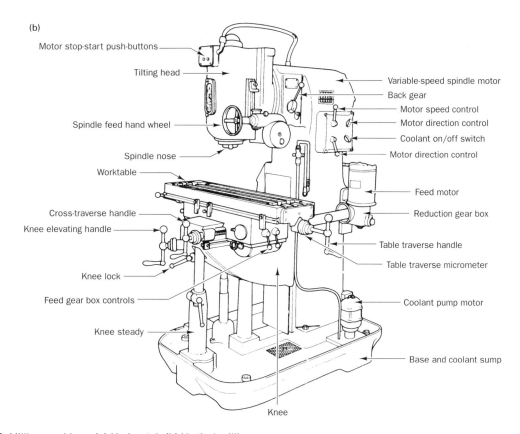

Figure 3.39 Milling machines: (a) Horizontal; (b) Vertical milling

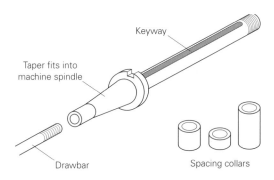

Figure 3.40 Horizontal milling machine arbor and collars

Using a milling machine

Setting the spindle speed

Required spindle speeds for given diameters of material are calculated in exactly the same way as for turning and the nearest available spindle speed is then selected on the milling machine. Approximate cutting speeds for selected materials are given below:

- Aluminium 80–110 m/min
- Brass 70–100 m/min
- Bronze (phosphor) 35–70 m/min
- Cast iron (grey) 25–40 m/min

Poor mounting   **Good mounting**

Overarm

Arbor   Cutter

Steady

Excessive   Excessive
overhang   overhang

Overhang reduced
to a minimum

Intermediate
steady

**Bad mounting –
poor rigidity, arbor may bend**
Lack of rigidity could lead to chatter,
inaccurate work and poor surface finish

Good rigid cutter mounting
Note overarm has been
moved back and cutter
positioned near machine
column

Using two yokes
The rigidity has been
increased by using two yokes
to cut a wide workpiece

Figure 3.41 Reducing overhang on horizontal arbor

- Copper 40–70 m/min
- Steel (mild) 35–50 m/min
- Steel (medium carbon) 30–35 m/min
- Thermo-setting plastic 35–50 m/min

Feeding the worktable
With horizontal milling, there are two ways of feeding the
work table and work under the cutter (Fig. 3.44).

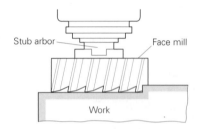

Stub arbor   Face mill

Work

Figure 3.42 Face mill fitted to spindle nose

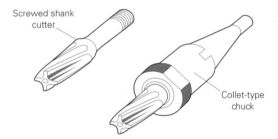

Screwed shank
cutter

Collet-type
chuck

Figure 3.43 End mill and collect chuck

- **Up-cut or 'conventional' milling** is the most common.
  As the cutter is trying to push the work away, it is very
  safe to use. However, it can lift work from the
  worktable and the cutting teeth tend to rub on the
  surface of the work before starting to bite, causing tooth
  wear and blunting of the cutter. It can also lead to wear
  of the feed mechanism as this is always working against
  the main cutting force.
- **Down-cut or 'climb' milling** should only be attempted by
  skilled operators, with a machine designed to operate in
  this manner. There is a tendency for the cutter to climb
  on to the work piece, resulting in excessive vibration and
  possible damage to the arbor. It has several advantages.
  The feed mechanism and cutter are working in the same
  direction – the feed mechanism only has to operate as a
  brake. The teeth of the cutter do not rub as they start to
  cut and the cutting action forces the work down onto the
  work table rather than lifting it up.

Cooling
As with turning, emulsified oil coolants are used, although
where the cutting action is severe in heavy duty machines,
undiluted soluble oil may be used. Make sure that the return
drain and filter from the work table do not become blocked
with swarf!

Milling operations and choosing the cutter

All milling cutters have a series of wedge-shaped teeth,
ground with rake and clearance angles. The variety of
operations and choices of cutter are best described by an
illustration, as shown in Table 3.18.

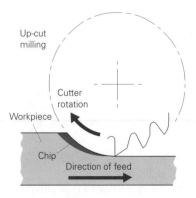

Up-cut
milling

Cutter
rotation

Workpiece

Chip

Direction of feed

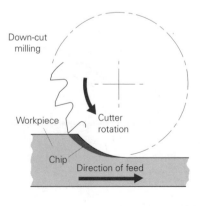

Down-cut
milling

Cutter
rotation

Workpiece

Chip

Direction of feed

Figure 3.44 Up-cut and down cut-milling

Table 3.18 Different milling cutters and their uses

Name of cutter	Type of milling machine*	Description	Uses	Illustration
Slab	H	A cylindrical cutter also called slab mills and roller mills	Produce wide, flat surfaces	
Side and face	H	Circular shape with teeth around the outer edge and on the faces	Light facing and cutting slots and steps	
Slotting cutter	H	Circular and thinner than the above. Teeth around the outer edge only	Narrow slots and keyways	
Slitting	H	Similar to slotting cutter, but thinner still	Narrow slots and cutting material to size	
Face mill	V	Circular with teeth around outside and on end face	Produce accurate flat surfaces as every part of every tooth on the end face passes over the whole surface	
Shell end mill	V	Smaller than face mills and mounted on a stub arbor	Producing flat surfaces	
End mill	V	Cylindrical with teeth around outer edge and end face	Light facing operations, profiling and milling slots	
Slot drill	V	Similar to end mills but with two cutting lips	Accurately milling slots and keyways	

* H= horizontal; V = vertical.

Safety notes

- Before using a milling machine make sure that you have been fully trained, that you are familiar with the use of all the controls and that you know the emergency stop procedure.
- Check loose clothing. Wear safety glasses.
- Do not use rags, cotton waste or a brush near a revolving cutter.
- Keep hands well away from moving cutters.
- Milling cutters have extremely sharp cutting edges. Care must be taken when handling them. Stout leather gloves give good protection.
- Multi-toothed cutters, together with swarf thrown out, make milling a potentially dangerous operation. Make sure that cutter guards are in position before engaging the spindle clutch and that the guard is not removed until all operations are completed and the machinery stationary.

Setting up on a horizontal milling machine

Finally, it is worth taking a look at the step-by-step procedure for setting up work on a horizontal milling machine:

- Select type and size of cutter.
- Select an arbor to hold the cutter.
- Clean the arbor taper and spindle.
- Screw a draw bolt into the taper and tighten the locking nut.
- Decide on the best method of holding the workpiece.
- Clean some spacing collars.
- Fit cutter and spacing collars on arbor – with the cutter as near to the spindle as possible.
- Check the cutting direction.
- Fit an arbor support bracket as near to the cutter as possible.
- Tighten all locking nuts.
- Check that all tools and loose materials have been cleared.
- Ensure that safety guards are in place.
- Select the correct speed and feed.

Joining and assembly processes

The most commonly used of these processes are:

- Crimping
- Soldering
- Welding
- Adhesion
- Wiring

Crimping

What is it?
Crimping involves pinching or pressing together, especially a tubular or cylindrical shape in order to seal or join together.

How is it done?
Crimping can be done with a simple hand-held crimping tool. It is commonly used for making connections in power circuits, when cable lugs and plugs are crimped onto cables (Fig. 3.45).

How does it work?
The sleeve of the lug or plug is slipped over the cable and then indented by a small pneumatic or hydraulic press, or by a hand-held crimper. Quicker than soldering, it also does not involve heat, which can damage insulation.

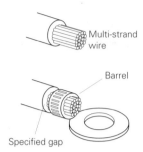

Figure 3.45 Crimped terminal

Soldering

What is it?
Soldering is the process of melting solder into a gap between metal parts to form a joint. It is suitable for joining most metals, especially copper, brass, tin-plate and steel. **Soft soldering**, using a relatively weak alloy of tin, lead and antimony, is best where strength is not required, nor is there likely to be vibration or heat on the joint. **Hard soldering** gives a much stronger joint using harder solders and much higher melting temperatures.

How is it done?
Surfaces to be soldered are first **cleaned**, removing grease and oil with a cloth, and oxidised material with wire wool or an emery cloth. A **flux** is then applied to both surfaces. This prepares the surfaces and allows the solder to flow and stick to them. It also prevents oxidation around the joint. **Solder** is then heated using an electric soldering iron or solder gun (soft soldering) or a brazing torch (hard soldering), and is applied to both surfaces, which are firmly held together. The soldered joint is allowed to cool and any active flux residue is cleaned off.

We shall look at the processes of **soft** and **hard soldering** in more detail. The principle is the same for both processes, but different fluxes, solders and heating methods are used.

Soft soldering

Soft solder is a low melting point alloy of tin and lead and a little antimony, to improve fluidity. It is particularly used for copper, brass and mild steel for joints in plumbing, sheet metal fabrications, and electrical and electronic circuits. The composition of the solder varies for different types of work, as shown in Table 3.19.

The type of flux also varies according to purpose. It is supplied as a paste or a liquid. There are two categories: 'active' fluxes', prevent oxidation, possess a cleaning action and are corrosive, or 'passive' protective but non-cleaning (see Table 3.20).

General method of soft soldering
The main operations in the procedure are shown in Fig. 3.46.

1. Clean surfaces to be joined.
2. Apply flux to surfaces to be joined.
3. Heat the copper 'bit' of the soldering iron.
4. The heated bit is now cleaned, fluxed and coated with solder. This is known as 'tinning'.
5. The heated and tinned bit is now drawn along the fluxed surfaces of the components to be joined, transferring solder to the components – 'tinning' the surfaces.

Table 3.19 Uses of Soft solder of different compositions

BS type	Composition (%)			Melting range (°c)	Uses
	Tin	Lead	Antimony		
A	65	34.4	0.6	183–185	Electrical and electronic circuits. Supplied as wire with a core of resin flux
K	60	39.4	0.5	183–188	Sheet metal work mainly stick form, also wire or ribbon
F	50	49.5	0.5	183–212	Sheet metal work mainly stick form, also wire or ribbon
G	40	59.6	0.4	183–234	Sheet metal work mainly stick form, also wire or ribbon
J	30	69.7	0.3	183–255	Plumbing mainly stick form, also wire or ribbon

Table 3.20 Characteristics of 'active' and 'passive' fluxes

Flux Type	Metals	Characteristics
Acidified zinc chloride (Bakers fluid)	Steel, tin plate, brass, copper	Active, therefore wash off after use.
Dilute hydrochloric acid	Zinc and galvanised iron	Active, therefore wash off after use
Resin fluxes (either a paste or contained as a 'core in electrician's solder)	Electrical conductor and terminal materials	Passive
Tallow	Lead and pewter	Passive
Olive oil	Tin plate	Passive, non toxic for food containers

Additional solder may be added, if required. The solder is not just 'sticking' to the surface, but is forming a permanent bond by chemically reacting with the surface to form an amalgam that penetrates into the surface of the metal. Note, the components should be supported on wood, during tinning, to prevent heat loss.

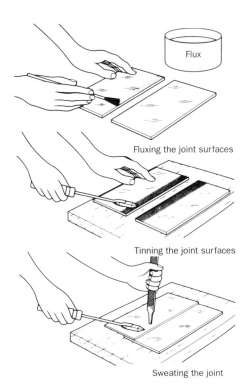

Fluxing the joint surfaces

Tinning the joint surfaces

Sweating the joint

Figure 3.46 Soft soldering procedure

6. The tinned surfaces are overlapped and heated using the soldering iron, which is drawn slowly along the join. Pressure is applied on the join and the solder gradually melts. When allowed to cool, the surfaces have joined together. This process is known as 'sweating'.
7. Any active flux residue should be washed off, and a rust inhibitor applied around the joint.

Electrical cables and components

Cables
1. Lugs for soldering on electric cables are generally ready loaded with solder.
2. Strip back the insulation.
3. Apply passive resin flux to the bare copper.
4. Insert copper wire into lug and sweat until molten solder appears around the edge.
5. Avoid overheating, which may damage surrounding insulation.

Components
- Usually supplied with leads and terminals ready tinned.
- Tinned copper wire or copper-printed circuit board is used for making the circuit.
- Place component in position.
- Apply heat with bit loaded with sufficient resin-cored solder to make the joint.

Safety notes
Care should be taken when working with hot materials and corrosive liquids:

- Wear heat-resistant gloves.
- Eye protection should be used when using active flux, which can spit on heating.
- Protective clothing should also be worn.

Hard soldering

Hard solder gives joints that are more ductile and have greater strength than soft solder. It has a much higher melting point than soft solder and heat is applied from a blowtorch fed with a mixture of air and natural or propane gas.

The solder used must have a lower melting point than the metals it is joining. The two types used are silver solder and brass solder, known as 'brazing spelter' and the process as 'brazing'. Their characteristics are given in Table 3.21.

Different fluxes are used, but most contain sodium borate, known as borax. They are generally supplied as powder, and are mixed with water to form a stiff paste.

Table 3.21 Characteristics and uses of Hard solders

BS type	Type	Composition (%)				Melting range (°C)	Characteristics and uses
		Silver	Copper	Zinc	Cadmium		
3	Silver solder	50	15	15	20	620–640	More expensive, not quite as strong as brazing spelter. Lower melting point makes it suitable for brass and copper, mild steel and cast iron
10	Brazing spelter	–	60	40	–	885–890	Strong, cheaper, suitable for copper, mild steel and cast iron. Widely used for joining steel tubes, and malleable cast iron fittings of bicycle frames

General method of hard soldering
1. Clean surfaces with emery cloth and degrease with acetone or methylated spirit.
2. Paint the borax flux on the joint.
3. Wire up or cramp the pieces together, leaving a very small gap.
4. Place the work on the brazing hearth (Fig. 3.47), surrounded by firebricks to reflect the heat back.
5. Heat with blowtorch to an even 'cherry' red. Note, as all work should be at the same temperature, thicker pieces need heating first.
6. Dip the end of the spelter rod (solder) into the flux and apply it to the joint.
7. When the rod reaches the correct temperature, a small amount will be drawn into the joint by capillary action.
8. After the work has cooled, the flux residue, a glassy film, may be cleaned away with a wire brush or emery paper.

Safety notes
You will be working with high temperatures and you should:

- Wear a face shield to protect your eyes, especially against sparks.
- Wear leather gloves to protect hands.
- Wear a leather apron to protect your body.

Welding

What is it?
Fusion welding is a process where the edges of two pieces of metal are heated to a high temperature until they melt and fuse together. Additional material may be added from a filler rod, which has the same composition as the materials being joined. The joint produced should be equal in strength to the parent material.

How is it done?
The heat is produced by one of two basic methods:

1. **Oxy-acetylene welding**, where oxygen and acetylene gas burn to produce heat. The gases are stored under pressure in steel cylinders and released through a regulator to a welding torch. Each regulator contains two pressure gauges, indicating internal cylinder pressure and line pressure to the welding torch. Temperatures may exceed 3000 °C.
2. **Manual metal arc welding**, where the heat source is an electric arc, like a prolonged spark, which is struck between the electrode and the metal being joined. The equipment is light and mobile, running from mains electricity. A transformer supplies the low voltage and high current to the electrode, which makes the arc with the metal being joined The electrode is also the filler rod, melting as welding proceeds. The current returns to the transformer via an earth clamp, either on the work piece or on the metal topped welding bench. Temperatures may reach 6000 °C.

We shall consider each of these methods in turn, having looked first of all at the general principle of welding.

Figure 3.48 shows the principle of fusion welding, and Fig. 3.49 illustrates a variety of welds.

Edges to be joined should be free of scale and rust and may need to be ground to an angle as in Fig. 3.49 to assist weld penetration.

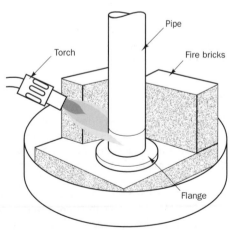

Fire bricks or other suitable insulating materials are packed around the component to be brazed. This helps to contain and reflect the heat supplied by the torch.

Figure 3.47 Hard soldering

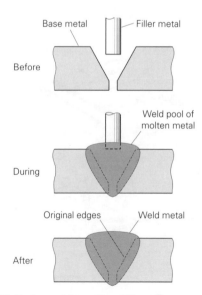

Figure 3.48 Fusing welding with a filler rod

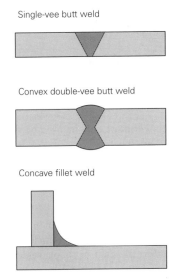

Single-vee butt weld

Convex double-vee butt weld

Concave fillet weld

Figure 3.49 Variety of welds

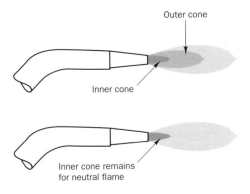

Outer cone

Inner cone

Inner cone remains for neutral flame

Figure 3.50 Obtaining neutral flame

Oxy-acetylene welding (gas welding)

The heat and characteristics of the flame can be varied to suit the thickness of metal being welded, by changing the size of nozzle connected to the blow pipe and by adjusting the gas supply from the cylinders.

- Before using a new gas cylinder any dirt or dust should be blown away from the internal screw thread by opening the valve momentarily.
- The screw thread on the regulator should be wiped clean to ensure that no oil or grease is present. *Note:* **These can burst into flames in the presence of high-pressure oxygen** – a process known as spontaneous combustion.
- Follow the guidelines given by the makers of the oxy-acetylene equipment to select the correct **nozzle size** and **line pressure**.
- Light the gas flame by first turning on and lighting the acetylene and then slowly turning on the oxygen.
- You will see two inner cones in the flame. Increase the flow of oxygen until the outer of these disappears, leaving a sharply defined inner cone (Fig. 3.50). This is the recommended flame for welding mild steel, cast iron and aluminium and is known as the **neutral flame**. It is the point at which the oxygen supply is just sufficient to burn all the acetylene.
- You are now ready to start welding, having made sure that the work is fixed securely with the correct gap and with a fireproof backing strip to support the weld.
- Remember that no flux is required as the molten metal is protected from atmospheric oxygen by the burnt gases, but you will be using a filler rod.
- Two welding techniques are used: leftward (forward) welding and rightward (backward) welding. These are illustrated in Fig. 3.51.

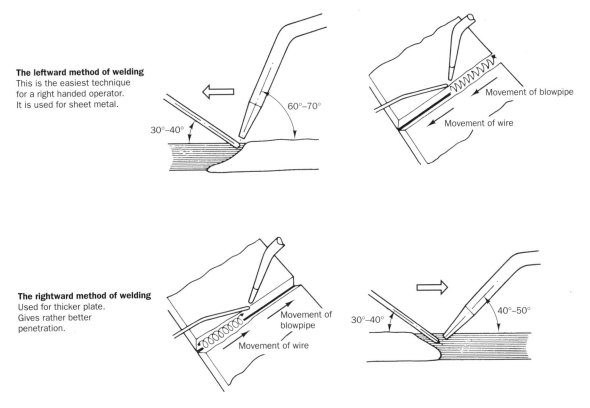

The leftward method of welding
This is the easiest technique for a right handed operator. It is used for sheet metal.

30°–40°   60°–70°

Movement of blowpipe
Movement of wire

The rightward method of welding
Used for thicker plate. Gives rather better penetration.

Movement of blowpipe
Movement of wire

30°–40°   40°–50°

Figure 3.51 Oxy-acetylene welding technique

- **Leftward welding** is used for thinner materials and bevelled plates up to 6 mm thick, cast iron and non-ferrous metals. Notice that the slight sideways movements of the blow pipe, pre-heats the material.
- Rightward welding is used on material over 6 mm thick, and here the movement of the blow pipe is circular.
- The heated area of the weld is called the *weld zone*. Because of the very high temperatures involved, the parent metal around the weld zone can be altered, becoming weaker and more brittle. It is therefore important that the speed of travel in the weld is neither too fast, where the weld does not penetrate deeply enough, or too slow, where the parent metal may be damaged! Correct speeds for different thickness of metal can only be achieved through practice!

Metal arc welding

As with gas welding, the makers of arc welding equipment give data for current settings and sizes of filler rod for different thickness of welding.

For arc welding, a flux is required to protect the weld by depositing a coating on it. It also stabilises the arc and makes the process easier. It is supplied in the form of a coating surrounding the electrode, which burns away, creating a gaseous shield. Striking the arc is the first step in the actual welding technique and this requires some practice!

The recommended technique for arc welding is illustrated in Fig. 3.52.

After welding, a layer of slag remains on the joint. This should be chipped away with a sharp-pointed hammer.

Safety notes
- Protective clothing must be worn when welding, including a leather apron and substantial footwear.
- Goggles or a safety visor must be worn. These should be appropriate to the method of welding, with filters to protect against harmful radiation produced.
- Ensure adequate ventilation.
  In gas welding:
  1. Check for gas leaks using a detergent solution only.
  2. Should flashback occur (the return of the flame through the blow pipe), first turn off the oxygen, then the acetylene.

3. Acetylene gas bottles must be stored and used in an upright position.
In arc welding:
1. Position screens or curtains so that other people cannot inadvertently see.
2. Have the position of the return lead checked before switching on.

- Welding equipment must only be used by skilled persons or under close supervision.

Specialised welding processes

The basic welding process has developed a lot in recent years and is a common feature of a range of industrial processes, notably in the manufacture of motor vehicles, where we have become accustomed to the sight of robot welders.

MIG and TIG welding

Both of these are electric arc welding processes, using an inert gas, which forms a shield around the arc.

MIG welding (Metal Inert Gas)
This is a popular, versatile form of welding, rapidly taking over from oxy-acetylene gas welding for repair work. It also lends itself to production welding using robots. The arc is struck between the workpiece and a continuous wire electrode being fed through a torch. An inert gas, usually argon or an argon-based mixture, flows through the torch, forming a shield around the arc, preventing oxidation and the formation of slag. By adjusting the mixture of gases, most metals can be welded by this process, including aluminium, copper, carbon and alloy steels, magnesium and titanium.

The continuous wire electrode provides the filler rod in one of two ways – spray or dip transfer (Fig. 3.53).

Spray transfer is suitable for fast welding of thick material. It uses high current and high voltage to cause a stream of metal droplets to leave the wire electrode and be deposited in the weld.

Dip transfer is suitable for thin sheet material as it uses less current and generates less heat than spray transfer. The wire electrode is repeatedly dipped into the molten weld pool

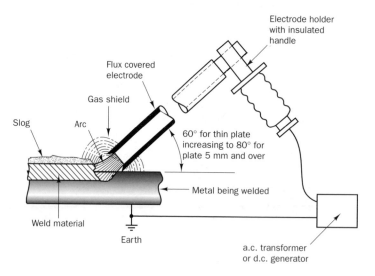

Figure 3.52 Arc welding technique

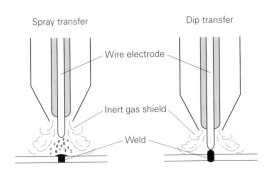

Figure 3.53 Spray and dip transfer: MIG welding

causing a brief short circuit, resulting in a rise in current and a small piece of wire electrode melting.

TIG welding (Tungsten electrode Inert Gas)
An inert gaseous shield, usually pure argon, forms around an electric arc struck between the workpiece and the tungsten electrode. Although it evaporates slowly, the tungsten electrode is not intentionally consumed. This is a process suited to difficult materials such as aluminium alloys and stainless steels.

Spot and Seam welding

These are examples of **resistance welding**, where an electric current flows through a high resistance to produce enough heat for welding to occur. It is the same principle as in a hair dryer or electric fire. These types of welding are used widely in the manufacture of car bodies.

Spot welding
Two sheets of metal are sandwiched between two electrodes, which are made from copper and have cooling water flowing inside them. Electric current flows from one electrode to the other, passing through the two sheets of metal. Most resistance to the current occurs at the joint line between the sheets and it is here that heat is generated and welding occurs. The process is repeated a number of times, as the sheets to be welded pass between the electrodes, to produce a series of 'spot' welds (Fig. 3.54).

Seam welding
Where the electrodes are in the form of a wheel, consistent pressure is applied along the joint and a **seam weld** is formed (Fig. 3.55).

Adhesion

What is it?
Sticky stuff! This is the process of fastening together two or more solids by the use of glue, cement or other adhesive. The strength of the joint depends on the ability of the adhesive to stick to the materials being joined (adhesion) and the internal strength of the adhesive – its cohesion.

How is it done?
A wide range of high-strength, synthetic adhesives have been developed in recent years and they have become an alternative to traditional methods of joining such as soldering and welding. A correctly designed bonded joint is very strong and this method is now commonly used in the motor vehicle

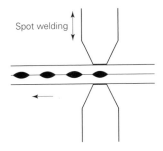

Figure 3.54 Spot welding

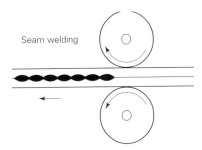

Figure 3.55 Seam welding

and aircraft industries. The choice of adhesive depends on the nature of the task. Manufacturers' instructions should be followed carefully.

Step by step

1. Consider joint design in general, as large a contact area as possible is desirable. Figure 3.56 illustrates a range of typical joints. The joint design should avoid cleavage and peel stresses as it is more likely to fail here than in shear and tension stresses (Fig. 3.57).
2. Prepare surfaces by removing grease, dirt or corrosion and lightly keying surfaces with a file or abrasive.
3. Select appropriate adhesive and apply carefully, following instructions and ensuring that the environment where bonding takes place has the correct temperature and humidity. Two-part adhesives must be accurately mixed and blended together. Methods of application include dispenser brushing, spraying, roll coating, knife coating, silk screen coating and melt coating. A guide to the selection of adhesives is given in Table 3.22.

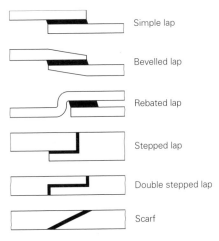

Figure 3.56 Typical bonded joints

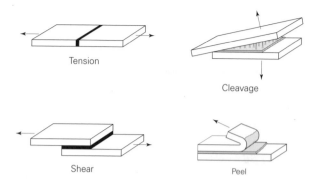

Figure 3.57 Stressing of bounded joints

4. Coated surfaces are brought into contact and held in position usually under pressure.
5. Most adhesives need to be cured to obtain full strength in the assembled joints. This may require some combination of heating, application of pressure and time. Again, follow instructions carefully!

Why use adhesives?

Use adhesives when:

- Rivets would look unsightly or rivet holes would weaken the structure.
- Access to a joint with welding or soldering gear is difficult.
- Heat would distort, or mark the materials being joined.

Some distinct advantages are:

- Similar and dissimilar materials can be joined.
- As adhesives are electrical insulators, they will reduce or prevent electrolytic corrosion where dissimilar metals are joined.
- Joints are sealed and fluid tight.
- Stresses are transmitted across the joint uniformly.
- With some adhesives, bonded joints tend to damp out vibrations.

However – it's not all good news:

- Successful joining of the surfaces can be difficult. Careful thought must go into the joint design.
- A faulty joint can be difficult to correct.
- A glued joint often requires time to strengthen and requires holding together, whereas a weld has immediate strength.

Safety notes

- Wear hand protection – adhesives can be difficult to remove and can cause skin irritation.
- Use in a well-ventilated environment – particularly when using solvent-based adhesive.
- Be particularly careful to avoid 'super glue' coming into contact with skin – the glue will readily bond skin to skin or skin to objects.
- Keep flammable adhesives well away from flames.
- Where possible, use an adhesive gun, which avoids wastage and the evaporation of flammable and toxic solvents.

Wiring

What is it?

Here we are looking at the methods of joining up electrical circuits, using either soldering or crimping techniques, both of which we have already looked at.

How is it done?

Small-scale electrical circuit work may be mounted on a circuit or matrix board. This is made from laminated plastic, pierced with a matrix of equally spaced holes. Pin tags are fastened into the holes at appropriate places, and components are soldered to them.

For larger scale electrical work, connections are made using wires, running around the workpiece, and joints are either soldered or a terminal is crimped and bolted – a technique common in the motor vehicle industry – or clamped.

Table 3.22 Adhesive selection guide

Category	Representative types	Physical forms	Joint properties	Joint materials	Type of job
Super glues	Cyanoacrylates	Low viscosity liquid	Brittle gluelines with metallic substrates. Thin gluelines, only 5 °C to 80 °C	Plastics, metals, fabrics, paper, rubber and 'skin'	Small, light structures with smooth, non-porous, close fitting surfaces, which require rapid assembly
Toughened adhesives	Acrylic and epoxide (epoxy)	Liquids, films, and pastes	High strength, toughness. Can be used on surfaces with thin oil films	Metals, glass, ceramics, wood, concrete and thermosetting processes	Structures subject to high stresses, heat and moisture
Two-polymer types	Phenolic–nitrile, phenolic–neoprene, phenolic–polyvinyl acetal and epoxide (modified)	Liquids, films, and pastes	Generally higher strength over a broader temperature range than other types. Also good resistance to chemicals	Metals, glass and thermosets	Structures subject to high stresses or heat and moisture. Used in motor vehicle and aircraft industries
Anaerobics and toughened anaerobics	Polyester-acrylic resins	One component, solvent-less, low viscosity liquids or pastes	Only harden in the absence of Oxygen. Temperature range: −50 °C to 150 °C.	Metals, ceramics, glass and thermosets (may attack thermoplastics)	May be used as 'assembly' and structural adhesives over small areas

Soldering joints

- Keep the joint clean, as a high tin content, low melting temperature solder, with a resin core flux, is used. This passive flux protects the joint, but contains no corrosive chemical to clean it.
- Avoid overheating. This can soften thermoplastic insulation and destroy devices such as diodes and transistors. Some form of heat sink is often required when soldering solid-state devices.
- Where possible, to give strength, secure a joint mechanically, by twisting the lead around the tag before soldering. The soldering ensures electrical continuity.
- Components can be removed by re-heating the joints with a soldering iron.

Where small-scale circuit work is being undertaken, it is appropriate to use a printed circuit board (PCB) or stripboard. Both of these have a thin layer of copper on one side, which means that joining wires are not needed.

Heat treatment

A number of heat treatment processes have been developed for metals and alloys. These can change their properties, making them harder and tougher, or more malleable and ductile. Both the temperature to which the metal is raised and the rate at which it is allowed to cool are critical to these processes. We shall consider two processes hardening and tempering.

Hardening carbon steel

What is it?
This is a process for hardening carbon steel, whereby the steel is heated to a bright-red (medium carbon steel) or cherry-red (high-carbon steel) temperature and then cooled, or quenched in water or oil to give it the desired properties.

Table 3.23 The effects of hardening carbon steels

Type of steel	Carbon content (%)	Type of quenching	Effect
Low carbon	<0.3%	–	None
Medium carbon	0.3 up to 0.5%	Oil	Toughening
Medium carbon	>0.5 up to 0.9%	Oil	Toughening
Medium carbon	>0.5 up to 0.9%	Water	Hardening
High carbon	>0.9%	Oil	Hardening

How is it done?
The steel must have a carbon content of over 0.3%, otherwise there will be no effect. The amount of hardening depends on the carbon content and the rate of cooling. Having heated the steel, it is then immediately cooled uniformly by dipping it, end on, into the quenching bath. Quenching in water is more violent than in oil and it gives maximum hardness. Oil quenching leaves the steel tougher and a little less brittle. Oil must be used for high-carbon steels as the violent water quenching will cause cracking.

The effects of hardening carbon steels are summarised in Table 3.23. Also some fairly common problems occur when using this process. These are summed up in Table 3.24.

Safety note when using oil for quenching
- Use high flash point quenching oil.
- Use a metal quenching bath with an airtight lid, so that any flames can be smothered.
- Keep the bath covered when not in use, so that foreign bodies and moisture do not get in.

Tempering carbon steel

What is it?
Tempering is a process which removes some of the hardness and brittleness of hardened steel, while producing a tougher, more elastic product that will still maintain its cutting edge.

How is it done?
Hardened steel is re-heated to between 200 °C and 600 °C, depending on its final use, and again quenched in oil or water.

Step by step

- The workpiece must be clean and is polished to brightness with emery cloth, after hardening and before tempering.
- It is heated gently and uniformly to its correct temperature. This depends on the tool or article being produced, for example, a lathe tool, which is subject to steady pressure, can be left harder than a chisel, which is subject to intermittent blows, or a screwdriver, which is subject to torque stresses.
- Tools with a single cutting edge are heated away from the tip, allowing the colours to run along the work.
- The temperature to which the steel is re-heated is judged by the colour of the oxide film, as set out in Table 3.25.
- The workpiece is quenched as soon as it reaches its correct temperature

Table 3.24 Common problems occuring when hardening carbon steel

Fault	Detail	Prevention
Underheating	Steel will not harden	Ensure that steel reaches its critical temperature
Overheating	This is commonly thought to make the steel even harder – it doesn't. Carbon content and rate of cooling govern hardness. Overheating means longer cooling time and less hardness. It also weakens the steel	Don't overheat!
Cracking	This can be caused by sharp corners, screw threads, holes near the edge of a workpiece, and sudden changes of section	Plan carefully at the design stage. Avoid rapid cooling of high carbon steel. Quench workpiece vertically and keep it moving to avoid waterline cracks
Distortion	This is caused by lack of balance or symmetry in the shape of the workpiece, or by lack of uniform cooling, or by change of grain structure of the steel causing shrinkage	As this can be difficult to overcome, precision components should be made slightly oversize and then be finish ground after hardening

Table 3.25 Effect of temperature when steel reheated

Temperature (°C)	Hardness – toughness	Temper colour	Uses
220	HARDEST	Pale straw	Lathe tools, scrapers, scribers
230		Medium straw	Turning tools
240		Dark straw	Twist drills
250		Brown	Taps
260		Brownish-purple	Press tools
280		Purple	Cold chisels, saws
290		Dark purple	Screwdrivers, chuck keys
300		Blue	Springs, spanners
450–600	TOUGHEST	–	Crankshafts

Chemical treatment

Chemical processes are used to clean workpieces, to remove material and to give surface finish. Processes include pickling in acid to remove scale, and de-greasing in chemical solvents. We shall focus on two processes known as *etching* and *plating*.

Etching

What is it?
Etching is the process of removal of unwanted copper from printed circuit boards. It may also be carried out to prepare a surface for coating with paint or other protective surface.

How is it done?
The work to be etched is coated in an etching solution. The composition of this solution is dependent on what is to be removed. In the case of a printed circuit board, copper is to be removed and ferric chloride is the etchant.

Step by step: producing a printed circuit board

1. The circuit is drawn by hand or designed using a CAD (computer-aided design) package.
2. The circuit drawing is photographed to produce a negative (remember that in a negative the light and dark areas are reversed).
3. The copper-coated laminated plastic (Tufnol) or fibre glass circuit board is coated with a photoresist by spraying or dipping.
4. The negative is placed in contact with the circuit board and they are exposed to ultraviolet light, which passes through the transparent parts of the negative. These areas exposed to the ultraviolet light will become the circuit.
5. The circuit board is developed in a chemical solution to harden the exposed areas.
6. The photoresist is stripped away from the unexposed areas.
7. The circuit board is placed in the etchant solution, which eats away the copper where it is not protected by the hardened photoresist. The copper that remains is the designed circuit.
8. The circuit board is washed to stop the reaction.
9. The remaining photoresist is now removed to allow for the soldering of components into position.

An alternative, lower technology method of etching follows!

1. Make a tracing of the planned circuit.
2. Turn the tracing paper over and place it on the copper clad circuit board. Go over the lines of the circuit, firmly with a pencil, to transfer it to the board.
3. Go over the lines on the circuit board with an etch resist pen or cover them with etch resist transfers.
4. Place the circuit board in the etchant solution for 10 to 15 minutes.
5. Remove the transfers, if used, then wash the circuit board and clean with wire wool.

Safety notes
- Ultraviolet light is harmful to skin and eyes.
- Protective clothing and eye protection should be worn as ferric chloride solution is highly corrosive to skin.
- Harmful fumes are given off, therefore the process should be carried out in a well-ventilated area.

Surface finishing

Polishing

What is it?
A fine abrasive powder is used to remove a very thin film of material from the near-finished workpiece. The powder may be dispersed in a liquid or made up as a paste.

How is it done?
- The abrasive to be used is applied to a soft fabric (often on a rotating wheel or pad) and rubbed on the surface of the workpiece.
- Finer and finer grades of abrasive are used in sequence.
- Polishing is finished with a natural or synthetic wax.

Painting

What is it?
A protective film is brushed or sprayed onto the workpiece.

How is it done?
- The workpiece is cleaned and degreased using an organic solvent. Sandblasting or immersion in acid (pickling) may also be used.
- Paint is then brushed or sprayed onto the workpiece in a well-ventilated area. Dipping of the workpiece is also an option for large items such as entire car bodies. Metal items may also be electrostatically charged to attract the fine droplets in a paint spray to ensure even coating. Paint type and uses are given in Table 3.26.

Grinding

What is it?
Similar to polishing, a coarser grade of abrasive is used which is bonded to a rotating wheel. The amount of material removed is considerably greater.

How is it done?
- Surface grinding produces flat surfaces. The workpiece is moved backwards and forwards against the rotating grinding wheel.
- Mounting the workpiece in a lathe-like attachment produces cylindrical surfaces. Both the grinding wheel and workpiece rotate against each other.

Table 3.26 Paint types and uses

Paint type	Components	Uses
Oil based	Pigment + Natural oil, e.g. linseed. May also be emulsified in water	Wood and metalwork. Can be used indoors or outdoors
Enamels	Pigment + Polymer resin	Metal work only as the coating must be heated to melting temperature
Catalytic	Pigment + Polymer resin, solvent and chemical hardener (catalyst)	Wood and metal work. Can be used indoors or outdoors. Solvent evaporation allows catalytic hardening of the polymer resin. This makes the paint more durable than oil-based paints.
Lacquers	Pigment + Polymer (cellulose, shellac, polyurethane, etc.), organic solvent	Wood work - thin, smooth, shiny finish. Metal work - coating of wire used in motor windings and transformer coils; vehicle body finishes

Plating

What is it?

Metal plating is usually used for corrosion protection but may also have decorative applications. There are three main processes that may be used.

How is it done?

- Hot dipping – The component (usually steel) is dipped into molten zinc (galvanisation) or tin (tinplate).
- Hot spraying - The molten coating metal (aluminium, cadmium or zinc) is sprayed onto the surface of the component.
- Powder bonding – The component is rolled in a heated (250–450 °C) drum containing a mixture of metal powder and its oxide. The powder alloys to the component metal as a thin surface film. If zinc/zinc oxide is used the process is called **Sherardising**. If aluminium/aluminium oxide is used the process is called **Calorising**.

Electroplating

What is it?

The process of depositing a thin metal film on the surfaces of the workpiece.

How is it done?

- The component is held in a bath of coating metal salt solution as the cathode in an electrolytic circuit
- The coating metal is also placed in the bath as the anode
- The current is turned on and the coating metal is deposited atom by atom on the component surface
- Common metals used in electroplating include chromium, silver and gold.

3.4 Tools and equipment

You should be able to **select** and **use** appropriate tools and equipment to produce an engineered product. There are many factors affecting the choice of tools and equipment including:

- What process needs to be performed?
- Is the process a manual or machine process?
- What accuracy or tolerances are required?
- How long should the process take?

Table 3.27 will help you to make decisions about what tools or equipment should be chosen to perform specific processes.

We will divide the tools in Table 3.27 into two categories:

1. Those used to apply physical force:
   - Hammers
   - Files
   - Hacksaws
   - Soldering irons

2. Marking and measuring devices:
   - Scribers
   - Engineer's straight edge
   - Engineer's square (try square)
   - Steel rule
   - Micrometer
   - Multimeter

We will look at each in turn.

Tools used to apply physical force

Hammers

What are they?
These are hand-held tools comprising a head of high-carbon steel, hardened and tempered to a straw colour on the striking face and pein only (Fig. 3.58). They come in all sizes.

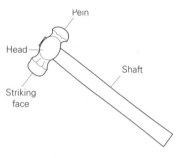

Figure 3.58 Hammer

What are they used for?
They are used for applying force to a part or component of a construction.

How are they used?
Hammering is carried out by holding the shaft of the hammer in the hand and raising the head of the hammer above the component to be struck. A suitable force is applied to the shaft with one's hand to cause the hammer head to be lowered and impact the component being constructed.

Choosing the right hammer

There are four different types of hammer (Table 3.28). They are each used for different purposes. Whatever their purpose you must also carefully choose the correct size of hammer. This is most important because:

- If a hammer is too big it will be awkward to use and you will not be able to exercise proper control.
- If it is too small it will have to be wielded with such force that, again, proper control cannot be exercised.

In both these circumstances choice of the incorrect size will result in an unsatisfactory job and also the possibility of injury.

Table 3.27 Tools and equipment required for specific processes

Process	BY HAND tools	BY MACHINE equipment
Marking out	Scriber, engineer's square, engineer's straight edge, steel rule	
Measuring and testing	Engineer's square, engineer's straight edge, steel rule, micrometer	Multimeter
Material removal	Files, hacksaw	Lathe, milling machine, drilling machine
Joining and assembling	Hammer, crimping tool, wire strippers	Soldering iron, welding equipment (gas/electrical arc-mig /tig), hot melt glue gun
Heat treatment	Tongs, quenching bath	
Chemical treatment		Etching tank, plating tank
Finishing	Abrasive papers, paint brushes, aerosol can	Buffing machine, dip coating tank, spray paint equipment, spray gun compressor, surface grinding machine, barrel polisher

Table 3.28 Uses of different types of hammer

Type of hammer	Diagram	Description
Ball pein		This is a general purpose hammer. The ball pein is used for riveting
Cross pein		The pein is at right angles to the shaft. This type is used for riveting in awkward places
Straight pein		The pein is in line with the shaft. This type is used mainly for bending sheet metal
Planishing hammer		It is used for beaten work. The faces must be kept polished and free from defects

Hints for safe operation

Like any other tool it is important that hammers are kept in good condition.

Before using a hammer make sure that:

- The head is not cracked or chipped.
- The head is firmly and securely fitted.
- The shaft is not split or rough.

When in use make sure that:

- The components being struck are not damaged.
- A soft-faced hammer is being used when machined surfaces are to be struck. Alternately, a soft metal drift should be placed between the hammer head and the component being struck.

Files

What are they?
Files are made from high-carbon steel which has been hardened and tempered so that a cutting edge can be made on it. The main parts of the file are labelled in Fig. 3.59. Files are classified by length, profile, the kind of cut used to produce them and also its coarseness, and, finally, their use. When made, the tang is left soft for strength as it fits into the handle. Files are forged to shape and then the teeth are machine cut, as in Fig. 3.60 and Table 3.29.

The coarseness or grade of these cuts is referred to by the terms: Bastard (coarsest), Rough, Second Cut, Smooth and Dead Smooth. The size of cut varies on each file with the largest having the heaviest cut.

Different types of file

The different types of file are shown in Fig. 3.61.

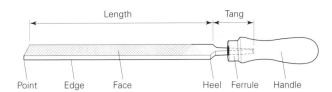

Figure 3.59 Parts of a file

Choosing the correct file

The following are criteria used for selection:

- *File length* – Select according to area of work
- *Shape* – Select according to shape of work
- *Type of work carried out*:
  General surfacing work – Hand file, flat file or flat surface of a half-round file
  Concave curves – Half-round file
  Slots and tight corners >90° – Square file
  Tight corners <90° – Triangular file
  Enlarging holes and round ended slots – Round file
  Narrow slots – Thin warding file

How to use a file

The correct use of a file is shown in Fig. 3.62.

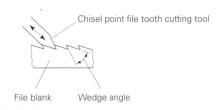

Figure 3.60 Cutting the teeth

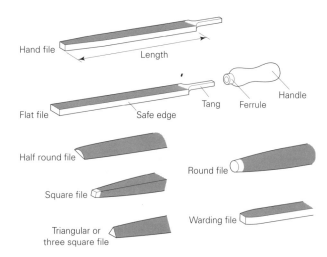

Figure 3.61 Different types of file

Table 3.29 Files: Types of cuts and their uses

Type of cut	Diagram	Cut produced by:	File use
Single cut	70° Tooth form of single cut file — Single cut file	Chisel type cutter – *First or over cut*	Not widely used except on soft materials such as brass, copper and aluminium
Double cut	45° 70° Tooth form of double cut file — Double cut file	Chisel type cutter – *Second or UP cut*	Used on tougher materials such as plain carbon steel and alloy steel. Also suitable for use on cast iron and most ferrous materials
Rasp	The tooth form of a rasp is made by a pointed cutter instead of the broad, chisel-type cutter used for a conventional file — Rasp	A pointed cutter	Rows of teeth staggered thus giving a smoother cutting action

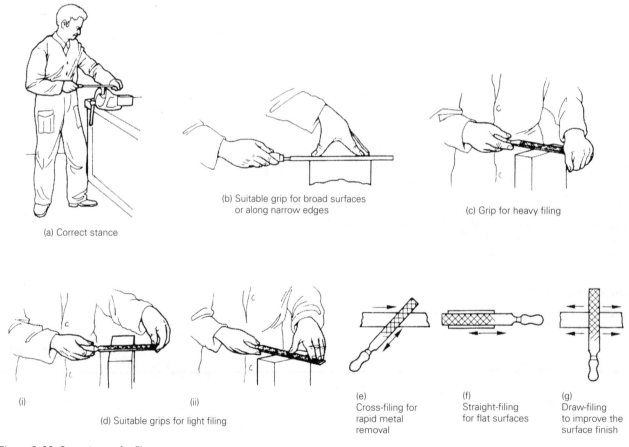

(a) Correct stance

(b) Suitable grip for broad surfaces or along narrow edges

(c) Grip for heavy filing

(i)

(ii)

(d) Suitable grips for light filing

(e) Cross-filing for rapid metal removal

(f) Straight-filing for flat surfaces

(g) Draw-filing to improve the surface finish

Figure 3.62 Correct use of a file

Guidelines

- Ensure that work is held firmly in a vice and that only a small amount of metal projects from the clamping jaws. This prevents vibration.
- Check that straight edges to be filed are held horizontally in the vice.
- Maintain a comfortable stance with feet well apart. This supplies a firm base from which to work (Fig. 3.62(a)).
- Look at the grip used for broad surfaces and along narrow edges in Fig. 3.62(b).
- Look at the grip used for heavy filing in Fig. 3.62(c). Note the application of pressure on the file with the palm of the front hand.
- For light filing, refer to Figs. 3.62(di) and (dii). You should hold the front of the file between the thumb and the forefinger to keep it horizontal. Cut on the forward stroke and take the pressure off on the return.
- For coarse filing, change the angle of the file frequently to keep the angle flat (Fig. 3.62(e)). This is used for quick material removal.
- For flat surfaces, use a straight file (Fig. 3.62(f)). Note that the pressure supplied to a file changes during the cutting stroke beginning at the tip of the file, balancing out and ending at the handle (Fig. 3.63). The weight is transferred from the back of the foot to the front.
- To improve the surface finish and to remove marks left by heavy filing, draw filing is used (Fig. 3.62(g)). Using a smooth file held at right-angles to the edge, push the file with both thumbs. A finer finish still is obtained by wrapping emery cloth around the file and repeating the process described above.

Maintenance of files

- Keep sharp new files for use on metals such as brass.
- Slightly blunt files become less effective but can be sharp enough for general use.

Hints for safe operation

- Never use a file without a handle.
- Do not use files on hardened high-speed steel.

Hacksaws

What are they?
They are general purpose saws for cutting metal. They are made of flat or tubular steel and will take blades of 150, 250 and 300 mm. The handle is screwed into a tubular bow or frame (Fig. 3.64). The blade is tensioned between two pegs attached to adjustable pins in the ends of the frame. Their tension can be adjusted with a wing nut. Note that blades are inserted with teeth facing forwards so that the cut takes place on the forward stroke.

Different types of hacksaw

There are two different types:

- Hacksaws – Frames are adjustable to fit 250 and 300 mm length blades.
- Junior – Frames are adjustable to fit 150 mm blades.

Blades also come in different types. They can be made of carbon steel or high-speed steel, but may be finished either with a hardened cutting edge or hardened right through. The

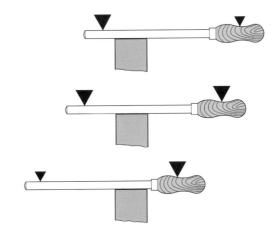

Figure 3.63 Changes in pressure supplied to a file

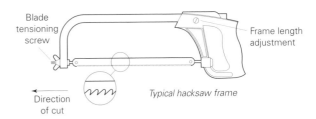

Figure 3.64 Adjustable hacksaw

soft-backed blades are less efficient, although they are tougher and less likely to break. The high-speed blades are more expensive than those of carbon steel, but last longer.

Another factor is the pitch of the teeth. This is the distance between two successive teeth. Alternate teeth also are arranged facing right or left, with every third or fifth tooth being straight. This helps to clear the chippings, thus preventing the teeth from becoming clogged.

What are they used for?
- This depends on the material being cut. The softer the material, the coarser the blade.
- The thickness and the shape of the construction should also be considered.
- The choice of blade for a particular piece of work is down to the teeth pitch. The largest possible should be chosen to give the maximum clearance for chips. Bear in mind, however, that at least two to three teeth should be in contact with the work – the thinner the metal being cut, the finer the pitch should be. If this is not considered, the teeth could be stripped from the blade.

For hand use, the best all round blade is one with about 1.5 mm pitch. For other purposes, the following can be used:

- Copper, solid brass and cast iron
  – 1.75 mm pitch
- Thin structural sections of silver steel and cast steel rods
  – 1 mm pitch
- Sheet metal and steel, copper and conduit tubing
  – 0.75 to 1 mm pitch

How to use a hacksaw

Reference should be made to Fig. 3.65.

1. As the blade is fitted with teeth, which are forward pointing, the work should be clamped in a vice to ensure that the saw is held vertical.

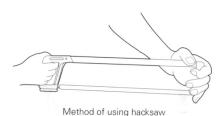

Method of using hacksaw

Figure 3.65 How to use a hacksaw

2. The frame should be held firmly by the student and the blade should cut on the forward stroke.
3. Slow, firm and steady strokes should be used.
4. Downward pressure applied on the forward stroke is released on the return stroke.
5. Solid metals should be cut with a firm pressure, while thin sheets need only light pressure.
6. Insufficient pressure at the beginning of a cut may cause the teeth to glaze the work, thus causing their wear.

Maintenance

Breakage of blades may be because of:

- Erratic and rapid strokes.
- Too much pressure.
- Blades that are not held tight enough in the frame.
- Work not held firmly in the vice.

Soldering irons

What are they?
Soldering irons comprise a metal bit, usually made of copper, which is heated either electrically, or with a gas flame.

What are they used for?
They are used for soft soldering, where strength is not required and the joints, once made, are not going to be heated or vibrated. This is a quick and easy way of making a joint in light items made from copper, brass and steel. They are also useful for making electrical connections in wiring.

Choosing the right tool

Descriptions and uses can be seen in Table 3.30.

Maintenance

- The irons must be kept clean and regularly tinned.
- If using an electric soldering iron, make sure the cable does not become kinked or frayed in any way.

Hints on safe operation

- Extreme care should be taken when working with hot surfaces and flames.
- Prepare your workspace carefully before you start. Make yourself aware of how near you are to other people.
- Keep a damp sponge available to test the temperature of the iron. Use it to keep your tools clean.
- Try to make sure that you are not disturbed by loud noises or by anything else that might shock you whilst working!

Marking and measuring devices

Scribers

What are they?
Scribers are implements made of high-carbon steel, about 120 mm long, with a finely ground-hardened and tempered sharp point – rather like a pen – with a point instead of a nib (Fig. 3.66).

What are they used for?
Scribers are used for scratching fine permanent lines onto the surface of work.

How are they used?
By looking at Fig. 3.67, it can be seen that they are held in the same way as a pen, having a knurled shank as a grip. They are used with guiding instruments, such as rules, engineers' squares, and radius gauges, for scratching a guideline. When using a square, make sure that you place the point of the scriber into the corner made by the square and the surface of the material you are scribing. To make sure that this is done, firstly place the scriber in position, then move the square up to it.

To enable the enscribed line to show clearly on the surface of the metal, a thin film of a contrasting colour is applied. This can be done in one of three ways, depending on the surface of the metal being marked:

- Whitewashing for surfaces of castings.
- Marking out inks for bright metal surfaces.

Figure 3.66 A typical engineer's scribe

Table 3.30 Soldering tools: description and use

Different tools	Description	Use	Heat source
Straight or hatchet bit	Solid piece of copper fitted to be big enough to conserve the heat and to keep the joint hot while solder melts	Traditional soldering tool	Gas flame
Small soldering iron	A small copper bit with a heating element incorporated	For electrical work	Electrical
Soldering torch	Used alone	Large joints	Gas cylinder
Soldering gun	With bit attachment, which is heated and cooled by a trigger	Traditional joints or thermoplastics and polystyrene	250 watt heating element

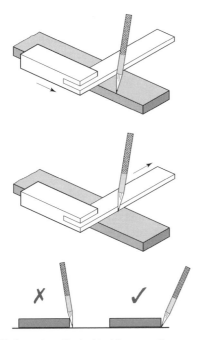

Figure 3.67 Correct method of holding a scribe

- Copper sulphate solution – for plain carbon steel. (*This solution is corrosive.*)

Maintenance

- Keep the scriber point sharp.
- As copper sulphate is corrosive, it will attack any metal instrument with which it comes into contact. Therefore wash the scriber under a running tap and dry it off, once you have used it in this way.

Hints on safe operation

- Never carry a scriber in your pocket.
- Always carry it facing downwards.

Engineers' straight edge

What is it?
It is an engineer's standard of flatness. This is one of the crucial features when checking a piece of work. A straight edge can be in the form of a steel strip for lengths up to 2 m (Fig. 3.68). For greater lengths, it can be of a ribbed cast iron design, with one edge straight (Fig. 3.69).

How is it used?
The steel straight edge is knife-edged. Use it to check flatness by placing the edge of the piece of work against it. Hold both up to the light. Any unevenness can be detected by light shining between them. Our eyes are able to detect a gap as small as 1/200 mm, so this is a reliable way of testing for flatness.

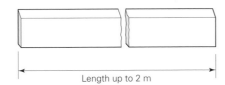

Figure 3.68 Steel bevelled straight edge

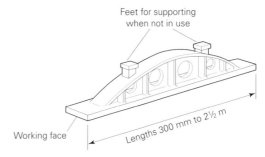

Figure 3.69 Cast iron straight edge

As the cast iron straight edge has an edge of substantial thickness, it can be used together with red lead paste, which acts as a visible indicator. This method can be used when it is difficult to hold long lengths up to the light.

First, smear the straight edge with a thin layer of paste. Wipe clean the face to be tested and place it in contact with the prepared straight edge. Move them about slightly to ensure a good contact and then separate. Where they have contacted, red lead paste will have transferred to the surface of the workpiece. If the surface is flat, red lead will appear all along its length.

Maintenance

- Care should be taken in handling a straight edge. It should not be used for any other purpose, such as a lever, as it could lose its accuracy.
- Make sure that it is wiped clean after use, removing all traces of red lead paste.

Hints on safe handling

- Handle carefully as these tools are heavy and the knife-edge could be dangerous.
- After using red lead paste, wash hands and nails thoroughly in soapy water.

Engineer's square

What is it?
A try square is the tool used by engineers for assessing squareness. Note in Fig. 3.70 that it consists of two components, which are hardened and tempered blades set into a short, thick bright steel stock. The two are at 90° to each other. The stock has a groove cut into the side of its

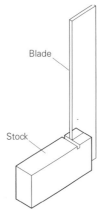

Figure 3.70 A typical engineer's try square

inside face which prevents filings and dirt from giving inaccurate results.

Try squares are available in a range of blade lengths from 75 to 1050 mm. They come in two types of grade: A – inspection and B – workshop (BS 939).

What is it used for?
A try square can be used for marking out lines which are right angles to a prepared edge. It can also be used for checking that surfaces are at right angles to each other.

How is it used?
It is used in one of two ways for checking squareness (Fig. 3.71).

1. For a small component, the stock is placed against the edge of the work and slid downwards until the blade comes into contact with the work. If the edge is not square, light will be seen between that edge and the try square blade, when viewed by the eye, as shown in the figure.
2. It is not always convenient to hold up a large component and try square to the light. A large workpiece is placed on a surface plate which is used as a datum surface. The use of feeler gauges tests the squareness of the workpiece face. The gap between the face and the try square blade will be consistent if the face is square to the blade.

Maintenance

- Care should be taken to maintain the accuracy of this precision instrument.
- Keep clean and do not drop.
- Lightly oil after use.
- Keep away from other bench tools to avoid the edge of the blade and stock from becoming burred
- Check for squareness.

Steel rule

What is it?
A steel rule is a precision tool, usually made of tempered steel, and it has a non-glare satin chrome finish. Steel rules are available in lengths up to 1 m but 150 (6 in) and 300 mm (12 in) are typical (Fig. 3.72). Rules usually have imperial and metric graduations, precisely etched on alternate sides. Metric graduations go down to 0.5 mm while imperial scales are down to 1/64 in.

What is it used for?
It is used in the workshop to measure the length of a component to only limited accuracy. This is because it is difficult to align the graduations accurately with the component being measured.

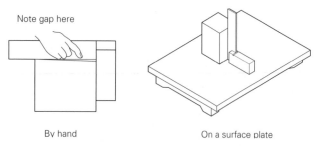

Figure 3.71 Testing a workpiece for squareness with a try square

How is it used?
- To overcome some of the problems of alignment, measure from the zero end set against a datum surface as in Fig. 3.73. Hold the rule on the edge so that the graduations touch the surface being measured.
- A less accurate way is to measure from the zero end, as shown in Fig. 3.74.
- A way of minimising errors when measuring the distance between two scribed lines is shown in Fig. 3.75.

Maintenance

- After use wipe rule clean and lightly oil to prevent rusting. Note that a dull surface is difficult to read.
- In use look after it carefully so that its edges and scales are not damaged.
- Never use it as a scraper or screwdriver.

Figure 3.72 A typical 150 mm (6 in) engineer's rule

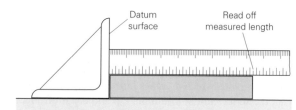

Figure 3.73 Measuring from a datum surface

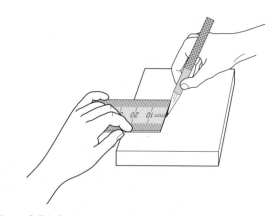

Figure 3.74 Quick method of measuring in from an edge

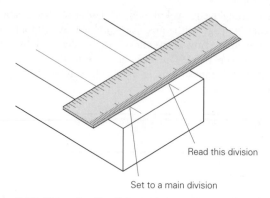

Figure 3.75 Measuring the distance between two scribed lines

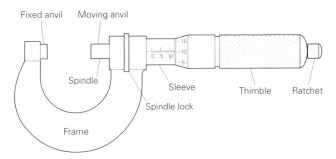

Figure 3.76 A standard 0.5mm metric micrometer

Micrometer

What is it?

It is necessary to be able to measure engineering work to greater accuracy than is possible to achieve using a steel rule. A micrometer is a precision instrument, which is capable of measuring to within 0.01 mm (0.001 in). It is designed around the principle that the distance moved by a nut along a screw thread is proportional to the number of revolutions turned by the nut.

Several different types are available, the most common being the external fixed anvil type, which is used for measuring outside dimensions. It comes in a range of sizes: 0–25 mm (0–1 in), 25–55 mm (1–2 in), and onwards in 25 mm intervals up to 450 mm (18 in).

The relevant parts of this micrometer are shown in Fig. 3.76.

What is it used for?

In addition to the external micrometer, which is used for measuring external dimensions, there are three other types. These are shown in Table 3.31.

How is it used?

- Firstly the correct size of micrometer needed must be identified.
- Note the lower limit.
- Screw the moving anvil so that the component to be measured is in contact with both anvils.
- Set the measuring pressure with the ratchet.
- Count the number of whole mm divisions visible on the sleeve.
- Add on 0.5 mm if a $\frac{1}{2}$ mm division can be seen.
- Total all the values recorded according to the above instructions, to get a final reading.

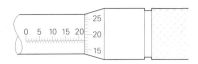

Figure 3.77 Micrometer scales

Results from example shown in Fig. 3.77.

- Lower limit 0
- Number of whole divisions on the sleeve 21
- 0.5 divisions on sleeve 00.5
- Thimble divisions lining up with zero on the sleeve × 0.01 00.18
- TOTAL 21.68 mm

Maintenance

- Make sure that anvils and workpiece are wiped clean before making a measurement. Do this by closing the anvil lightly on a piece of paper and sliding it out.

Table 3.31

Description	Diagram	Feature	Use	Accuracy and range
External adjustable micrometer		Range of precision anvils of different lengths used to replace the interchangeable fixed anvil. Usually comes with a set of precision checking gauges	To measure the outside of a feature	0.01 mm 0–100 mm
Depth micrometer		It is made up of: • a hardened ground base • a micrometer head • a set of interchangeable precision rods	To measure the depth of holes or slots	0.10 mm 0–300 mm (1–12 in)
Internal micrometer	INTERNAL MICROMETERS.	It is made up of: • a measuring head • 5 precision rods • spacer • handle Adjustable by means of the precision rods	To measure internal dimensions of the component	0.01 mm 50–200 mm (2–8 in)

- Never try to take a measurement when a machine is moving.
- Periodically check for zero error: this can be done by, first of all, cleaning the anvil face, then closing the ratchet. Check that the zero line on the thimble and the datum line on the barrel coincide. If they do not, mention it to your tutor.

Multimeter

What is it?

The multimeter is an instrument designed to measure potential difference in volts, current in amperes and resistance in ohms in both a.c. and d.c. circuits. There are two different types of multimeter: the **digital** meter and the **analogue** meter.

Digital meter

This gives a direct numerical reading and is, therefore, much easier to read. It has the added advantage of having no moving parts, which makes it more robust. However if the battery runs down then readings can be confused.

Analogue meter

This type of meter has a pointer and a scale from which readings are taken. There are a series of switches and knobs which allow different ranges to be selected.

How is it used?

Figure 3.78 shows how an analogue multimeter is connected to measure e.m.f. current and resistance.

Points to note when measuring resistance

- No current should be flowing in the circuit or component whose resistance is being measured.
- Set the switches or the buttons on the multimeter to the appropriate resistance range.
- Adjust the pointer to zero using the knob marked ohms or resistance.

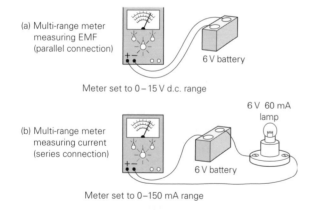

(a) Multi-range meter measuring EMF (parallel connection)

6 V battery

Meter set to 0 – 15 V d.c. range

(b) Multi-range meter measuring current (series connection)

6 V 60 mA lamp

6 V battery

Meter set to 0–150 mA range

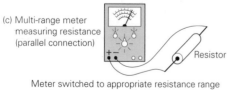

(c) Multi-range meter measuring resistance (parallel connection)

Resistor

Meter switched to appropriate resistance range
Ohmic value is read directly off meter scale

Figure 3.78 Uses of a multi-range meter

- Place the probes on either side of the item whose resistance is to be measured.
- The resistance reading can be taken directly from the meter scale.

Case study

In this section we will be looking at how materials and processes were selected for the manufacture of the following components of the Power Screwdriver:

- Cover
- Casing
- Gears
- The spindle

Cover

The material from which the cover is made needs to be:

- Tough, which is the property of a material which allows it to absorb energy. The cover needs to absorb quite a lot of energy from the mechanisms it contains.
- Easy to manufacture in large quantities – cuts costs.
- Relatively cheap, if the scrap material from manufacture can be recycled and used again, this will cut down the overall cost of the material.
- Environmentally friendly. Being able to recycle the material is environmentally friendly. A lot of manufacturers want to be able to claim that their products are 'Green Products', which means that they have considered the environment in some way.
- Easily available.
- Insulate the hand against electricity.
- Can have surface detail and inside detail.
- Relatively light which makes operating easier when weight is not a problem.
- Good outer surface appearance.
- Can be coloured.

When all these factors were considered, the choice was reduced to one of two materials:

- **Polyamide (Nylon)**, which is hard, tough, resilient to wear, has a low friction surface, is resistant to extremes of temperature, has good chemical resistance, electrically insulative, can be coloured, can be recycled easily and can be used in mass production processes.
- **Acrylonitrile–butadiene–stryrene (ABS)**, which has a high impact strength and toughness, is scratch resistant, light and durable, has a good appearance with a shiny surface finish, is resistant to chemicals, is electrically insulative, can be coloured and can be used in mass production processes.

Activity: Which one of these two plastics best suits the list of criteria stated above and why?

Manufacturing process

Both of the above plastics are thermoplastics, which can be easily moulded into a large variety of different shapes. The cover made from thermoplastic needs to be mass produced, which means that it is made in large quantities, fairly quickly and cheaply, but still has a good appearance. Remember also that the cover needs to be coloured in some way and has surface and interior detail. The cover itself is split into two halves, this allows the components – i.e the battery, switch mechanism and motor – to be easily placed inside when the power screwdriver is being assembled.

> *Activity*: Find out about the following processes and say which one would be most suitable for making the cover of the power screwdriver out of Nylon:
>
> * Hot extrusion
> * Vacuum forming
> * Injection moulding
>
> Gives reasons for your answer.

Casing

The casing of the power screwdriver houses the gears and the final drive shaft or the spindle, which is used to attach the screwdriver bits. The casing therefore has to resist large turning forces (torque) from the gears and spindle and also large thrust loads on the end as the user pushes against the spindle and bits to drive screws into the material.

The casing therefore has to resist both:

* Axial loads
* Radial loads

The casing also houses an internal annulus gear, which is formed on the inside surface. The teeth of this gear have to be accurate and must resist wear.

The spindle housed by the casing, forms a plain bearing, with a steel shaft rubbing against the casing, which needs to be a slightly softer material than steel. Also the power screwdriver needs to be relatively light so that the user does not tire while using it, and the weight needs to be spread evenly throughout its body. Therefore the material to manufacture the casing needs to be relatively light.

Choice of material

The material should be a lightweight metal, strong enough to resist axial and radial loads. It should have the ability to be formed accurately with internal and external detail. It should be softer then steel, readily available and cheap to mass produce.

Choice of process

The process should have the ability to produce complicated shapes with accurate internal detail. It should be able to use aluminium alloy as the process material, which needs to be mass produced, causing minimum waste.

> *Activity*: Find out about the following processes:
>
> * Metal die casting
> * Turning and machining
> * Sand casting.
>
> Decide which process would be the most appropriate to meet the product requirements. Give reasons for your choice.

Gears

Planetary gears

If the planetary gears were heavy, they would exert large centrifugal forces as they rotate. Therefore the planetary gears need to be as light as possible. They have to be accurately made and be able to resist wear when rubbing against the annulus and sun gears. They also exert turning forces and need to be strong enough to withstand these forces without distorting in any way.

As one of the main mechanisms in the power screwdriver, they should be as efficient as possible, avoiding loss of efficiency through frictional forces and heat production caused by gear surfaces rubbing against one another. It would be desirable for the material to have a low coefficient of friction.

The gears also need to be cheap and have the ability to be mass produced with accuracy.

> *Activity*: Find out about the following materials and processes and decide which material and process are best suited to the production of the planetary gears. Explain your decisions.

Materials
* Nylon
* ABS
* Aluminium alloy

Processes
* Injection moulding
* Die casting.

Sun gears

These are made from steel as they have to take three times the torque of each planetary gear and therefore have to be stronger than the planetary gears. They are made by a process called **rolling**, which is a forming process, that presses the material into the required shape using a specially shaped roller. The main reasons for the use of this process are:

* Steel is malleable and ductile and can be rolled into shape.
* A lot of components can be produced from one rolled section cut up into individual parts.
* There is no waste material.
* It is a quick mass production process.
* The correct accuracy or tolerances can be achieved.

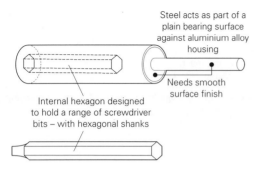

Figure 3.79 Power screwdriver-spindle

The spindle

The spindle is made from steel (see Fig. 3.79). It has two different diameters: a smaller 6 mm shaft and a larger 13 mm housing. The surface finish is very smooth as the shaft forms part of a plain bearing surface. The inside of the larger diameter housing has a central hexagonal hole.

Activity: Two different processes were used to make this component. One process was used to manufacture the outer shape or exterior profile, with the two diameters and smooth bearing surface. The other was used to manufacture the internal hexagon shape.

External shape
- Centre lathe – single point cutting
- Rolling.

Internal Shape
- Boring
- Broaching

Find out about each of these processes and say which is the most appropriate for each of the internal and external shapes. Gives reasons for your selection.

3.5 Health and safety

You must be aware of health and safety issues relating to the use of materials, components, tools and equipment required for your engineering activities.

Following safety procedures and instructions

Health and safety is probably the most important element in the working life of all those working in industry. Engineers often work in an environment which can be very dangerous. Only when dangers are recognised and understood can appropriate measures be taken to protect against personal accident and injury, ill heath or damage to equipment.

Safety procedures specific to the following have already been described elsewhere in this chapter:

- Marking and measuring tools and techniques.
- Material removal.
- Material forming and joining.
- Heat and chemical treatment of materials.
- Material finishing techniques.

Over the years, governments have passed safety laws ensuring that people observe health and safety measures while at work. The most important of these laws is the Health and Safety at Work, etc., Act 1974. This act covers virtually everyone in all kinds of work For more specialist engineering legal information about processes or operations, you may need to refer to one of the following acts or regulations:

- The Factories Act 1961
- Eyeshield Regulations 1974
- The Electricity at Work Act 1989
- COSHH (Control of Substances Harmful to Heath) 1995
- Manual Handling Operations Regulations 1992
- Personal Protective Equipment Regulations 1992
- Provision and Use of Work Equipment Regulations 1992

Keeping a safe place of work

Risk assessment

To avoid accidents and harm in a situation, you need to think about:

- Hazards
- Risks
- Risk assessment
- Risk control.

A hazard is anything that might cause harm or damage. The chance of a hazard causing harm or damage is called a **risk**. You can work out how big the risk is by thinking about whether the harm or damage is likely to happen. This is called **risk assessment**. **Risk control** is the action taken to ensure that the harm or damage is less likely to happen.

It is important that you learn to look at situations in this way, so that you can take appropriate risk control actions. Consider the following example:

- Identify the risk – The substance with which you are working is considered hazardous.
- Assess the risk – The hazardous substance produces dust; you would need to work out the exposure levels, how much of the substance is used; how much dust is produced and the type of working environment in which it is used.
- Control the risks by isolation or substitution, i.e. use another material or substance.
- If this is difficult, then use an extraction system, which will extract the dust.
- If this is difficult, provide adequate ventilation.
- If this is difficult, then wear personal protective equipment, e.g. a CE marked dust mask or respirator.

In all areas of manufacturing it is important to think about and reduce risks to yourself and others. It is helpful to think about safety in three ways:

- Safety with materials
- Safety with people
- Safety with equipment and machinery

Safety with materials

Handle materials properly and with care.
Be particularly careful when handling hot materials.
Wear gloves when handling hot or sharp materials, grip with tongs if appropriate.
Be very careful with sharp ends or edges remove them whenever possible.
Put materials giving off fumes in a well-ventilated area, fume hood or spray booth.
Dispose of waste and scrap materials properly.
Clean up spills quickly and thoroughly.

Safety with people

Think about the way you work and think about others.
Concentrate and avoid accidents.
Be properly dressed, use protective clothing. Do not wear loose clothing.
Secure hair and clothing if necessary.
Use safety equipment, e.g. goggles, face mask respirators if necessary.
Think ahead about possible consequences before starting any action.
Make sure you know the correct and safe procedure for operation of tools and equipment, ask if unsure or receive the correct training or instruction if required.
Injury. For even minor injuries seek first aid attention.
Be aware of specific safety rules applying to tools equipment and materials you are using.
Think about how risks can be avoided or reduced. Help others to avoid risks.

Safety with equipment and machinery

Before using tools and machinery

- Is it the right tool or machine for the job?
- Do you need training to use the tool or machine?
- Are there any by-products produced which will affect others, e.g. dust or fumes?
- Is any special clothing or safety equipment needed?
- Are the machines or tools in good condition; do they need repair or adjustment?
- Prepare the area or equipment before starting work, clean it down if necessary.

Using tools and machinery

- Secure the workpiece thoroughly.
- Make sure that guards and covers are in place.
- Be aware and keep clear of moving and or cutting parts.
- Stop the machine before making adjustments.
- Do not leave a working machine unattended.

You must have a clear understanding of:

- What to do in case of an accident.
- Who is in charge of first aid.
- Where first aid can be found or administered.
- What to do when an alarm sounds.
- What to do if there is a fire or emergency, e.g. where the fire exists and how to proceed.

After using tools and machinery

- Return all tools and equipment to their correct places.
- Leave equipment clean and safe and ready for the next person to use.

Activity: For a given product specification and a list of the processes/tools and equipment used to produce the product, identify any health and safety issues related to the product's manufacture.

3.6 Production plan

The production plan gives details required to make a product. You must be aware of the main features of a production plan and produce one for an engineered product.

A production plan should give information about:

- The main stages of production of a product.
- The sequence of actions involved in the manufacturing processes.
- When and where the materials and components you have selected are needed in the process.
- When and where the equipment you have selected is needed.
- The quality checks required.

Identification of the main stages of production

Before you can develop a production plan you must identify the main stages of production, which your product will have to go through.

Preparation

This will involve the preparation of tools and equipment/machines as well as the preparation of materials used to manufacture the product. Generally preparation can involve:

Material preparation

- Ensure that all materials and components required by the specification are available in the appropriate form and quantity.
- Check the condition of materials and components including size, type, physical state and defects.
- Assess any problems and suggest solutions.
- Clean up materials and components – involving degreasing, removing corrosion, exterior coatings and packaging.
- Use the specification to measure materials accurately to minimise waste. Measure their size, weight and quantity.
- Mark up materials using correct marking procedures and tools. Mark up materials economically to minimise waste, e.g. consider the best layout of component shape on the material, always work from a datum edge or surface.
- Rough cut materials if necessary, or divide them into appropriate quantities or batches.

Tool and equipment/machine preparation

- Check the condition of tools and equipment, e.g. routine maintenance.
- Set up, calibrate and adjust tools and equipment to required specification dimensions.

Processing

Generally, processing involves:

- Being conversant with the production methods required by the specification.

- Obtaining the correct training in appropriate processing methods and techniques if necessary.
- Using processing methods accurately.
- Checking for quality.
- Ensuring that the correct health and safety procedures are adhered to at all times while processing.

Assembling

Generally, assembling involves joining individual parts to produce the final product.

- Ensure that processing and assembling are planned efficiently to maximise the use of time.
- Subassembling parts and then final assembly of product.
- Being conversant with the joining methods required.
- Obtaining the correct training in appropriate joining methods and techniques if necessary.
- Using joining methods accurately.
- Checking for quality.
- Ensuring that the correct health and safety procedures are adhered to at all times while assembling.

Finishing

Generally, finishing involves producing the finish required by the specification, including:

- Being conversant with the finishing methods required.
- Obtaining the correct training in appropriate finishing methods and techniques if necessary.
- Using finishing methods accurately.
- Checking for quality.
- Ensuring that the correct health and safety procedures are adhered to at all times while finishing.

With many products a number of components are processed separately before finally coming together for assembly and final finishing. An individual component can go through all the main stages of production and be assembled or attached to the other components of the product after it has been finished. In these cases it is desirable to develop separate process planning sheets for each component and then a separate one for the final assembly and finishing operation.

A process planning sheet is made up using the following information:

Process description	Materials/ Components	Machine/ Equipment	Tools	Quality indicator	Estimated time

- Process description – Gives a brief outline or simply the name of the process to be used.
- Materials and components – States the type, grade and form in which the material or components are supplied.
- Machines or equipment – Gives the name of the machines or equipment to be used in the outlined processes.

Op. No.	Description	Equipment
1.	Chuck bar, in centre lathe.	3 jaw chuck
2.	Rought turn all diameters and face end	Turning tools 0–25, 25–50 micrometers rule, odd leg calipers.
3.	Drill & Ream ⌀12.0 Hole.	Centre drill, drills. ⌀12.0 Reamer.
4.	Part off.	Parting Tool.
5.	Face of length.	Vernier caliper.
6.	Mount on Mandrel	⌀12.0 Mandrel. Mandrel press.
7.	Set between centres in centres lathe.	Catchplate, carrier.
8.	Finish turn all diameters, chamber and undercut.	Turning tools, depth micrometer.
9.	Set in milling machine using Vee block against vice jaw (horizontal or vertical)	Vee block, machine vice ⌀8.0 cutter.
10.	Centre cutter – take trial cut.	
11.	Mill to depth & open up slot to size.	Slip gauges.
12.	Set in vee block & mark out position of topped hole.	Vernier height gauge. Surface plate, centre punch.
13.	Drill and tap 2.B.A hole	Tapping size drill, set 2.B.A. taps, tap wrench.
14.	De-burr, check all dimensions.	File.

Figure 3.80 Planning sheet

- Tools – Gives the names of tools required for the different processes including any type of tool for measuring and testing.
- Quality indicator – This includes information about specific values to be achieved, e.g. critical dimensions, property values such as hardness, information about textures and surface finishes and other quality measurements.
- Estimated time – Gives the processing time required per item or if larger numbers are required per batch.

Figure 3.80 gives an example of another type of planning sheet, which has been developed, working directly from the product specification and or an engineered drawing of the specification.

Production scheduling

A production schedule is an effective way to plan the sequence of production and makes the best use of the time you have available. The processes involved in manufacturing have to be organised into a smooth flow. Your planning should start from the time the product must be finished. In order to produce a production schedule you will need to make some calculations.

Processing times

In industry, information can be provided about the average time any one process takes to complete. This information has been collected over a long period of time and experience of a large variety of process practices. In a similar way, if you have had experience of any of the processes in your production plan, you may be able to estimate the time that process would take to complete.

Another way to determine a process time, is to complete a trial run. This is very useful, especially if you have not used a specific process before. It is wise to practise the process before you apply it to the engineered product. In industry you would be expected to complete a training course to show that you are proficient in the use of the process you will be required to operate.

To produce a production plan you will need to work out process times for each of the main stages of production, e.g. Preparation, Processing, Assembling and Finishing.

Sequence of activities

In planning the sequence of activities required to make a product, it is often helpful to use a block diagram, or flow chart (see Fig. 3.81). This shows the sequence of processes required to make the component parts of a product and how some of the component parts are brought together for a subassembly and then how these subassembled parts are brought together for their final assembly and finishing. This type of chart is often called a production process layout.

Another useful way of planning activites is to use a Gantt chart (Fig. 3.82). You can use the production process layout to determine the order of production and you can then use the Gantt chart to illustrate or plan how long each part will take. A Gantt chart will give you an overview of the whole production process, showing what needs to be done and when it should be done.

How quality will be checked and inspected

In any process there are points at which quality assessments and measurements are made. For example measurements could be made on the following:

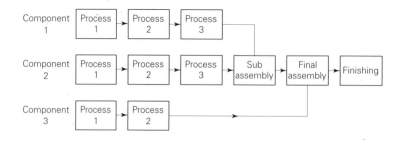

Figure 3.81 Flow chart

Figure 3.82 Gannt chart: a simple schedule

Inputs and outputs

Inputs to the process

Inputs can include the materials used, the components used, tools and equipment used, the person operating the process. Quality checks can be made on the materials to check for defects and checks on accurate measurements and marking out. The quantity of materials and form in which they are supplied can also be checked.

Components can be checked to assess whether they are functioning correctly, whether they are damaged and whether they are supplied in the correct form and quantity.

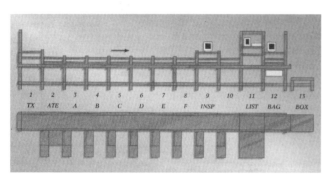

Line position		Time
Line position 1	Place transformer on PCB, secure with tie wrap and solder. Fit voltage label on transformer.	1 min 30 s
Line position 2	Place PCB on automated test jig. Run test.	3 min 10 s
Line position 3	Prepare chassis – bend to shape – fix warning label. Add feet, fixing pillars, PCB insulator, acoustic damping pad. Secure PCB with screws. Plug in display to PCB.	2 min 30 s
Line position 4	Secure earth lead to CD mechanism – screw and crinkle washers. Fit CD mechanism to chassis – four snap rivets. Remove protective plastic film from LCD display. Secure gaskets and windows over display. Check display operation. Fit laser warning label to outside of chassis.	1 min 58 s
Line position 5	Fit buttons. Fix front panel to chassis with fasteners.	2 min 44 s
Line position 6	Fit rear panel to bottom of chassis using 2 washers and 2 screws. Secure phono connecting socket to rear panel with 2 screws. Secure connectors and phono sockets to rear panel with 4 screws. Fit blanking rivet into earth hole above mains inlet. Fit laser label to space provided on rear panel.	2 min 40 s
Line position 7	Repairs bench.	
Line position 8	Pass unit onto the off soak test area for testing.	
Line position 9	Fit cover gasket to CD drawer mechanism. Front panel check. Voltage/bar code labels. Inspect the unit – internal check and rear panel check.	1 min 39 s
Line position 10	Fit cover plate to chassis. Use 4 screws for the chassis side and 4 for the rear panel. Check alignment of chassis.	1 min 30 s
Line position 11	Listening test.	3 min 5 s
Line position 12	Clean the unit. Put in polythene bag and add documentation and accessory pack.	2 min 40 s
Line position 13	Box and dispatch.	
	Total time for unit	**23 min 26 s**

Figure 3.83 Planned production line

Tools and equipment can be checked for smooth operation, damage and accuracy. Routine maintenance can be carried out, e.g. oil and water supplies, etc. Equipment can be recalibrated if necessary.

Operators can be assessed. They should be able to demonstrate that they can operate tools and equipment accurately.

The process

Quality checks should be made at critical control points throughout the process to ensure that the product at all stages of production is meeting the specification requirements.

Critical control points are monitored by quality control systems , where 'go/no go' or 'yes/no' decisions are made. A product cannot 'go' to the next stage of production without meeting the appropriate quality indicator set out in the specification.

Critical control points generally occur after each main stage of production, but they can occur throughout each main stage if necessary.

Look at Fig. 3.83 to see how critical control points (monitored by control systems including testing and inspection techniques) have been planned in the production of a CD Player.

Outputs from the process

The main outputs from the process are the product itself and waste materials. The product should be tested and checked against the original specification, to see if all specified requirements are met. Waste should be controlled, disposing of it safely or recycling it in some way. Both of these processes should be monitored to ensure compliance with health and safety regulations.

Quality control loop

Quality is achieved when the results of these measurements (input, process and output) are interpreted and used to shape future work practice (Fig. 3.84).

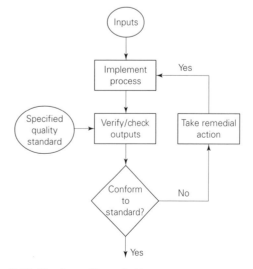

Figure 3.84 Simple quality control loop

Table 3.32 The differences between Quality Control and Quality Assurance

Quality Control when making a component part	Quality Assurance when making a component part
Use information in the specification to measure and mark the dimension onto the material	Use information in the specification to measure and mark the dimension onto the material
	Check this measurement with the correct measuring instrument
	Check that this measurement is the same as that given in the specification
Cut the material along the marked line	Cut the material along the marked line
Measure the cut material to see if it is the same dimension given in the specification	Measure the cut material to see if it is the same dimension given in the specification
The component part will either be the correct size, in which case it will pass and move onto the next stage of production, or it will not be the correct size in which case it will fail and have to be reworked	Quality is assured and the component will be the correct size

Quality control and quality assurance

You should know the difference between quality control and quality assurance. When producing your electro mechanically engineered product you should try to assure the quality of your product.

Quality control involves the inspection of the product after a part of the production process has been completed e.g after the preparation stage or after the assembly stage. Quality control is used to detect when a product is not up to standard or does not meet the specification.

Quality assurance, on the other hand, is a planned series of actions, which are used to make sure that the product meets the agreed standards. Quality assurance takes place before, during and after production. The aim of quality assurance is to make sure that the product is right first time.

To understand this more clearly look at Table 3.32. To assure quality in your product you will have to consider very carefully *each part* of the production process and *each component*.

3.7 Measure and compare engineered product with the specification

You will be able to measure and compare the final engineered product to the product specification. This includes:

The required dimensions

Use the measuring instruments and the techniques outlined in this chapter to measure and compare your product against the dimensions given in the specification, these include : engineers squares, try squares, rules, micrometers and multimeters

The required tolerances

After measuring your product with the correct tools and equipment, make a note of the results and then check these dimensions with those given in the specification. Do they fall within the tolerances stated in the specification. If the answer is no, then identify where the errors were made and suggest how these errors could have been avoided.

The required finish

The specification should state the texture, pattern or in other words the surface finished required by the product. It should also state the level of finish and may give the upper and lower limits of surface roughness required.

You should check the surface roughness table shown earlier in the chapter to see if the correct processes have been used to achieve the appropriate range of surface roughness. This will give you a very basic idea of whether the correct surface finish has been achieved, another way to check the finish is to use surface comparison blocks, which come in a boxed set and represent typical surface roughness values as produced by various workshop processes. Comparison is made by drawing your fingernail across the test blocks until a match of feel is achieved.

If the correct surface finish has not been achieved, identify where the errors were made and suggest how these errors could have been avoided.

The required quality

The quality indicators outlined by the specification are: standards, legislation, aesthetics and surface finish and performance. We have already looked at standards and legislation, surface finish and aesthetics.

Performance

To evaluate the product's performance you have to ask the question: Does it do what it was designed to do? To find the answer to this question you will need to test your product.

Testing performance

Think about what you want to test and ask yourself the following questions:

- Why you are testing? (reason)
- What you are testing? (part)
- What you want to find out? (properties or capacities)

The type of test will depend on what you are trying to find out. Here are a few possibilities:

- Apply a constant force.
- Apply a steadily increasing force.
- Repeatedly apply and remove a force.
- Apply an oscillating force.
- Expose the item to specific physical conditions.

You may need to measure inputs such as:

- Loads, force torque.
- Number of operations, e.g. stroke or cycle.
- How long input is applied, physical conditions, e.g light, level, temperature level, etc.
- Starting dimensions.

You will need to measure the effects of the test such as when failure occurs. Does it occur at a particular load, after a certain number of strokes or under certain conditions. You might need to measure how long it takes for something to happen, the maximum loading achieved or change in the dimensions of the product.

Comparison with the specification

To compare your product against the specification you should be able to answer the following questions:

- Did the product fully meet the specification? If not, what were the differences? Could you make changes or modifications to resolve these differences?
- Is the outcome reliable? Does it continue to meet the specification when used repeatedly?
- Is it safe? Have you checked it against the specified standards and legislation?
- Was the product completed within the given time?
- Does the appearance of the product meet the aesthetic features required by the specification?
- Have you systematically tested the product?
- What did you do with the results?

> *Exercise*: Measure and compare drawing or photograph of a component part of a product, with the working drawing produced for the original product specification. Highlight any differences.

Index